The Year of the Lord's Favor

The Year of the Lord's Favor

Preaching the Three-Year Lectionary

Sherman E. Johnson

The Seabury Press / New York

1983
The Seabury Press
815 Second Avenue
New York, N.Y. 10017

Printed in the United States of America

Library of Congress Cataloging in Publication Data

Johnson, Sherman E. (Sherman Elbridge), 1908–
    The year of the Lord's favor.

    Bibliography: p. 256
    Includes index.
    1. Bible—Homiletical use.   2. Bible—Liturgical
lessons, English.   3. Lectionaries.   I. Title.
BS534.5.J63   1983   251   83-9081
ISBN 0-8164-2359-8

To Massey Hamilton Shepherd, Jr.

He has lived mentally and spiritually through the whole history of the People of God; he has participated in the life of the world and of the Church today; he has brought present and past together as he has lived in and with the liturgy and private prayer; thus he has been able to give many students and colleagues the wisdom that brings new life through Jesus Christ our Lord.

Contents

Table of Conversion

Sundays after Epiphany and after Pentecost

The method of designating the Sundays "of the Year" or "ordinary time"—the Sundays after Epiphany and after Pentecost—differs in the various Churches. The following table shows when a given proper occurs according to the nomenclature of the various systems.

After Epiphany

Roman Catholic "Of the Year"	Lutheran, Presbyterian, Methodist After Epiphany	Episcopal After Epiphany
Y1 (Baptism of the Lord)	1 (Baptism of the Lord)	1 (Baptism of the Lord)
Y2	2	2
Y3	3	3
Y4	4	4
Y5	5	5
Y6	6	6 (= Proper 1)
Y7	7	7 (= Proper 2)
Y8	8	8 (= Proper 3)
Y9 (does not correspond to propers in other churches; any of Y6-9 may be after Pentecost)	Last Epiphany (Transfiguration)	Last Epiphany (Transfiguration)

After Pentecost

Roman Catholic "Of the Year"	Lutheran, Presbyterian (after Pentecost)	Methodist	Episcopal No. of Proper
Trinity Sunday	Trinity Sunday	40. Trinity Sunday	Trinity Sunday
Y9	2	41. 5/29-6/4	4
Y10	3	42. 6/5-11	5
Y11	4	43. 6/12-18	6
Y12	5	44. 6/19-25	7
Y13	6	45. 6/26-7/2	8
Y14	7	46. 7/3-9	9
Y15	8	47. 7/10-16	10
Y16	9	48. 7/17-23	11
Y17	10	49. 7/24-30	12
Y18	11	50. 7/31-8/6	13
Y19	12	51. 8/7-13	14
Y20	13	52. 8/14-20	15
Y21	14	53. 8/21-27	16
Y22	15	54. 8/28-9/3	17
Y23	16	55. 9/4-10	18
Y24	17	56. 9/11-17	19
Y25	18	57. 9/18-24	20
Y26	19	58. 9/25-10/1	21
Y27	20	59. 10/2-8	22
Y28	21	60. 10/9-15	23
Y29	22	61. 10/16-22	24
Y30	23	62. 10/23-29	25
Y31	24	63. 10/30-11/5	26
Y32	25	64. 11/6-12	27
Y33	26	65. 11/13-19	28
Y34 (= Christ the King=Last Pentecost)	27 (Last Pentecost)	66. 11/20-26	29 (Christ the King)

Preface

This book has been written for working preachers and seminary students in the hope that it may help them to preach honestly and effectively from the Holy Scriptures, using the lectionaries that have been set forth since 1970.

Observers of the American culture know that the Bible is no longer familiar to the vast majority of the population. Its words do not evoke an immediate response as they did when Abraham Lincoln wove scriptural phrases into his Second Inaugural. The preachers are partly responsible for this failure. Not only is the content of the Scriptures not well known, but its central message has not come through clearly to the people.

Much preaching has been topical and related only peripherally to a text or passage. Even in denominations that claim to be Bible-centered, the messages delivered on Sunday too often reflect only those parts of Holy Writ that appeal especially to the preacher.

Theologians and biblical experts have diagnosed the sickness that infects the American pulpit and have suggested remedies. Several of their books are listed in the bibliography appended to the present volume. Part of the answer to the problem is a faithful and intelligent use of the lectionaries. This avoids the tendency to ride hobbies and it can expose the rich and manifold glories of the Scriptures.

The Bible is not a "resource" to be consulted or exploited when one has a particular purpose in mind. Instead it is the Church's collection of writings that speak first to the mind and spirit of the homilist, and through him or her to the People of God. Good preaching comes out of study of the text, daily relationships with people inside and outside the Church, theological and non-theological reading, and the interior life of meditation and prayer.

This book is designed to give a historical and theological orientation to the lectionaries and to the passages which they specify. It is suggested that the book be given a first reading. The next step might be to make a tentative plan for preaching during a season of the liturgical year or at least for a few weeks. The reader is then advised to return to the relevant sections of the volume and also to study the pericopes more fully in one of the excellent commentaries on the lectionary that are now available. This can be supplemented by use of standard commentaries on the separate books and other helps to understanding the Bible. A passage of Scripture should be seen in its widest context, historical, theological and liturgical.

The present book is divided into three parts. The first of these is an introduction to the lectionaries and their relation to the Scriptures. Here an attempt is made to disclose the nature of religious speech, particularly as it is used in public worship, to relate this to the canon of Scripture, and to suggest principles of interpretation.

Part Two, the Cycle of the Great Story, explains how the lectionaries set forth sacred history, beginning with Advent and continuing through Trinity Sunday. No attempt is made to discuss every pericope in detail; the purpose is rather to see the passages as related to basic theological themes of the Bible. Thus there are sections that deal with the biblical view of history, the covenants, prophecy and apocalyptic, the meaning of the Incarnation, the Cross and Resurrection, the gift of the Holy Spirit and the return of Christ, the nature of biblical proclamation, the human condition, God's action in relation to this, and the response of the believer.

These themes inevitably recur in Part Three, which discusses pericopes in Sundays "of the Year" or "ordinary time," between Epiphany and Lent and after Trinity Sunday. These chapters are arranged topically, but in such a way that the sequence of the Sundays is followed so far as possible. Chaps. 12–14 aim to set forth the Good News, the positive message of Jesus, which can be distinguished to some degree from the Church's witness to him that is reflected in the gospels. Chap. 15 compares Jesus with the prevailing Judaism of the time, particularly in controversies over observance of the law. The miracles, which require separate treatment, are discussed in Chap. 16. Two chapters (17–18) deal with the letters of Paul, and Chap. 19 considers the ethics of the post-

apostolic period. Finally, Chap. 20 chooses pericopes that bear especial·
ly on prayer and the interior life. Since a passage may be discussed at
more than one point, readers are urged to use the index of scriptural
references. This and a select bibliography are included at the end.

One conviction that lies behind this book is that the formation of
attitudes may be the most important function of preaching. The Bible
of course contains much instruction, warning and encouragement, and
all these have their proper function, but homilies that end only in
exhortation (usually in vague and general terms) may lead merely to
resistance or to feelings of guilt that produce no good result.

A change of attitude is more productive. The prophets, psalmists and
wise men of the OT, and Jesus himself in his ministry and teaching,
reflect a particular point of view. For us it is a subtle and delicate art to
foster an attitude to life that takes seriously a loving and just God who
cares about all his creation in all ages. The preacher who wishes to
practice this art must first orient himself or herself in this direction, and
then use not only preaching but also the arts of worship, pastoral care
and church administration to this end.

The specific literary and historical judgments that are given here are
based on modern critical methods and represent, I believe, a wide
consensus of Catholic and Protestant scholars, even if they are not
universally accepted. Perhaps I may add my own testimony that a long
ministry of teaching in theological seminaries in which these methods
were used has deepened my faith and my appreciation of the power and
beauty of the Scriptures. My greatest wish is that these pages may
somehow communicate to readers the excitement and joy, the discovery
of being under judgment by the Word of God and at the same time
being liberated by the gospel; the sense of continuity with the past and
the expectation of the future that have been my experience in teaching
and preaching from the Scriptures.

There are frequent minor variations between the several lectionaries
in the extent of a given pericope; in such cases the longest form of the
pericope is often cited. When only one lectionary prescribes a pericope
different from the rest, this is sometimes ignored. In general, the pas·
sages discussed are those of a majority of the six.

OT quotations are from the Revised Standard Version; those from the
NT are the author's own translation.

Mr. Howard E. Galley, Jr., of the Seabury Press, has made many
improvements in this volume through his careful editing, and it has been

a pleasure to have his counsel. Professors David G. Buttrick, Godfrey Diekmann, O.S.B., Donn Morgan, Shunji F. Nishi, and Massey H. Shepherd, Jr., have given me helpful suggestions. Others who have encouraged me in this project are Deans Frederick H. Borsch, O.C. Edwards, Jr., and Ronald W. Graham. The Ven. Paul E. Langpaap, D.D., provided me with early information on the NACCL lectionary. To many others, living and dead, I am indebted, not least to my wife Mary, who has encouraged, sustained and cheered me throughout.

—————————·Part One

The Lectionary and Its Relation to Scripture

The Importance
of the Lectionary

·1

The beginning of Jesus' public ministry is portrayed in a most dramatic way by the author of the Gospel of Luke and The Acts of the Apostles. The scene occurs in the synagogue at Nazareth, shortly after Jesus had surmounted the temptations in the wilderness. The attendant handed him the scroll of the prophet Isaiah, whereupon Jesus read a passage from the 61st chapter:

> The Spirit of the Lord is upon me,
>   because he has anointed me
>   to proclaim Good News to poor people,
>   he has sent me to announce release to captives
>   and sight to the blind,
>   to set the bruised at liberty,
>   to announce the year of the Lord's favor   (Luke 4:18f.).

He then gave the scroll to the attendant, sat down, and spoke to the congregation: "Today this scripture is fulfilled in your hearing."

At a later time, Judaism had a fixed lectionary in which there were two lessons for each Sabbath, one from the Torah (the Pentateuch) and one from the Prophets. We cannot prove the theory advanced by some Jewish scholars that this system existed as early as the time of Jesus, but St. Luke the evangelist may have assumed that the Lord was using the prophetic reading prescribed for the day.

"Today this scripture is fulfilled in your hearing." This states exactly

3

one of the purposes of a Christian lectionary. It is to take a pericope from the ancient book and to let it speak directly to the people. They are to hear it in such a way that it expresses what was uttered in the past and is also a word directed to them in their own situation.

No one knows just when and how lectionaries came into use in the Christian Church. According to some recent theories, three of the gospels—Mark, Matthew and John—were constructed on the plan of the Jewish liturgical year and intended to be read in sequence, but this cannot be established. Nor is there any clear evidence that the Church adopted the Synagogue's scheme for reading the OT.

We have in fact very little information that is earlier than the fourth century. In the eastern Church continuous reading was apparently the prevailing custom, as it is still in the Nestorian and Jacobite churches. The Greek Orthodox adopted a semi-continuous scheme in the ninth century. The earliest western lectionaries date from the fifth century. Certain books of Scripture were associated with specific seasons of the year, and there are traces of continuous reading. In early spring, when fields and vineyards were being prepared (Septuagesima and the Sundays following), sections such as the parables of the Laborers in the Vineyard and the Sower were read. Festivals interrupted whatever sequences there were, and certain pericopes clustered around saints' days. Two lessons, one always from the gospels, were standard practice in the west, but sometimes there were more.

During the middle ages there were gradual changes. The traditional lectionary, which had local variations by the sixteenth century, became the basis for the reforms adopted by the Roman Catholic, Lutheran and Anglican communions. The Missal of 1570, adopted in connection with the Council of Trent, made some changes in the ancient pattern. Luther took over most of the historic readings but added some new lessons at the close of the Church year. One of his purposes was to encourage preaching from the pericopes. After the Reformation the Lutheran lectionaries tended to vary somewhat in the several national churches. The Book of Common Prayer of the Church of England took most of its readings from the Sarum Missal, the standard of the diocese of Salisbury, which was also in use in some other parts of England.

All of these lectionaries were similar to one another, and on a one-year cycle. As a result, many passages of Scripture were never read at the Eucharist in the liturgical churches. Some pericopes, such as Gal. 4:21–31, read on the fourth Sunday in Lent, were so obscure that the average reader could not understand them without explanation.

John Calvin favored a single reading at each service, and this custom was followed by many of the Reformed churches. The more radical Protestant churches rejected lectionaries altogether.

Lectionaries Now in Use

The principal reason for having a lectionary is the conviction that it is the right of the people to hear many parts of the Bible read in public in a systematic way. If the choice of readings is made wisely, worshippers can be enriched by a comprehensive view of the Christian faith and the moral teaching that accompanies it, can be refreshed and encouraged by the manifold spirituality of the Scriptures, and can learn the story of God's people, their struggles, defeats, triumphs, restoration, and new life, all of which is part of the heritage of present-day Christians. There is also a negative value: a congregation can be preserved from the limitations and idiosyncrasies of the individual minister.

Until 1969, the Roman Catholic Church used the lectionary of 1570. The *Ordo* that is now in use was a consequence of the reforms of the Second Vatican Council and went into use on November 30, 1969. It provides a three-year cycle with abundant readings from the OT as well as from the NT. The Presbyterian (1970), Episcopal (1970, 1976), Lutheran (1973, 1978), and Methodist (1979) lectionaries are variants of it, but all, including the Roman, have been influenced by the principles of the Liturgical Movement, in which scholars, clergy and lay people of several communions have participated.

A lectionary accepted by all the churches is much to be desired. To this end, the Consultation on Common Texts, an association representing most of the major churches in the United States and Canada, has commended a lectionary for trial use until 1986, prepared by the North American Committee on Calendar and Lectionary. This will be referred to as NA.

All of these lectionaries have been consulted in the preparation of this book, and references are given in the index. Where the extent of the pericopes varies, the longer form is often cited.

The authority of the lectionary is different in the several communions. In some churches it is prescribed by canon law, while in others its force may be advisory. Since these lectionaries are so broadly based and—like the Bible itself—free from particular confessional interests, a leader in worship is wise to follow them, except when special events and circum-stances demand a change.

Scripture is a gift that is entrusted to us, and it has a right to be read in such a way that it will be most effective. The lector must understand what he or she is reading and must read clearly; when the passage is eloquent, it should be presented eloquently; joyfully when joyful; always with a sense of its high seriousness, and so that the personality of the reader does not obtrude too much upon it. It is an increasing custom to invite lay persons, men and women, including the young, to read the lessons, but the readers should be carefully selected and properly trained for the privilege.

Many parts of Scripture preach themselves if they are read well, and need little or no exposition. Others just as clearly call for historical and theological background for their understanding. In addition, the homily is an integral part of public worship, and we shall argue that liturgical preaching is essential to effective use of the lectionary.

The Liturgical Year

The lectionaries are based on the Christian calendar, which begins not on January 1 but on the Sunday nearest to St. Andrew's Day, November 30. The liturgical year can be divided into two roughly equal parts, the special seasons that commemorate events in sacred history, and "Sun-days of the year" or "ordinary time."

From the first Sunday of Advent through the feast of the Epiphany, and from Ash Wednesday through the Day of Pentecost, themes for the readings are set by the seasons and the events commemorated by them. The Sundays after Epiphany and after Pentecost are "ordinary time," except that the first Sunday after Epiphany celebrates the Baptism of Jesus, and in some churches the last Sunday of that season the Transfigur-ation. The first Sunday after Pentecost is devoted to the Trinity, and the last to the kingship of Christ.

Much of the "ordinary time" is given over to course reading. For example, parts of Matthew and Romans are read in partial sequence in Year A; Mark, I and II Corinthians in B; Luke and various epistles in C. The Gospel of John, other books of the NT, and the selections from the OT, are read where they seem most appropriate. The Psalms are gener-ally harmonized with the lessons.

Special readings are provided also for saints' days and other com-memorations that may fall on any day in the week. These vary in the different churches and, although they are obviously important, will not be discussed in this book.

At some points the Christian year corresponds to the Jewish year. Thus Easter comes approximately at Passover season, which is followed after fifty days by the Feast of Weeks or Pentecost. The date of Christmas came to be fixed at December 25, not far from Hanukkah (Chislev 25), which is also among other things a winter solstice festival. This parallel development came about partly by historical accident, but both liturgical years bear witness to a tendency common to many religions to have a cycle of annual festivals and fasts. In primitive religion this is part of the "myth of the eternal return," as Mircea Eliade calls it; that is, the belief that the eternal order is an unchanging, recurring cycle. Judaism and Christianity have found this useful, for there is that which does not change. In addition the annual cycle is helpful psychologically and educationally.

Principles behind the Lectionary

Behind the lectionaries there is a principle basic to Christian theology from the beginning, that the New Covenant and the Old Covenant are intimately related. Sometimes this is stated in the maxim, *Novum testamentum in vetero latet, vetus testamentum in novo patet;* that is, the NT is latent in the Old, the OT lies open (patent) in the New.

From the early centuries on, this principle has influenced preaching and teaching. At times it has been carried to such absurd lengths that much of the Hebrew Bible was deprived of its true and original meaning and used merely as a quarry for prophecies of Jesus Christ and the time of salvation. Yet there is genuine continuity between Judaism and Christianity, and the process of finding the connections began with the NT writers themselves. As we consider proper methods of interpretation, we shall summarize the ways in which the NT uses the OT.

The lectionaries now in use try to apply the concept of continuity in a way that is honest to historical fact and to the true meaning of the OT. One way to state the principle by which pericopes are placed together is to say that the two testaments interlock with one another. Sometimes the NT passage reinforces the message of the OT and carries it further, at other times it contrasts the old and the new, and often simply alludes to stories and insights found in the Hebrew Bible.

Christians, by faith, see in the Scriptures one continuous story of God's dealing with humanity which reveals his nature and purpose.

Ideally the lectionary should help members of the Church to see this clearly and thereby receive guidance for thinking, prayer and action. The purpose of the Bible is not to teach us natural science or history, or to satisfy our curiosity by predicting the future, but rather to unite us to God through Christ. A consideration of how the Scriptures are used in the lectionary may show us how this purpose can be accomplished.

The Lectionary and the Spiritual Life

It may not be immediately apparent but it is nonetheless true that the lectionary can foster the personal development of the priest or minister. Some clergy are under obligation to celebrate or concelebrate the Eucharist daily or to recite such offices as Morning and Evening Prayer. The lectionary provides a systematic method of reading the Scriptures. To take a little time of silence and to meditate on each pericope, and mentally to offer a brief prayer, is a good way to begin the day. Many men and women, in many parts of the world, are doing the same thing at every moment.

It is hard to describe what happens as a result of these devotional exercises, but we who have engaged in them for a number of years are convinced of their value. One becomes better acquainted with the text and perceives meanings and applications that have not previously been noticed. The effect on the subconscious mind may be even more profound, for the minister has formed the habit of coming quietly into the presence of God. This, together with the critical and exegetical study of the Bible, which ought to be a part of sermon preparation, forces close attention to the text, tends to make one think religiously about other aspects of the day's work, to reflect on what is to be seen all around and to ask what God thinks about it. As a result, prayers of aspiration, thanksgiving and intercession can arise naturally and spontaneously throughout the day. We are often distracted, sometimes depressed or fearful or angry, but systematic reading of the Scriptures brings us back to the quiet place where our heavenly Father is always present.

Good preaching does not come just from finding a text or passage, studying it with commentaries and other helps, looking for illustrations, and making applications. Prayerful use of the Bible reminds the preacher that he or she represents the Church and is responsible to it and to the word of the Scripture and therefore must not intrude with his or her prejudices and peculiarities. Yet the homily comes also out of personal conviction. Sensitive preachers have listened to the Scriptures and have let them be woven into the fabric of their thinking about the people whom they meet and the life of the community and the world. A good sermon is germinated over a period of time, often in ways of which we are not quite conscious.

The Canon of Scripture

One of the purposes of the lectionary is to find unifying strands in a religious literature containing great varieties. It does so by selection and arrangement. But such a process had already gone on while the Scriptures were in the making. The Bible is a collection of collections of books, and what is contained in each of them was determined (as it is in the case of the lectionaries) by the consensus of a religious community.

The Old Testament (i.e., books of the Old Covenant; see II Cor. 3:14) is the name that Christians give to the Hebrew Bible. It is a deposit of traditions, some of which go back at least as far as the time of Moses, that contains all the surviving literature of an entire people down to the time when Ezra returned from exile, and most of its subsequent writing down to about 164 B.C., a period of roughly a thousand years.

Yet it is not just a national library. It is a selection made for the purposes of a community of faith. That community determined its limits by excluding other writings, now mostly lost; and it edited the books, gave them their present shape, and arranged them in order. Hebrew traditions were at first oral, and the first extensive writings, the court history of David and the document conventionally called J which underlies much of the Pentateuch, were evidently composed about the time of Solomon. Traditions from the north, known as E, were later added to J.

Many laws, formulae used in worship, and proverbial sayings already existed, but the first attempt to codify the traditional law, so far as we know, was in the book discovered in the time of Josiah (II Kings 22:8–13), which makes up most of the Book of Deuteronomy. It was evidently produced in the northern kingdom of Israel and brought to Jerusalem by refugees after the destruction of that nation. The first stage in making up the OT canon was the collection of the Torah or Pentateuch during the exile. This was the work of priests, who took over the functions previously exercised by scribes of the royal court of Judah. They made the Pentateuch into a story beginning with creation and continuing through the death of Moses, relegating sources that dealt with later events to another collection, and into this narrative they wove legal and other materials. The purpose was to guarantee survival of the Jewish people, now mostly in exile, as a religious community and to prevent its assimilation. The Torah gave the people its identity, reminded them of their origins and early history, and provided a basic guide for community and individual life.

In ancient times only a few people were literate. Writing occurred when something had to be preserved, and a religious canon was formed only when there was tension or controversy that required a fixed standard. During the period of the Hebrew monarchy, such prophets as Amos, Hosea, and Isaiah were often in conflict with the priestly and royal authorities. Their message was a direct insight into the will of Yahweh and also a call to return to the ancient traditions of the period before the monarchy. Deuteronomy was the first attempt to bring prophecy and legal traditions together as a basis for unity and peace.

The point becomes even clearer when we realize that it was priestly scribes who brought together the second part of the canon, containing the Former Prophets (historical books, Joshua through Kings) and the Latter Prophets (Isaiah, Jeremiah, Ezekiel and the book of the Twelve). Prophets are always hard for a community to digest, even when as in the case of Jeremiah the prophet is in the deepest sense loyal to the community; and the canonical process involved editing and amplifying the prophetic writings and domesticating them to a degree. The respect shown the prophets is, however, significant; and as a result the canon preserves the tension between the prophet on the one hand and the royal establishment, priest or scribe, on the other. We should not think of this as a contest between prophets and priests—some prophets were also priests and they did not oppose priesthood as such—rather it was a matter of some prophets and priests against other prophets and priests. It is characteristic of the canon (in the NT also) that irreconcilable viewpoints are put side by side and not always harmonized. This reflects respect for tradition and responsibility to the community. Those who made any part of the canon hoped that matters would now be in equilibrium, but the process had to be repeated.

There is great variety in the Latter Prophets, and the books written in the Persian period after the exile show that prophecy was gradually transformed into apocalyptic, a process that we shall discuss later. When the prophetic canon was closed and it was believed that prophecy had ceased, the impulse which had given rise to prophecy manifested itself in apocalyptic and in the interpretation of what was now regarded as Scripture. This can be illustrated by the way in which the prophetic books were edited and by the tone of Malachi, which concludes the canon.

The third part of the Hebrew canon is known as the Writings. The Psalms are the heart of this collection, and the other most important element consists of the wisdom books: Proverbs, Job and Ecclesiastes. Ruth and Esther tell of two famous women; the Song of Songs is a collection of love and marriage songs; the Lamentations speak of the exile and destruction of the Temple. Daniel is an apocalypse. Ezra-Nehemiah recounts the return to the Holy Land, and the canon concludes with the two books of Chronicles, which are a priestly rewriting of history down to the time when Cyrus ordered the return of the exiles. By making this arrangement, the collectors reinterpreted history so as to idealize the reigns of David and Solomon and teach that the priestly arrangements of the second, post-exilic Temple had been ordained by these kings.

The theological purpose of this collection was to integrate a rich wisdom tradition, much of which was as old as law and prophets, into the Bible as a whole and to harmonize it with prophecy, the legal tradition, and worship. Apocalyptic, represented by Daniel, had replaced prophecy to some degree, but its assumptions did not fit well with the majority tendency of Judaism to adjust to conditions in this world and to observe the law in daily life. Other apocalypses were rejected, but Daniel's strict loyalty to the law made the book suitable for reading. The Jews were able to include all these books because of the tradition that they had been written by David, Solomon, Jeremiah and other worthies who lived no later than the time of Ezra.

It is often assumed that a council of rabbis at Jamnia (Jabneh) decided on the limits of the canon late in the first century A.D. after the fall of Jerusalem, but this is no more than conjecture. All that can be said is that a consensus emerged not earlier than this date.

Thus in the time of Jesus the canon of Writings was still open-ended. The Dead Sea Scrolls show that the Essenes had a larger collection. The Old Greek version, usually known as the Septuagint, which was produced by Alexandrian Jews in the third century B.C. and later, contained several books that are now called Apocrypha or deuterocanonical books. This was the Bible of the early Christians and it has come down to us only through the Christian Church. It has an arrangement of the books that differs both from the Hebrew canon and present-day Christian Bibles.

The Alexandrian canon, with slight variations, continues in use in the Orthodox and Roman Catholic communions to this day. At the time of the Reformation, Martin Luther contended that only books in the Hebrew canon should be deemed authoritative, and the Protestant churches have followed this rule, except that in the Church of England fourteen deuterocanonical writings were included as Apocrypha, to be read in church but not used to establish any doctrine.

The NT likewise grew gradually. The four gospels and ten letters ascribed to St. Paul were probably the nucleus, and they were made official in response to the heresy of Marcion. Acts and the Pastoral Epistles were soon joined to them. For a few centuries there was no complete consensus. Some churches included some of the so-called Apostolic Fathers and so had more than the present twenty-seven books, while others had fewer. Our present collection was determined by general agreement and largely because of the influence of two Church Fathers, St. Athanasius, bishop of Alexandria, and St. Jerome, the translator of the Latin version known as the Vulgate. The decisions of councils had little to do with it.

The Canon as Norm and Authority

The canons of the OT and NT grew out of the consensus of a worshipping community that desired to have a definitive collection of books as a guide to faith and life. A careful reading of the Bible shows, however, that even if there was an attempt to put these books in a certain theological and historical perspective by means of selection, editing and arrangement, the several writings contained conflicting reports of historical fact and opposing points of view.

Attempts to smooth out the Bible, either ancient or modern, so that it speaks with a single voice, simply will not work. They result in a blurred, confused picture or in a particular theological line that an individual theologian or a community defends by selecting some elements and disregarding or distorting others. In addition, the canons were framed by living communities that developed and never stood still.

Thus Judaism was never able to use the Hebrew Bible without the help of an oral tradition that was continually amplified. Before the NT canon was agreed upon, there was a Christian tradition of interpreting the OT and even of such NT books as were deemed authoritative. Just as in the case of the Septuagint, the NT had fringes for a long time, and there were local churches that read some of the Apostolic Fathers and other books. The second century writings that have been preserved to us, as well as Jewish writings that were never in any Bible, not to mention other literature, are essential for a full understanding of the NT in its setting.

Since all parts of the Scriptures are the deposit of a living tradition, and since like extra-biblical tradition they contain such divergent viewpoints, the famous controversy between Catholics and Protestants over the authority of Bible and tradition is now seen in a different light. Scripture is not prior to tradition, nor on the other hand is tradition prior. The two stand together and are part of one process. For all churches the canon has unique normative value, but it has no single theological point of view except in the broadest sense. Rather it exhibits the variety of insights that can guide the churches and their members. It is not a theological treatise but a group of books written from faith and for faith (Rom. 1:17). The canon as a whole must be taken seriously, but so must the many parts that make it up.

In Chap. 4 we shall discuss principles of interpretation, but at this point we may begin by asking whether some parts of Scripture are more important than others. It is tempting to try to find a "canon within the canon" that is a guide to the rest, especially since the critical method often makes it possible to distinguish earlier traditions from later ones and to trace the development. For example, the biblical theology movement that was influential in the 1950's regarded the message of the eighth and seventh century prophets as the heart of the OT. There has long been an attempt to recover the earliest form of Jesus' teaching and to regard this, or the message of Paul, or both (somehow harmonized) as the norm by which the rest of the NT is to be understood and assessed.

It is necessary to isolate the various stages, because otherwise there is no historical perspective, but in the case of the OT there are values in the legal and wisdom traditions that we neglect to our peril. And, while the earliest forms of Jesus' teaching do have unique value for us, his teaching as it stands in the gospels is formulated so much in the light of the Church's faith that we can only approximately arrive at his original words. The later books of the NT disclose the Church as it tried to understand the revelation and apply it to community life, and these Christians are our forebears.

The Bible needs to be read with a historical understanding that has in view both the earliest recoverable traditions and also the canon as it stands. The lectionaries are so broadly based with respect to the NT pericopes, that they are a "canon within the canon" only in the sense of selection, and are a fair sampling of biblical literature. They are not quite so successful in presenting the wealth of the OT.

Principal Themes of the Old Testament
A fresh look at the OT causes one to observe that it contains an amazing variety of content and literary forms. Stories, laws, proverbs, prophecies, psalms and prayers seem almost to be jumbled together. The deuterocanonical books continue this variety almost to the time of Jesus. The NT has a narrower range, both in time and content, but it represents most of the Christian writing that has been preserved to us from the earliest days of the Church.

Is there a central thread, something that might be used as an organiz-ing principle and a guide to reading, that runs through all these books? Or, if there are several threads, which are the most important?

The impression one gains from the lectionaries is that those who devised them have a special interest in the messianic elements which Christian tradition has always used as prophecies or foreshadowings of Jesus Christ. Although this is important as part of the Church's message, it is only one strand of the prophetic and apocalyptic parts of the OT.

It has been said that the principal theme of the Scriptures is God and the Church (more accurately, the People of God). To Christians this means the Hebrew or Israelite nation before the exile, the Jews, and the Christian community. But this obvious statement does not carry us very far.

The covenant is a concept that runs through the entire Bible, even though it is not the only way in which the relationship between God and his People is expressed. Covenants, it was believed, were established through Noah, Abraham, Moses, David and Jesus. A covenant is something like a contract or treaty, but it is not an agreement between equals. God is supreme, and the People accepts the covenant or rejects it, observes its terms or is unfaithful to them. But God is always faithful, and in the end he will restore and redeem his own People. This concept is taken up into the NT faith that a New Covenant has been inaugurated by Jesus. It is essential to grasp these convictions if we are to understand the books of the Bible.

Closely connected with the covenant idea is the conviction that the Scriptures represent also a dialogue between God and the People. The OT contains many passages in which the Hebrews believe that God has spoken directly to them. The Word of God is as important as his covenant, and the early Christians heard him speaking through Jesus Christ. The Word as recorded, however, came through many different kinds of prophets, and their oracles do not always match.

Hebrew prophets and people spoke to God; they prayed to him, appealed to him, and argued with him. The Word of God which the great prophets discerned called the nation back to its true and original vocation, but there were other prophets (Jeremiah called them false) who believed that God would always protect the kingdom against its enemies, and they supported the established order, tinged as it was with paganism. The dialogue went on among the people themselves. Job refuted the theology of his well-meaning friends, and in this controversy wished that there were an arbiter who would stand between him and his Maker, so that in the end the rightness of his cause might be proved.

In the gospels there are many dialogues between Jesus and his disciples, the crowds, and his opponents. The letters of Paul show the Apostle in frequent controversy with his churches and with other men who claimed to be apostles and who invaded his mission field. The varieties of Christology in the NT are attempts to understand the deeds and person of Jesus and they grew out of discussions among Christian teachers, as we can see by reading between the lines.

These ways of looking at God—through covenant and the ongoing dialogue—may be foreign to many of our hearers. They may be more familiar with the statement that the OT shows the development of an ethical monotheism that is presupposed and continued in the New. There was a development, though the exact lines of it are debated, but "ethical monotheism" is an abstract concept that does not do full justice to the fact that the writers of the Bible found God living and active and involved in human history.

Most of the moral teaching of the OT is related to the faith that God has established the covenant. At Sinai, Yahweh set forth a Torah. The Hebrew word *torah,* however, has a reference wider than that of our word "law," for it includes all religious teaching and tradition; yet it is true that many of the commandments have a strongly legal and juristic character. The prophets presupposed and accepted the traditional law, but it underwent continual reinterpretation, and by the time of Jesus a tradition of oral law stood alongside it.

Jesus rejected the authority of this oral tradition and gave his own radical interpretation of the written Torah in the light of God's will as he perceived it. Paul regarded the law as having an ambiguous position. In itself it was good and just and holy, but the law by itself could not bring salvation, and those parts of it that set Jews apart from other nations were not binding on Gentile Christians and were in fact likely to divert them from that faith in Christ which saves. The moral demands of the Torah were still valid but their application was always to be governed by the principle of love, the consideration for others that binds the community together.

Hebrew worship at first developed partly out of the traditional prac-tices of the neighboring nations. There were several types of sacrifice and national festivals appropriate mainly to an agricultural society. The latter are still reflected in the Jewish and Christian liturgical calendars.

A process that perhaps began with Moses purged these festivals of pagan elements and interpreted the scheme of worship in the light of the covenant. Animal sacrifice seems strange to the modern Christian, yet some types of it were communal meals in which the relationship of the worshipers was, so to speak, reinforced. In Judaism the Sabbath and the major festivals have functioned to maintain Jewish identity and to keep religious faith alive. The Psalms have always been used in Christian worship. The OT contains a large cultic element, and this must always be borne in mind if we are to understand the religion in which Jesus grew up. As to sacrifice, it was reinterpreted by Christians, especially in the Epistle to the Hebrews, as a type of the perfect sacrifice of Christ.

In the OT there is also a strand of tradition that might be called secular, insofar as anything could be in this culture where sacred and secular are not separated. This is wisdom. Originally wisdom is simply reflection upon human experience, handed down from one generation to another. The Book of Proverbs, with its maxims of prudence and morality, is the classic example of this. Hebrew ethics derived from wisdom as well as from law. The sapiential literature is that part of Scripture in which revealed truth and human wisdom touch one another, and wisdom is celebrated as one of the oldest gifts of God and thus a source of revelation. The prophets often quote traditional maxims but use them to make a more profound application (e.g., Amos 3:3-8). Psalms such as 1, 15 and 112 exhibit a blending of law and wisdom. Wisdom elements are numerous in the priestly tradition, which also combines prophecy with wisdom, and the early rabbis are often called "sages." Jesus was like the prophets in adapting wise sayings to his specific message (Matt. 5:25f.; 6:24; Mark 4:25; Luke 14:7-11).

The Book of Job contains sharp criticisms of the prevailing theology of reward and punishment. There is no more persuasive or beautiful statement of the Deuteronomic doctrine than the speeches of Eliphaz, which apply this not only to the nation but also to individuals, as Ezekiel had done. Job, who knows that he is righteous and that his sufferings are undeserved, rejects this solution. So little of Job is included in the lectionaries that congregations might never hear parts of the book. Yet the homilist must ponder its ideas if he or she is to be prepared to treat the themes of justification, the problem of evil, and even of God as lord of history and creator.

Ecclesiastes (Qoheleth) is even sharper in denying that goodness, diligent toil, and wisdom itself are necessarily rewarded. All is vanity; he seems to say that what is best is to enjoy life and the work that one does (Eccl. 5:18f.). This unique book, often called cynical or skeptical, was preserved because it was attributed to Solomon, and it was made acceptable by the addition of a postscript (12:9-14) and probably other comments within the body of the book. One may ask how Qoheleth can be considered part of the biblical revelation. This is possible only if revelation is understood as a process of dialogue, and in that case the function of the book is to raise difficult questions that can dispose of cheap and easy answers and lead to deeper understanding.

Apocalyptic is an element of the OT that develops after the exile. Israel's faith in the covenant involved hope in the future of the holy People. As the northern kingdom and then Judah went into exile, this hope came to have an increasingly miraculous aspect and emerged as apocalyptic prophecy. It was believed that no matter what disasters the nation might suffer, God would restore its fortunes. This was usually, though not always, thought to be achieved through a Messiah, an anointed king descended from David.

The principal themes of the OT—the covenants, the interaction in history between God and his People, wisdom, law, worship and the Messiah—are summed up by St. Paul in Rom. 3:1f. and 9:4f. as the special privileges and glories of the Jew. These themes underwent various reinterpretations during Hebrew and Jewish history. The early Christians saw the prophecies fulfilled in an unexpected way that partly affirmed but completely changed the expectations of the ancient Hebrews. Jesus, as understood by the NT writers, was the Messiah, but not the kind of king dreamed of in the eighth century B.C. or by most Jews in the first century of our era.

Yet as we prepare to preach on an OT passage we must not read it only from a Christian point of view. The OT must be understood for what it is, and the descriptive historical method is a necessary background for honest preaching. When we proceed to the next stage, that of asking what the various parts of the Bible mean to us and to our people, it is Jesus and the OT prophets who are the most reliable guides.

Basic Themes of the New Testament

It seems so obvious that one hardly needs to say it: the central interest of the NT that determines everything else is the life, death and resurrection of Jesus Christ, and its basic doctrine is a Christology that takes various forms. Only second to this is the doctrine of the Holy Spirit, which arose to explain the remarkable experiences of the early Church. We have to remind ourselves of this, because the NT simply presupposes the knowledge of God and his activity that is found in the OT, and it does not have to repeat the message of the Hebrew Bible. Jesus looked to God the Father and spoke of him; otherwise the NT looks to God as known in Christ and in the Holy Spirit. It is necessary to emphasize this, for Christology does not stand by itself and it cannot be separated from the entire biblical doctrine of God.

Yet it is certainly true that the other great themes of the NT, i.e., the atonement, justification by faith, the redemption of mankind, the new understanding of the moral and spiritual life, and the future of the universe, all are intimately related to Christology and the doctrine of the Holy Spirit. For all its diversity, the NT in this respect is a unity.

If there is another thread that runs throughout the NT, it is the attempt of the early Christians to understand the relation between the old and the new. In a later chapter we shall discuss the typology and allegory which they applied to the OT and thereby found a bridge between the Old and New Covenants. Paul used this method; throughout his letters he was concerned with the problem of the identity, new yet old, of the Christian and the Church. His theology was more profound than the typology that he used from time to time, which was only one way to express it. The process of understanding the new event that God was creating in the world began with Jesus himself, in his proclamation of the Kingdom of God, his parables, and his controversial sayings. Thus it is not enough to preach Christology; it is also necessary to grasp and proclaim the message of Jesus.

·3

Worship:
The Context
of Preaching

T he Scriptures come to us from a worshipping community. In Judaism and Christianity, preaching in the sense of proclamation, prophetic judgment, and the building of right attitudes and action, was usually related to worship. It appears from the gospels that Jesus preached and taught in the open country, in streets and public squares, and from a boat, but sometimes in the synagogues. Luke's account of his visit to Nazareth suggests that his message may have been directly related to the liturgy of the day. It aroused hostility, yet there were those who marvelled at the words of grace that he spoke.

The principal purpose of the homily is to serve as an integral part of public worship. The participants are to be brought into the presence of God. Faith is awakened or strengthened, and love becomes more fervent. The worshippers should be able to go out into the everyday world with a new perspective, ready to bring the vision they have seen and the word they have heard into their many relationships. This is particularly the purpose of eucharistic worship.

This is not always recognized, for we have been in churches where the sermon had scant relation to the rest of the worship, which consisted of miscellaneous "opening exercises" preceding the sermon. What was said may even have had little to do with the Bible. Twenty to thirty minutes were spent in teaching doctrine, exhorting to moral conduct, taking a stand on current issues, dealing with personal problems that the hearers might have, or even promoting the immediate concerns of the institution. All of these have their place but they are subordinate to the main purpose of the homily.

If we are to understand the true function of preaching, it is best to reflect on the nature of worship. Worship is an activity common to all mankind, in every place and time. Here one should think not only of the great world religions but also of the so-called "primitive" ones, for certain elements are shared by all.

Human Language

Worship is a particular kind of human speech, and it implies a world view, a way of looking at reality. This is evident in the very fact that it is addressed to the unseen God and speaks of this God revealing himself to human beings. Since it is possible to deny that there is a Being who can thus be worshipped, and yet prayer is such a universal activity, a theology of worship should properly consider the nature of language and the function of religious speech as part of it.

Although there are many languages on earth, articulate speech is an endowment of all humanity and more than any other factor distinguish- es human beings from other animals. It constitutes humanity as a whole and also each individual. When the infant begins to speak, he or she creates a world; that is, the child is now in communication with other objects and persons. Its experiences and relations can now form a coherent whole; this is its world. The world exists objectively, to be sure; but the subjective, experienced world of each individual is that which he knows, directly or indirectly, and it is language that organizes this world for him. The member of a completely isolated tribe in New Guinea lives in a much smaller world than does the inhabitant of a large city in a western nation, but everyone has a world in which, in a sense, he is at the center.

When human beings began to name things, classification and identification became possible, and through communication they were able to control the environment as never before. The ancient Hebrews showed their consciousness of the unique power of language by telling the story—not really naive—of how God brought all the animals to Adam to see what he would call them (Gen. 2:19-20). Once something is named—a new chemical compound, a newly discovered species of plant, or a pathological condition—it is distinguished from all other objects, and the scientist has a certain control over it. No wonder that the ancients ascribed magical power to the name.

Language consists of action words (verbs) and relation words as well as nouns. The human mind is able to make a syntax and create coherent sentences; language and thinking seem to be two aspects of one operation. We may suppose that the earliest human beings, as they exercised their new powers, found the world full of wonders.

Words are, after all, symbols that point to something else, and a single word can refer to more than one object, action or relationship. The meanings of words are extended by metaphorical use. The verb "run" denotes an activity of our bodies, but we say that water or an electric motor "runs." The Latin word for "run" gives us "current," which can mean a current of water or electricity or refer to events that are now "occurring." This basic use of language makes classification and abstraction possible. It leads to the images of poetry and the speech of worship and also to logical, discursive speech.

Many primitive people even today are animists who regard nearly all objects as living or possessed by spirits. That which they can name must have life. In a prescientific society many events were mysterious and their causes were ascribed to the activities of spirits or divine beings who could sometimes be influenced by the spoken word.

Logical reasoning and science became possible when human beings observed that one event regularly follows another. This is reflected in speech, so that special words and constructions are evolved to express new concepts. The Greeks in the sixth century B.C. began to develop a scientific vocabulary. The ancient Hebrews were rational people also, but the vocabulary of the OT uses vivid pictures and metaphors and tends to be concrete rather than abstract. Hebrew speech made no distinction between the natural and the supernatural. The truths perceived by the Israelites were expressed in myth, that is, sacred story.

Scriptural speech and religious speech in general can be understood better when one reflects on the many kinds of speech, oral and written, with which we are familiar. We have, for example, stories, songs, poems, political speeches, commencement addresses, advertisements, legal briefs, personal and business letters, and scientific monographs. Each of these reflects a different situation that calls for a specific form and often a special vocabulary. The Scriptures likewise contain a variety of forms, each of which has its own purpose.

Sacred Story

Although these various forms are used in the Bible for worship and instruction, they were in the same kind of language that people used in daily life as they spoke with one another and dealt with mundane problems. The difficulty faced by modern readers of the Scriptures is that their language, and that of many forms of worship, is foreign to everyday ways of speaking and to scientific and historical discourse. We have specialized our speech to a much greater degree than did the ancients.

The very idea that God *is,* and that there can be prayer and worship, presupposes that there is reality beyond that which can be photo-graphed, tape-recorded, weighed or measured. What we know by ordi-nary verifiable means is real, but the Scriptures know of another dimension to reality.

Although men and women live in one world, they experience many different kinds of worlds. Whatever their relationships may be—famil-ial, geographical, national, and cultural—these constitute their subjec-tive world, and we are acquainted with the cultural shock sustained when one is forced to adjust to a different world.

Worship, in Christianity or in any other religion, can be said to create a "virtual" or ideal world. Religious people prefer to say that it brings them into this world, which truly exists and makes sense out of the chaotic world of ordinary experience. Through worship they are taken out of everyday time and space into the true existence where they properly belong. A cultic calendar, such as that of the Jewish and Christian years, and a specially built temple are symbols of this.

Worship is always connected with what is technically called a "myth." This word, which properly means "sacred story," is a neutral term that neither affirms nor denies the truth of the story. The myth almost always tells how the world and humanity came into existence and what they were like in the beginning. It indicates also how human beings lost the happy condition they had in that primitive time, and directs how life is to be lived. Recitation of the story is an essential part of the liturgy, and together with the actions and prayers that accompany it, is the means by which worshippers are brought back for the time being into the ideal space and time where they truly should be.

The sacred story of the Hebrews and the later Jews and Christians was not, however, completely mythical. It was based also on historical mem-ory, and as we find it in the Scriptures history was interpreted as controlled by actions of God in rescuing his People from Egypt, gathering the tribes, establishing a covenant with them, and leading them in the battles by which they won the Promised Land. This is not the kind of history that scientific historians write; it is sometimes called "saga," but it is part of what we are calling sacred story. Just so the stories of creation are not those of modern science and should not be confused with it. But both saga and creation myth were based on faith in the one God. They determined the self-understanding of the People of God and influenced them in their historical actions as well as in their worship.

The creation story in Gen. 2:4b—3:24 can be classified as a "myth" in this sense. One should compare it with the later priestly account in Gen. 1:1—2:4a, which belongs to a more developed stage of theological thought and is in strong contrast to Babylonian and other creation myths from the ancient Near East. The Scriptures contain other stories of sacred time that tell of events significant for the establishment of a holy People and the laws and worship that give them identity. Such are the Exodus from Egypt and the giving of the Law through Moses, and the supreme example for Christians is the story of Jesus' birth, ministry, death and resurrection. In fact the whole Bible, from Genesis to Revelation, has sometimes been called a comprehensive myth, although it contains a great deal besides.[1]

Two examples will illustrate how Jewish and Christian worship have patterns similar to that of primitive people in many parts of the world. The Jewish Seder, celebrated at Passover time, makes the participants contemporaneous with the events of the escape from Egypt. The liturgy emphasizes throughout that it is *we* who were rescued, and everyone hears the definite command: "In each and every generation a man must regard himself as though it were he who came forth from Egypt." There is also the promise of the future: "This year here; next year in Jerusalem!"

Similarly the Christian liturgies for Holy Week and Easter bring the worshipping community into the time of past events and make these more than just a memorial. We "proclaim the Lord's death, until he come" (I Cor. 11:26). Eastern Orthodox piety often speaks of the liturgy as bringing heaven and earth together. One lives in a different time and a different space.

[1]Northrop Frye, *Anatomy of Criticism* (Princeton: Princeton University Press, 1971), pp. 316-326. See also his book *The Great Code* (New York: Harcourt Brace Jovanovich, 1982).

In primitive religion the sacred time is in the indefinite past, and there is no sense of an ongoing history or development. Time is, so to speak, cyclical; it repeats itself, and in theory the tradition never changes, though in fact it does.

We can understand this sentiment because in our faith we desire that which is permanent, secure and absolutely real. Religious people are conservative in that they wish to conserve cherished values, even though they may differ as to what those values may be. Those who accept even the most radical and innovative religious movements believe that they are coming back to something that is in danger of being lost. The Jewish oral tradition, which continually adapted the Torah to new circumstances, was in theory given to Moses on Mount Sinai. Christians believe that there is a "faith once delivered to the saints."

But life and history never stand still. It might be supposed that the myths of primitive societies would prevent change and progress, but just because the myths and rituals are in symbolic language and so are open to various interpretations, the myth itself can stimulate human beings to creativity. The true world is not closed but open because the symbols—often operating through the unconscious mind—work on the religious imagination. Prophets and holy men renew and revivify the older symbols through prayer, meditation and sudden insights.

Judaism—and consequently Christianity—broke out of the cyclical notion of reality because it had a sense of history that is lacking in Babylonian, Syrian and Egyptian mythology. God's saving acts are rooted in ordinary history, history that has an indefinitely extended line and a purpose. The story of creation in Genesis is of course prior to history, but otherwise the religious, poetic, imaginative interpretation is applied to events that from any point of view actually took place.

Liturgical time, as we see it in the Jewish and Christian calendars, is circular and brings us back, year after year, to our origins. In Christian worship the cycle of the Lord's birth, life, Cross and Resurrection permits us to identify ourselves with him and morally to follow his example. But this does not divest history, past and present, of its reality.

The Power of the Word

A liturgy depends on sacred story but it also includes response and action on the part of the worshipping community, expressed in prayer, praise, and other acts. These do not "change God's mind," even though the OT sometimes uses such language (Exod. 32:14), but the Christian has faith that God hears prayers and that something important is accomplished by the act of worship. That it affects the believer personally is beyond doubt; other results must be left to the loving kindness of God.

Certainly speech can be, to use the term of some philosophers, performative. When a judge delivers a verdict of "Not guilty," the legal and sociological situation of the person at the bar is changed. In theological speech it is said that when God justifies (acquits, vindicates) the sinner the decision cannot be questioned. God is just, and the sinner is now a righteous person who has a future. To take other examples: when a president signs a bill, or the partners at a wedding say "I do" and the minister says, "I pronounce you husband and wife," a significant act has occurred.

Much religious speech has this character. "God said, 'Let there be light,' and there was light" (Gen. 1:3); "the Good News . . . is a power of salvation" (Rom. 1:16). Hence the Fourth Gospel proclaims, "In the beginning was the Word" (John 1:1). *Logos* here may allude to a Stoic doctrine, but the earliest hearers of this gospel would have thought first of God's Word in Genesis.

Metaphorical Speech

Sacred story and liturgy are the product of the religious imagination; or, to put it in theological language, they spring from faith. God and his activities, and the realm in which he operates, cannot be described by scientific speech, but only by analogy. Hence sacred story functions through symbols and metaphors, which have a richer and wider meaning than the words and pictures in which they are expressed. From the point of view of educated western people, and particularly Christians, the world view and symbols of primitive religion seem strange and only a partial view of reality, but they are not necessarily crude or unsophisticated, because they are charged with meanings which an outsider can apprehend only with difficulty. The Jewish and Christian sacred stories differ from others in that they refer to one God and are largely rooted in historical event.

Throughout the Scriptures much of the language is metaphorical and poetic. This is especially so in the tradition of Moses, the prophetic books, the Psalms, and the teaching of Jesus, for it is supremely in such instances that the encounter takes place between God and humanity which we call revelation and inspiration.

This encounter results in story, prophecy, praise, prayer and liturgy,

and is embodied in a tradition that is finally written down in the Scriptures. The process of this encounter and the words that point to it have
analogies in the creation of poetry, music, painting and sculpture. Frequently the artist does not have a preconceived plan when he starts to
create. The poetic images, or the forms, or the melodies and harmonies
emerge as the artist uses his materials and confronts the workings of his
own mind. The finished product is seldom achieved at a single sitting;
the maker cannot tell precisely how his inspiration comes; in a sense the
work of art creates itself, though not without the artist's own intelligence
and taste. That which is created also modifies the artist; as a result he
may have new insights and emotions and be a different person.

Something like this must have been the experience of the prophets.
They began with their faith in Yahweh as just, good and loving, with
a particular care for his People. They were conscious of the pervasive
evil that impelled Israel and Judah to be unfaithful to the covenant, and
they listened to the word of God that came into their minds, often
without consciously asking for it. This experience transcended common-
ly received ideas and was so intense that often it could only be expressed
in symbolic and mythical language, and this they put in the artistic forms
of contemporary folk poetry.

We may say that this was a product of the religious imagination when
we think of its human side and use psychological language. Certainly not
all imaginative contructs are of equal value; they can include fairy tales
told mainly for amusement or as the projection of impossible desires;
they can even be hallucinations. In the eighth and seventh centuries
there were false prophets, some of whom were sincere but wrong-
headed. The true prophets were true because their vision was based on
the nature of Yahweh himself, and this was recognized by those who
came later, and supremely by Jesus himself. What has just been said
of the prophets can be applied to those who told the stories of Genesis and Exodus. They looked at the same world that others observed,
and in and beyond it saw the activity of the living God and heard
his words.

The faculty that makes possible the creation of story and prophetic
oracle does not dispense with that rational faculty of the human mind
that we call cognitive and that deals with physical facts and scientific
data. It is one and the same person who is logical and imaginative. The
prophets and Jesus did not live in a dream world, and their sayings
include a good measure of practical wisdom. But they were able to see

the world and life from a different perspective, and this we can call revelation.

This perspective is possible because the story teller or prophet is questioning the Unknown. He or she is both thinker and worshipper and seeks guidance, understanding and judgment. The voice (or some-times the vision) that arises in the mind presents a picture of ultimate reality that can be communicated, and it also transforms the person who is seeing and believing. Henceforth that person belongs to the God who is partly known and partly hidden, and to his order, but the prophet must also live in the everyday world with those who have not yet heard the message.

The prophets were inspired, but not mechanically; the vision and the voice were mediated through their reasoning minds, and they spoke some things that everyone could understand, although there were those who found some of their sayings baffling or offensive.

Worship and the Lectionary

The revelation, the new perspective, is never the private possession of the prophet; he knows that it is intended for the community. The worshipping community is constituted by a sacred story which gives it its particular character, and this is imbedded in a liturgy which is cele-brated at specific times and brings the people into contact with the divine and into what is regarded as the true time and space intended from the beginning.

We do not know exactly how the ancient Hebrews first developed their liturgy, but there are clues to this in the Book of Exodus. Like all ancient peoples they offered sacrifices and had seasonal festivals, but these were given their new specific meaning by the story that told of the covenant that God had made with them and the consequences that followed. Such psalms as 78, 89, 103–107, 114, 132 and 136 show that the story was recited in worship, and the Passover Seder is one of the significant forms of the story in Jewish tradition. The Eucharist recalls God's action in Jesus Christ and makes it an immediate experience for the participants. By implication, the story includes God's encounter with the people of the Old Covenant, but the degree to which this is explicit varies with the several eucharistic rites.

The liturgy itself brings the people into the place and time where the living God encounters them, and from this they can go out into ordinary life sustained by a new vision and a fresh word. The function of liturgical preaching is to assist the other parts of the liturgy so that the participants may hear and understand the sacred story.

Therefore the sermon should take account, when possible, of all the pericopes that are read on a given occasion and relate them to the action of the liturgy. Two problems that are involved in this must be mentioned here and will be discussed more fully in what follows.

First, any lectionary includes what the Church, at the time when the scheme is devised, considers most important for the people to hear. But this is not the whole of Scripture and does not contain the whole story; therefore the preacher needs to bear in mind the total message, even as he or she prepares to preach on a specific passage. That is why this book attempts to provide a simple theological introduction to the Bible as a whole.

Second, while the interpretation given in the homily should serve a liturgical purpose and be relevant to the needs of the hearers, it must also be historically and theologically honest. Not only is this essential to our integrity as servants of God; it is also practical. Even though not every hearer is a university graduate, the general level of eduction in a typical congregation is such that the creation stories in Genesis cannot be treated as scientific accounts, and the same can be said of many other elements in sacred story. When such passages are to be expounded, the homilist must look for the symbolic truth that lies behind the story. Scripture contains many different literary forms, each of which has a specific purpose and manner of speaking, and this affects the way in which each is to be interpreted. Because the Bible is so often misused, the preacher needs to consider sound methods of interpretation and employ them.

Interpretation

·4

We preach from the Scriptures in the context of worship. These Scriptures might be said to have resulted from preaching, at least in many cases, but such preaching was different from what is customary now. Often it was a story or the oracle of a prophet, a song or a proclamation. In most cases these messages were handed down in oral tradition and only later combined into books. The books were not written to be used in our preaching; the audience and the circumstances of writing were quite different from our own situation. Yet we use them, and in a deeper sense they use us; they determine our vocation and constitute us as preachers and leaders of worship.

A great opportunity is offered us, but the art that we practice is a delicate one: to be honest in interpreting the Scriptures and at the same time to make them instruments of God's purpose in our time and place. Whatever we do by way of application must be in harmony with the purpose of the biblical passage.

Exegesis, when narrowly defined, is the attempt to arrive at the meaning of a book or part of it, as nearly as possible as its author intended it to be heard. The first step in this is the establishment of the most probable text and then its translation. A version in English or in any other language involves judgments about variant readings, grammar and lexicography, and usually this cannot be made without reference to various passages in the book, other books of Scripture, and frequently other literature as well.

To go beyond this, and to interpret what is translated, involves two kinds of pursuits which usually go on simultaneously and can be separated only in theory. These are critical examination of the text itself and

31

interpretation of it in its wider context in Scripture and in the culture in which the biblical book was written.

Internal examination of the text properly begins with redaction criticism and form criticism, which are distinct but related methods. The final author of each book (for example, the gospels) had a distinct purpose in writing for his audience. This can be determined from the organization of the book and by comparing it with other literature. In the case of Matthew and Luke this is relatively easy, for they used Mark as a source. Although we do not have Mark's sources before us, the comparison with the other two makes Mark's specific interests stand out, and to some degree we can separate his editorial work from the materials he used. Accordingly, the theological purposes of the authors can be discerned, and we can see how they adapted the tradition to the needs of the Church. Often this is illuminating to homilist and hearers.

The gospels are a unique species of literature, designed to proclaim Christ and awaken faith. This is especially true of Mark and John. Matthew adds to this a strong interest in catechetical instruction for leaders and people, while Luke comes nearer than the others to writing a "life of Jesus"; that is, he thinks of his story as a part of sacred history, beginning in the OT and continuing into the apostolic age. Matthew also has this motive, but it is not quite so prominent. Redaction criticism can be applied to other books of Scripture also.

Form criticism goes back of the written books to study the traditions contained in them. The literary forms of the tradition were originally oral and each form had a specific function, or situation in life. A psalm or oracle of a prophet has a function different from that of a legend, a proverb, or a law, and because it is poetic and metaphorical the oracle or hymn should not be understood as ordinary prose. By isolating these pieces from materials that have been added, it is possible to distinguish stages of tradition. In the case of Jesus' teaching, the life situation of his ministry is not identical with that of the early Church, and the process of form criticism brings the distinctive character of his message into sharper focus.

Since form criticism deals not merely with literary forms but also with setting in life, it requires inquiry into secular history, archaeology, and the religious and cultural background of the text. Fortunately the preacher does not have to do all of this for himself, because of the excellent commentaries, dictionaries, atlases of the Bible, and other helps that are available. The point we are making is that to understand a biblical passage we must look at a tradition that is present in more than one stage, often several. We cannot often speak of the "original" meaning of a story or saying, only the earliest that is recoverable.

On which stage of the biblical tradition should the homilist focus his meditation and preaching? The earliest recoverable or the interpretation given it by Synagogue or Church? In every case he or she will have to make the decision. It is often helpful to disclose both to the hearers. When one discusses a parable or saying of Jesus, the two are usually closely woven together, but his original thought and intention (so far as we can discern these) are likely to be more arresting and important than later interpretations; yet this does not imply that his early Christian followers have nothing to teach us. In studying the text, the preacher should try to bear the whole tradition in mind.

Exposition

Sometimes a preacher moves back and forth between exegesis and exposition without being conscious of what he or she is doing. Exposition is the art of taking these ancient stories, prophecies, laws, or pieces of wisdom, and applying them to the issues and needs of human beings in our communities. There always has to be a distinction between "what was said then" and what God says now, and often it is well to admit this frankly in the homily itself.

One can argue that exposition is a proper part of exegesis, and that the process of interpretation is not complete until a connection is made with present-day life and thought; otherwise the sacred text remains only an archaeological discovery. Henry Cadbury published a book entitled *The Peril of Modernizing Jesus*[1] but he also wrote an article, "The Peril of Archaizing Ourselves." What is urged here is simply that the homilist be clear about the process and not confuse his own applications with the intent of the text. Scripture itself contains exposition of previously existing texts. One example of this is the way in which Wisd. 15:18—18:19 interprets the story of the plagues on the Egyptians.

We can illustrate this further by examining the parable of the Sower (Mark 4:3-9) and its application (4:13-20). When Jesus spoke the parable, the point may not have had anything to do with the seed that fell among thorns or on stony ground, for the emphasis was not on that part of the story but on the marvelous harvest on the good land, which symbolized

[1]New York: Macmillan, 1937.

the surprise and joy of the Kingdom that God was bringing. To understand this in the context of Jesus' ministry is strict exegesis.

The interpretation that Mark gives does not fit that context. It presupposes the situation of the Church's second generation, when some
Christians do not remain firm in the face of persecution or have worldly
cares and delight in riches. We cannot say dogmatically that Jesus could
not have foreseen such a situation, but the passage looks like an early
attempt at exposition, the adaptation of the parable's message to a new
situation so that it becomes an allegory of different kinds of soil. It is
a good sermon, even though it may not have been what Jesus originally
intended, and in that sense it is the word of God, but it is moral
catechesis rather than proclamation of the coming Kingdom.

Exposition, then, is building a bridge between "what was said then"
and "what must be said now." This is the task of hermeneutics, and
exposition should be based on a sound hermeneutical principle.

At first glance one might think that a simple algebraic formula would
suffice: a is to b as x is to y, with a representing the biblical situation and
b our own, x the original meaning of the passage and y the solution
called for. But it is not that simple. Too often the method results in
nothing but a moral maxim that everyone knows anyhow, and the text
is emptied of its true life. The Scriptures require a theological reading.
If the understanding of the parable of the Sower given above is correct,
the application should be one which puts us into the position of Jesus'
original hearers. We may have no vivid faith that God will make his
Reign effective on earth, but he speaks to us that it is at hand and that
it will be more glorious than we can conceive. This is a challenge to
reflect on what God's Reign might be and to perceive, so far as we can,
the signs of his powerful presence. Such signs were to be seen then; are
we willing to look for them now? The seed has been sown.

Theological Understanding

Liturgical preaching is necessarily theological. When we use this word
we are not thinking of something abstract or technical (though philosophical theology has an important place in our thinking) but of ways
to let the text speak God's word to us.

Exegesis can contribute directly to this. As Gerard Sloyan has said,
the "primary literal sense" of most of the important passages in the
Bible is a poetic or symbolic meaning. The biblical writers were not
primarily concerned with history or prediction, and to suppose that

their language is literally, historically "true" is to misjudge their purpose. They were conveying symbols of a God who is partially revealed and partially hidden.

In Chapter 2 we discussed the themes that run through the two testaments. These are the basic insights of the Bible, and the lectionary is most effective when symbols used in the OT harmonize with those in the New. The symbols underwent reinterpretation in the OT and this continued in the NT, as we can see from the concept of the covenant.

Jesus proclaimed the Reign of God, which is implied in the OT. He intended to fulfil the Law and the Prophets, not to abrogate them; but with his teaching a new element came into Judaism. When we isolate his sayings from the interpretations added by the tradition and the gospel writers, we find that he nearly always took the OT at face value and interpreted it in its own terms (see, e.g., Matt. 4:4, 7, 10). At times he heightened its demands (Mark 10:2-9; Matt. 5:21f., 27f., 38-42) or gave the moral commandments precedence over the cultic. Thus he followed the main line of OT teaching rather than its details and (as he and we believe) disclosed God's original intention. Some theologians call this the *sensus plenior* or fuller meaning of Scripture.

The Cross and Resurrection amounted to a revolution, and the early Church was faced with the problem of understanding how the old and the new related to one another. Interpretations of the OT that owe something to the Jewish methods of the time play an important part in early Christian literature.

A passage in I Cor. 10:1-13 exhibits clearly the point of view of several NT writers. I have said rather bluntly that the Hebrew Bible was not written originally for our purposes, but Paul saw it otherwise. The gifts of God to the Hebrews in the wilderness, and their rebellion and punishment, he says, were examples and warnings *for us;* that is the first point. Second, the interpretation here, as elsewhere in the NT, is governed by Christological faith; the rock that gave water was Christ, and it was he whom the Israelites put to the test. The other most important principle is eschatological: Christians are living in the final age; to us "the ends of the ages have arrived" (10:11). This is not found universally in the NT but it is prominent.

The early Christians employed several patterns of interpretation. One of these, the fulfilment of prophecy, is stated directly in Luke 4:18f. and in a whole series of passages in Matthew, and implied in such passages as the annunciation to Mary (Luke 1:31-33, which draws on Davidic messianic prophecies and language from Judg. 13:3).

Typology is closely related to fulfilment. I Cor. 10:1-13 is one of the classic examples of this, and Paul says that the events of the Exodus were types. Some of the most cherished parts of the NT use the method, and it is important to recognize it, for the lectionaries carry on the tradition. The antitypes partly match the OT types but completely transform them. Matthew finds the wonderful birth of Jesus suggested by the Greek translation of Isa. 7:14 (Matt. 1:23). Joseph, the husband of Mary, corresponds to Joseph son of Jacob, who went down into Egypt; the return of the Holy Family to Palestine matches the Exodus, and Jesus-Joshua comes into the Promised Land (Matt. 2:13-23).

Typology is implicit in the use made of the Servant Songs of Second Isaiah, and is used to show that Jesus announced good news to the Gentiles, healed diseases, and suffered death on behalf of God's People. The pattern often contrasts the partial character of the Old Covenant with the perfection of the New, as in the Epistle to the Hebrews, or reverses what happened in the past (Rom. 5:12-14; I Cor. 15:45f., Adam and Christ; see Luke 9:51-56 for another reversal). Typology can, however, distort the purpose of the OT and even the tradition of Jesus' teaching, as in Matt. 12:40 where Jonah in the belly of the whale is made a type of the Resurrection. The point of the original pericope, as we can see from the parallel, Luke 11:29-32, is that the "sign of Jonah" is the preaching of repentance; Matthew did not need this type to reinforce faith in the Resurrection.

Allegory is different from typology in that the story subjected to this treatment has no importance in itself. Every one of its details means something else. The point of the story can be stated in prose and the narrative dispensed with altogether. The rabbinic tradition contains many such stories, whose form resembles the parable of the Weeds (Matt. 13:24-30, 36-43). Paul calls the story of Sarah and Hagar an allegory and interprets it as such (Gal. 4:21-31). The law in Deut. 25:4, forbidding one to muzzle the ox while it threshes out grain, was meant to be obeyed literally, but the Apostle substitutes another meaning (I Cor. 9:8-10).

Allegory is only one of many species of writing found in the Jewish books called Midrashim, which are collections of interpretative material based on passages in the OT. *Midrash* means investigation, study, or interpretation. It is evidently the "searching" of the Scriptures mentioned in John 5:39. The midrashic method of expounding an earlier text so as to make it relevant to a later situation began in the OT itself, as we remarked above. It is a free, homiletical exposition of the text that could include the telling of parables and other stories.

There are numerous examples of midrash in the NT. The stories of Jesus' nativity and childhood, though perhaps based on independent traditions, were influenced in their language and details by Jewish midrash on the birth of Moses and other parts of the OT, and the miracles in Mark are reminiscent of stories told about Elijah and Elisha.

Sometimes the midrashic method seems logical to us, but at other times fanciful, since it can depend upon peculiarities of grammar or spelling or some other single detail in the sacred text. From the NT one may observe Gal. 3:16-20 and John 10:34, and there are other quotations or allusions to passages that in the OT context had little or nothing to do with the point the evangelists were making (Matt. 8:17, 27:9f.; Luke 17:32; John 2:17).

The *arguments* based on midrashic method may not be logically compelling, but we would be poorer without the midrash. It imparts to the NT a poetic character, it stimulates the imagination, and reminds us that a truth that cannot be fully expressed in scientific discourse can be conveyed by symbols. The early Christians were fascinated by obscure places in Scripture that spoke of a rock or stone, especially because Jesus had given Simon Peter the name *Kepha* (Rock; Greek *petra,* Matt. 16:18; Mark 3:16; John 1:42). Among such passages were Ps. 118:22; Isa. 28:16; 8:14f.; and as a result we have a rich NT midrash in Mark 12:10f.; Acts 4:11; I Cor. 3:11; Eph. 2:19-21 and I Pet. 2:4-8.

Often, of course, the NT carries on the straight literal meaning of the Hebrew Bible (Matt. 18:16; Luke 2:23f.; 4:25-27) and frequently the Scriptures are used for moral and ecclesiastical teaching (Mark 12:29-33; Rom. 12:19f.; 13:8-10).

Beyond this, the NT writers have often discerned, as Jesus did, the *sensus plenior,* the purpose of God that lies behind the whole Scripture. This is a judgment that we can make only as Christians and by faith; it is imaginative but not frivolously fanciful. Even in their typology the writers were far from being misled in seeing a single purpose of God to judge, teach, rescue, lead, feed and heal his People, and from time to time preserve a remnant for the future. We can see instances of this in the Pentecost story (Acts 2:17-21; cf. Joel 2:28-32); in the use of the Servant songs, unique in the OT; and in the way in which chapters 9-11 of Romans deal with two opposing explanations of why most Jews rejected the gospel and finally come out with triumphant faith in the destiny of Israel.

The Lectionary as an Interpretation

A glance at the lectionary for Advent and Christmas will show at once that its framers have carried on and improved a tradition that goes back to the NT itself in putting together pericopes from the two testaments. This in itself is an implied interpretation and it is primarily Christological in outlook.

A lectionary is a selection, and many parts of the Scriptures are necessarily left out; those that are included are the ones deemed most useful for the People to hear. This has the force of making a "canon within the canon," and those who have devised it do not pretend that it is perfect. Happily, several of the Christian communions have agreed on its main lines and most of the specific readings. It is the best we can do at the moment. Recent writers have, however, criticized it because so many important OT passages have been omitted. Those that are prescribed are often brief, and many of the great stories and oracles of the prophets do not appear at all. Very often the OT reading merely subserves the theme of the NT pericope.

The remedy for these deficiencies is not to depart from the lectionary, but for the homilist to study the OT more fully so that he can bring his learning to bear on the passages from which he preaches. The program of the parish can also include classes of instruction in which at least some members of the congregation can gain a deeper understanding of Scripture.

Up to this point we have suggested some of the principles of sound interpretation, but we have not shown how they may be applied in preaching. This can only be done as we examine the pericopes of the Church year.

——————·Part Two

The Cycle of the Great Story

·5

Orientation to Advent

All parts of the lectionary, like the Scriptures themselves, are so inter-connected theologically that one could enter the web at almost any point. Advent, the season latest to be added to the Christian calendar, depends upon Christmas, and the theology of the Incarnation in turn takes its meaning partly from the event of Easter, for the Resurrection was the beginning of specific Christian faith. Since Advent opens the liturgical year, it is the place to begin; but all other parts of the cycle have to be presupposed.

At first glance, Advent appears to be a curious collection of various themes of "coming": the arrival of the forerunner John the Baptist, the announcement of Jesus' birth, the promise and threat of the Day of Yahweh, the general resurrection and the judgment. In the older lection-aries the narrative of the triumphal entry of Jesus into Jerusalem ("Palm Sunday") was also read in Advent. The season is a complex consisting of several symbols, in which the past and the future are brought into the present. The result is to arouse a faith that God in Christ is always coming, and that the proper response of the Christian is to keep alert, live in joyful hope, and be at work whenever the master of the house or the heavenly bridegroom should arrive.

The Festival of Christ the King
In the new lectionaries the Advent theme of the end of the age and the coming of new heavens and a new earth moves back into the last

41

three Sundays of the season after Pentecost or "ordinary time," so that this aspect of Scripture is fully exposed. There is so much variation in the pericopes for Sundays 32 and 33 of the Year in the six lectionaries that the reader must be referred to the commentaries on them, and only some of the passages will be discussed in this book.

The liturgical year concludes with the last Sunday before Advent. The Roman *Ordo* calls this the festival of Christ the King, and in the other churches it is essentially that even if it is not given that name. It is a fitting introduction to a study of the Advent season because it illustrates the use of important parts of the OT in the New and also the method of the lectionary in handling the Bible as a whole. The pericopes are almost identical in the lectionaries.

Year A. The parable of the Last Judgment (Matt. 25:31–46) is the magnificent climax of Matthew's eschatological teaching in chapters 24–25. The other parables of chapter 25 are read on the two Sundays of Year A preceding this. It must originally have been a parable of a King Messiah (verse 34), but the King is now given the title Son of Man. The judgment is not primarily on Jesus' disciples, who have been taught to feed the hungry and clothe the naked, but on all nations, and it holds out the promise that those who have not known the Son of Man will be accepted if they are found to have served him.

Roman Catholic commentators have been quick to point out that the emphasis of this Sunday on the lordship of Christ should not foster any temptation to "triumphalism" on the part of the Church. As Christians we can claim no special credit or pretend that we are better than everyone else. In particular we cannot reject Judaism, the religion of the OT, as an inferior religion, even though we believe that its full significance is revealed in Christ. Of course, all churches and religious groups run the danger of ascribing to themselves the glory and virtues that belong to their Lord. Matthew's parable of the Last Judgment and many other passages in the gospels exclude self-righteousness, and this implies re-nunciation of that transferred pride which while claiming little for one-self is complacent about the church to which one belongs. Paul, with bitter irony, told the Corinthians that they were behaving as though they were kings already (I Cor. 4:8), and he warned the Romans that Gentile Christians as wild olive branches must not vaunt themselves as superior to the old olive tree into which they had been grafted (Rom. 11:13–24). We have unspeakably great gifts of grace, but we are a pilgrim Church and a servant Church.

With the gospel reading there is the passage from I Cor. 15:20-28 which teaches that at Christ's coming the dead will rise, death will be destroyed, and he will establish his reign. Ezek. 34:11-24, the OT lesson, is part of the Shepherd chapter, which denounces the shepherds who have abused the flock and promises that God himself will seek out his sheep, feed them, and protect them. Elsewhere in the OT the shepherd symbolizes the King (I Kings 22:17; Jer. 10:21; 23:1-4). The prophet Jeremiah goes on to promise that a Davidic king will be the shepherd (23:5f.). Early Christians would have read this passage as a foreshadowing of the action of God in the ministry of Jesus.

Year B. The perspective of John 18:33-37 is different. Jesus, who is before Pilate, testifies that he is king, but not of this world; his function is to witness to the truth and to gather those who belong to the truth. Rev. 1:4-8, in John's letter to the seven churches, proclaims Christ's death, Resurrection and lordship over all the earth. This pericope echoes Zech. 12:10-14 and also Dan. 7:13-14, which is the OT reading for the day except in NA (Jer. 23:1-6, promise of faithful shepherds). In the Daniel passage one like a son of man comes to the Ancient of Days to receive dominion. The Episcopal lectionary adds verses 9-12, which the homilist should at least bear in mind. In Daniel the "son of man" symbolizes the Jewish nation as it will be in the future. More will be said later in this chapter about the pericope; the NT of course applies it to Jesus as Son of Man.

Year C. The gospel reading (Luke 23:35-43) suggests Christ's otherworldly kingship in still a different way. His royal power is manifested in his compassion for the individual. He has been mocked as king of the Jews, but the penitent bandit asks Jesus to remember him when he comes into his kingdom. The answer is that this man will not have to wait for the general resurrection but "Today you will be with me in paradise." In this sense the Reign of God is already established. Luke's eschatology has similarities to that of John, in that the decisive event has already occurred. It is also true that alongside the prevailing doctrine of the general resurrection there were Jews who believed that the martyrs already enjoyed blessedness in the company of the patriarchs. NA substitutes John 12:9-19.

The Roman, Presbyterian, Methodist, and NA read II Sam. 5:1-5, which tells of the anointing of David, on this Sunday. This looks forward to the pericopes of Advent. The others prescribe Jer. 23:1-6, which contains some of the themes of the Ezekiel passage read in Year A. The second reading, Col. 1:11-20, announces the lordship of Christ over the Church and the world and also his part in the creation of the universe. In this respect it anticipates the Christmas gospel, John 1:1-18.

The kingship of Christ must be understood, as in I Cor. 15, as prepara- tion for the Reign of God. This Sunday is also a key to the intention of all six lectionaries to proclaim Jesus Christ as Lord and Savior. The readings for the festival of Christ the King remind one only incidentally of the Cross and Resurrection, and they focus on the "last things," but the whole cycle of the history of salvation from Advent through Pente- cost is implicit here.

Interpretations of History in the Old Testament

The messianic and apocalyptic teaching of the last Sundays before Advent are, however, only one biblical approach to the theology of history. It must not be forgotten that the OT as a whole was the context in which Jesus and the early Christians looked at the relation of God to his People. Therefore the apocalyptic view that is seen in the festival of Christ the King should be set in the light of the Mosaic covenant, the royal theology that undergirded the monarchy of Judah, the prophets' response to this, and the gradual development of apocalyptic.

These understandings of national life and God's purpose for his People result from a combination of myth and historical memory. It was distinctive of Israel that it took past history seriously but also interpreted it through myths that were already part of the mental and spiritual life of the people.

The experience of some of the Hebrew tribes in their successful exodus from Egypt, their desert wanderings, and their conquest of the Promised Land determined how they understood their history and identity. The development of this world view is complicated, and here we can sketch only the broad outlines. We can say, however, that as they remembered these events, they had come to know Yahweh at Sinai and identified him with the high God who had been traditionally wor- shipped in various forms, but especially in two: the God of the patri- archs, and 'El, the Creator. The covenant established through Moses was made with a league of tribes.

These tribes were relatively independent of one another and during the conquest and settlement of Canaan they lived in a sort of rough democracy under charismatic persons (the Judges) who led them in war and arbitrated controversies. It was worship of Yahweh, who was their real king, that bound the tribes together, and in the covenant tradition he was thought of as the Divine Warrior. The Song of the Sea in Exod. 15 is the early and classic example of this tradition. The crossing of the Jordan near Gilgal was second only to the Exodus from Egypt in their memories and the two events are reflected in Ps. 114. Gilgal was important as a place of worship for the tribes in the early period. Josh. 24 looks like a "renewal of the covenant," but it probably records the moment when one or more tribes were added to the league at Shechem.

The monarchy was first established under Saul as a response to conflict with the Philistines. David completed the conquest and set up his capital at Jerusalem, which belonged to none of the tribes and was on the border between north and south. He was able to keep the allegiance of these fiercely independent tribes, and one example of his statesmanship was that he had two priests, one from the north and one from Judah.

Solomon built up a royal system like that of the neighboring kingdoms. His temple was designed on Syrian models, and he brought the realm into close economic, political and cultural relation with Syria. Elements of the myth and ritual of Canaan now became part of the Hebrew heritage. The Exodus-covenant tradition was historical, in that it based Hebrew identity on the acts of God in history, while Canaanite-Syrian myth thought of the supreme God as having created an unchanging order, as in the "myth of the eternal return" described in Chap. 3.

The royal theology that developed in the kingdom of Judah interpreted Yahweh as creator of the cosmos who now presided over a council of spiritual beings (Pss. 29; 82:1; 89:7). This mythical concept was purified by the insistence that Yahweh alone was to be worshipped, and it was reconciled with past history through belief in an everlasting covenant that God had established with David and his successors. Jerusalem was now the most important sanctuary—though archaeology has disclosed that there were shrines elsewhere, as at Arad—and according to a theory that is much debated, one feature of Temple worship was a festival of the enthronement of Yahweh. He was indeed king, but the earthly king was his son and representative (II Sam. 7:14). The cultus reinforced the royal institution.

The Judges had combined charismatic power with political leadership, and Samuel was the last in this line. In David's reign the prophet began to emerge as an independent figure who could declare the will of Yahweh and even call the king to account. When Jeroboam I revolted against Solomon's son Rehoboam and separated the richer northern part of the realm from Judah, it was partly because of the tyranny of royal officials but also a prophetic protest that appealed to the Exodus-covenant tradition with its rough tribal democracy under God. The kingdom of Israel was unstable. Under strong kings like Omri and Ahab, who followed pagan political and religious models, it was temporarily firm, but revolts and dynastic changes often followed. Men like Elijah and Elisha preserved the old prophetic and covenantal tradition, which appears most clearly in Amos and Hosea.

When the northern kingdom came to an end in 721 B.C., refugees from the north came into Judah and strengthened the prophetic movement that existed there. In Deuteronomy and the Deuteronomic editing of the historical books, Joshua through Kings, we can see a blending of this tradition with the belief in a permanent covenant made with David. The two traditions were always in tension with one another, as the prophecies of Jeremiah and the story of his life indicate all too clearly.

Certain parts of this development will now be considered in greater detail, but the above survey should make it clear that the OT does not have a single theology of history. The pericopes chosen for Advent and the three preceding Sundays warn against two errors. The attempt to calculate the future too precisely can lead to fanatical attitudes and behavior. But it is also wrong to neglect the warning of a coming crisis, which is constant in both prophetic and apocalpytic eschatology, and to live carelessly, as though there were no judgment, national or personal, to be faced. The eschatological teaching of Jesus is difficult to reconstruct because the early Church's expectation is so interwoven with it. Yet he often sounded the note of urgency—signs of the Reign of God were already present—and he taught his disciples to pray "thy Kingdom come." Other sayings indicate that he did not presume to second-guess what God was about to do.

The Covenant
The conviction that God, through Moses, established a covenant with the tribes lies behind the prophetic understanding of history. Merged with the later idea of a special covenant with David and his successors, it carries through into the NT and into Christian ecclesiology and ethics, even though it does not appear in all parts of the NT.

The model, or closest analogy, of the covenant idea is to be found in the international treaties of the ancient Near East between a great king and his vassals; thus it is not an agreement between equals. God offers it, and it is accepted or rejected. The Mosaic covenant has stipulations in the form of laws. If the covenant is violated, Israel is punished, but God is always faithful to his promises.

This means that God has chosen a particular people to be his own and to fulfil his purposes. When the OT canon is viewed as a whole, it appears that this People includes Abraham's descendants through Isaac, not Ishmael; through Jacob, not Esau. Ultimately the ten tribes of Israel were dispersed and mainly lost, and there remain Judah and Benjamin, but only a remnant of these. Yet Yahweh is God of the whole universe and is concerned for other nations too (Isa. 19:24f. and the Book of Jonah). The destiny of Israel, according to the covenant theology, is to follow God's will, not its own ambitions as such, and in later books of the Bible it is to be a light to the nations, an example of what a community should be.

This destiny has to be worked out in history. The faith that history has a theological meaning distinguished the Hebrew and Christian religions from most other religions of the world.

Jeroboam I, Son of Nebat, was considered a great sinner by the later biblical writers because he set up shrines at Dan and Bethel (I Kings 12:26-33; 14:7-16). Yet he acted partly at the instance of a prophet and believed that he was serving Yahweh. The Yahwistic and covenant tradition continued strong in the north. We have no writings from Elijah and Elisha, but it is clear that they protested against worship of the Baals alongside Yahweh, or of serving him with ceremonies derived from paganism. Elijah's denunciation of Ahab for the murder of Naboth and seizure of his vineyard (I Kings 21:1-19) illustrates the situation. Baalism, which Ahab's wife Jezebel promoted, was a religion of fertility and prosperity that upheld the existing order. Increase of royal power and concentration of wealth in the hands of the king and his friends had led to oppression of the poor and expecially the ruin of small farmers. This was a direct violation of the spirit of the covenant and the more egalitarian life of ancient Israel. Elijah was thus the forerunner of Amos and Hosea.

The Eighth Century Prophets

Although the oracles of the eighth and seventh century prophets are not well represented in the lectionaries, they are of great importance because of their realistic view of history and their assessment of the problems of their times. To say that more than any other part of the OT they express most purely God's purpose for the nation is a theological judgment, but it is one worth considering.

The experiences of the prophets which they interpreted as the word of God, which were discussed in Chap. 3, are related to mysticism and apparently arose out of meditations, in which the prophet's reason worked on his sudden insights. This can be illustrated from Amos, whose thoughts were triggered by a plague of locusts (7:1), a plumb-line (7:7) and a basket of summer fruit (8:1). It is significant also that these oracles are dialogues with God. Jeremiah and the Psalms contain many pleas and protests together with the divine answers. Abraham was said to have negotiated with Yahweh so that the people of Sodom might be spared (Gen. 18:22–33), and the Book of Job is the supreme example in the Wisdom literature of such a dialogue.

Out of the converse of Amos with God came oracles denouncing the oppressors of the poor (8:4–6), their idle luxury (6:1–7) and that of their wives 4:1–3). Their sacrifices are of no avail (4:4f.; 5:21–24), and their worship is profaned by ritual prostitution (2:7). Even the royal house of Jeroboam II is not spared, and Israel will go into exile (7:7–11).

Hosea, like Amos, saw no hope for the nation unless there should be a thoroughgoing repentance. He observed another factor that was to be disastrous for Israel: its alliances with foreign nations and preparations for national defense (Hos. 5:13; 7:11; 8:14; 10:13–15; 11:5).

Hosea stands in the tradition of covenant thinking, and one sign of this is that he uses the figure of the "covenant lawsuit" in which the sovereign calls witnesses to prove that the vassal has broken his promises (Hos. 4:1–6; cf. Deut. 30:19 and Mic. 6:1–8, which is the classic example of this type of speech). At the same time, he proclaims something that foreshadows Jesus' Good News. The covenant with Israel is like a marriage, and God in his love for Israel will woo back his erring wife (Hos. 1:2—2:20). The prophet uses a different figure when he speaks of his love for Ephraim (i.e. Israel) and calls him his son, whom he taught to walk (11:1–4).

Isaiah carried on the tradition of the northern prophets by denouncing the same evils, oppression of the poor which made a mockery of worship (1:10–17), pride and idolatry (2:8–22) and wanton luxury (3:16–24; 5:11f.). If Judah continues in its present ways, there can only be disaster (5:1–10). Isaiah's spiritual problem was complicated because he belonged to the southern kingdom and evidently believed in the covenant with David, whether or or not the messianic prophecies of 9:2–7; 11:1–9 are from his hand. On occasion he encouraged Ahaz and Hezekiah, but like Hosea he believed that the policy of alliances and military preparedness would lead to ruin (8:5–8). Assyria is the rod of God's anger (10:8–11) but that nation in its pride will go down to destruction (10:12–16), for it is only a temporary weapon in God's hands.

The historical and geopolitical situation is fairly easy for us to understand. The two small Hebrew kingdoms were on the narrowest part of the Fertile Crescent, the land bridge betwen Egypt and Mesopotamia. They were buffer states, and their resources and manpower could never match those of the great empires. The success of David and Solomon came only at a time when there was a power vacuum.

The prophets may have been conscious of these realities, but their interpretation of history did not rely on these alone. Instead they perceived that Yahweh had a unique purpose for his People, to keep the covenant and the law and to maintain freedom and justice. They were not to rely on military power or foreign alliances but to trust in God. This is a type of pacifism. If, in spite of this fidelity, they were to become subject to foreign domination, this would not mean annihilation. Their conquerors were no more than instruments of Yahweh to punish a rebellious nation, and when their purpose served they would disappear. There would always be a remnant, and in the end God was going to establish a reign of peace and justice.

But rulers and people behaved as nearly all other nation-states have done throughout the course of history. No one can tell what might have happened if the prophets had been heeded. Perhaps it is too much to expect that any nation will accept the risk of trusting in God, not merely for individual but also for corporate protection. Even the patriotic Isaiah may have been accused of conspiracy (Isa. 8:12); certainly Jeremiah suffered the danger and ignominy of being branded a collaborator with the enemy. Long after the Exile, the Maccabees, who began as liberators and high priests, made themselves kings and succumbed to the heady temptation to play the game of power politics.

Deuteronomy and Jeremiah

During the reign of King Josiah of Judah (640–609) a scroll was found in the Temple which evidently comprised most of the present Book of Deuteronomy (II Kings 22:8–13). It was a Torah, in the form of a farewell exhortation by Moses, which expressed the Mosaic covenant theology and evidently came from the northern kingdom. It contains no mention of David and his covenant, and the sacred mountains are Ebal and Gerizim, near Shechem.

The immediate consequence of the book's discovery was a thorough-going reform which Josiah undertook (II Kings 23:1–27). Later writers, known as the Deuteronomists, expanded this book and edited the historical books, Joshua through Second Kings, in the light of this theology. "The place which Yahweh your God will choose" (Deut. 12:5) was now understood to be Jerusalem, and the Deuteronomists edited the history to include God's establishment of an eternal covenant with David; thus the Mosaic covenant and the royal theology were reconciled. The other principal doctrine of the Deuteronomic history is that the nation is rewarded when it is loyal and punished when it apostatizes.

Jeremiah began his prophetic work during Josiah's reign, and it continued until after the fall of Jerusalem and the second deportation to Babylon (587/586). His denunciations of the nation's evil followed the pattern of those of Amos and Hosea. He probably welcomed the reform of Josiah, but came to see that it was inadequate because the later kings and their counsellors and prophets trusted blindly in the Davidic covenant and the sanctity of the Temple. It was not easy to protest against this, and Jeremiah more than any other prophet has left us a record of his complaints to Yahweh and the answers that he received. His sermon against the Temple, in which he spoke Yahweh's word that "I will do to this house which is called by my name . . . as I did to Shiloh" (Jer. 7:14), aroused such hostility that he barely escaped being put to death. Because he advised the king and people not to resist Nebuchadnezzar's invasion, he was branded as a subversive. After the final disaster, he wrote to the exiles in Babylon, urging them to seek the welfare of the cities where they lived and to carry on normal lives in their captivity.

The Deuteronomic doctrine of reward and punishment was now seen to be inadequate. Jeremiah heard a new word of the Lord, that the adage "The fathers have eaten sour grapes, and the children's teeth are set on edge" could no longer apply; God's justice will be meted out on an individual basis (Jer. 31:29f.). Yet there is still hope that the nation will be restored, for Yahweh promises a new covenant, written in the hearts of people (31:31–34).

The Beginnings of Apocalpytic

Next to the Exodus and the covenant on Mount Sinai, the Exile to Babylonia was the most important event in the formation of Judaism. It is probable that during the Exile the Pentateuch received almost its present form, the oracles of earlier prophets began to be collected, and the institution of the synagogue came into being. The nation was not destroyed, but it ceased to be an independent state. New prophets arose with messages for the people in their changed situation. The process by which apocalyptic arose is still debated, and various theories depend partly on the definition of that term. Nevertheless we can say that in the prophets of the sixth century there is a gradual shift from prophetic eschatology, in which the action of human beings helps to shape history, to apocalyptic eschatology, in which everything depends on God's action.

Ezekiel's prophecies belong to the early days of the Exile. He was a visionary, consciously possessed by the Spirit. The dialogue between God and his People continues, but it is now centered much more on the response of the individual. Israel is no longer a participant in international politics, and Ezekiel reflects the psychology of a minority nation in subjection to an empire. In his later oracles he moves in the direction of apocalyptic thinking, dreaming of an ideal temple, more cultically pure than the old one, with a miraculous river issuing from it, and a greatly enlarged Holy Land allotted to all the twelve tribes (Ezek. 40–48; cf. 37:15–28).

Hebrew thought was not abstract; the speech in which faith and revelation were expressed was concrete, pictorial, and imaginative. Myth and historical remembrance interpreted one another. In the prophets of the sixth century and later, the mythical understanding of history became more prominent.

The Second Isaiah (chapters 40–55) was the greatest of these prophets. Confontation with the powerful cults of Babylon led him to be the first to teach unambiguously that there was and could be no god other than Yahweh. His aspect as almighty Creator, which was originally a feature of cosmic and royal mythology, was now applied to his purpose to restore his People (40:21–31). Because of his universality he could use Cyrus, who permitted the return to the Holy Land, as his immediate instrument, his Messiah anointed for that purpose (45:1–7). The theme of the Creator is joined with that of the Exodus and conquest; the Divine Warrior will vindicate his People (51:4–11). The language of vindication or justification was later to be used by Paul to describe what happens to one who has faith in Christ.

The songs of the Servant of the Lord, a unique feature of Second Isaiah, gave a new dimension to the purpose and destiny of Israel. Here the nation is the Servant who announces God's will and is to fulfil it. David is mentioned only vaguely in 55:3f., a passage apparently meaning that Yahweh's promises to him are to be fulfilled not in an earthly king but in an everlasting covenant.

Many exiles did indeed return, and the prophecies of Haggai and Zech. 1-8 encouraged the building of the second Temple. These oracles express some hope that Zerubbabel, appointed by Persia as governor of Judah, would restore the Davidic dynasty, but this never came about. Persia found it expedient to have Judah ruled through high priests, and when Ezra instituted his reforms, the Zadokite priestly families which claimed descent from Solomon's priest took control of the cult, and Levites who had traditional claims to priesthood were deprived. Ezra and his followers emphasized obedience to the Torah and discouraged eschatological hopes.

For a minority at least, this led to a time of discouragement. The prophets who represented this minority resisted the power of the Zadokites and charged that the nation, far from fulfilling its promise, had become corrupt and sinful. This led to a new phase of prophecy characterized by apocalyptic eschatology, expressed in Third Isaiah (Isa. 56–66), a group of oracles by several persons but with similar themes, and also in Zech. 9-10 and Isa. 24-27.

Chapters 9-10 of Zechariah predict that God, as Divine Warrior, will come to execute judgment and bring back the rest of the exiles, and there is also the promise of a king who comes peacefully, riding on an ass's colt (9:9-12). Christians later understood this passage as a prophecy of Jesus' triumphal entry.

In Third Isaiah we can trace a progressive alienation, which culminates in 56:9—57:13 and 66:1-16. The latter is a bitter denunciation of the Temple and its sacrifices. The tone of chapters 56-66 is imperialistic; in days to come, aliens will serve not only God but also Israel (61:5-7).

Prophecy has definitely become apocalyptic in Zech. 11-14. The terrible oracles of chapter 11 and 13:7-9 predict that the "shepherds" (leaders of the people) will be punished, as in Ezek. 34, but in contrast to Ezekiel's promise the sheep will be scattered. Only a small remnant, refined like gold, will be left. The covenant, and the union between

Israel and Judah, have been annulled. The obscure verses referring to thirty pieces of silver (11:12f.), the price of a slave, were later applied to the story of Judas Iscariot's betrayal of Jesus (Matt. 26:15; 27:9f.).

Another passage, which speaks of mourning for a martyred prophet or leader (12:10–14), was used in Christian apocalyptic (Matt. 24:30; Rev. 1:7). In chapter 14 the order of nature itself is to be renewed, and all nations will come to Jerusalem to worship at the Feast of Tabernacles. This festival, in the days of the monarchy, may have celebrated the enthronement of Yahweh as king and was the most important of the three pilgrimage feasts. There is no longer any hope in the normal processes of history. Only Yahweh can set things right and bring the new world of which the prophet dreams.

Malachi has some relation to Zech. 9–14. This prophet ("my messenger") denounces the priesthood for its corruption and the failure of the priests to teach the people (chapters 1–3), prophesies the Day which will come, burning like an oven, to destroy the evildoers, and promises the messenger of the covenant, who will refine the sons of Levi like gold and silver. The sun of righteousness will arise with healing in his wings, and Elijah is to come before the great and terrible Day of the Lord, to reconcile children and fathers (chapter 4). The NT quotes the Elijah prophecy with respect to John the Baptist.

Daniel

Daniel is the classic example of an apocalyptic book. In the first place, it interprets past history through symbols and predicts a redemption that is soon to come. The book was composed during the revolt of Judas Maccabeus against the Syrian monarchy, and concluded after the Temple had been rededicated in December, 164 B.C. Thus, with the possible exception of some of the Psalms, it is the latest writing in the Hebrew Bible. The First and Second Books of Maccabees and Josephus' *Antiquities of the Jews* give most of the historical background.

Second, Daniel was written in the name of a person who, according to tradition, had lived several centuries earlier. Third, it shares two additional characteristics with other apocalyptic books. It was written when faith in humanity and in historical processes had failed; and it portrays an imaginative, ideal world.

The book may have been based partly on old tales of how a strict and pious Jew was persecuted in the reigns of Nebuchadnezzar and Belshazzar. The actual author of Daniel was a pacifist, and these stories were told to encourage Jews to trust in God for rescue rather than, perhaps, to resist as the Maccabees did. As the two wicked kings of the past came to an end, so would Antiochus Epiphanes, the king of Syria, who like them had defied the living God.

The first six chapters, then, purport to tell the story of an earlier century and they lead up to the essential part of the apocalypse. Here there is a capsule history of several kingdoms that are symbolized by a succession of beasts (7:1–8). This is followed by the prophecy of the future. One who is like a Son of Man (a human being, in contrast to the bestial kingdoms) is brought to the Ancient of Days, and there he is given an everlasting dominion that shall not pass away (7:9–27, a passage, part of which is read on the festival of Christ the King, Year B). This Son of Man is explained as meaning "the saints of the Most High," the Jewish people.

Thus a human and humane kingdom, never to end, will replace the inhuman empires of the past. The angel Michael will appear as defender of the nation, and a resurrection of the dead will ensue (12:1–4). This vindicates God's justice, for the martyrs of the Maccabean period had gone to their deaths not because they were sinners but precisely because they were righteous. Now for the first time we find that explicit doctrine of resurrection which came to be accepted by Pharisees and Christians alike.

Daniel, like Enoch, Jubilees, and other non-canonical Jewish books, is a tract written for a specific occasion. Its conclusion discloses its date. The "abomination" that has made the Temple desolate has been removed, and the Holy Place rededicated (12:11–13). The Maccabees did indeed triumph, took over the high priesthood, and established a kingdom that lasted till 63 B.C., but the dreams of the author of Daniel were never realized. The symbols and predictions of this book were intended for the late second century B.C. and are of no help in determining the future of the twentieth or twenty-first centuries A.D.

The Christians who formulated the gospel tradition read Daniel in their own way. Jesus had spoken of himself as "Son of Man," and they assumed that it was he who after his Resurrection came to the Ancient of Days (Mark 14:62; Luke 22:69). The apocalyptic thirteenth chapter of Mark and its parallels connected the "abomination of desolation" with the destruction of the Temple during the first Jewish revolt of A.D. 66–73, and took the prophecy of Daniel as assurance that Jesus was to return to judge the world and establish the Reign of God. This was perfectly natural; they lived in a time of crisis when many Jews shared the apocalyptic mood.

As we meditate and preach on the apocalyptic readings at the end and beginning of the ecclesiastical year, we may face two opposite dangers: to take the symbols too literally, or to dismiss them as archaic and irrelevant. Yet the majority of Christians repeat the Apostles' Creed, "He will come again to judge the living and the dead," or the Nicene, "He will come again in glory to judge the living and the dead, and his kingdom will have no end." It is essential to know what we mean by this symbol.

In one respect apocalyptic takes up an essential element of Hebrew prophecy. Yet it ignores the living dialogue between Yahweh and his people in history; that is, the essential part that must be played by human beings in shaping the destiny of their community. One needs to understand this in an age when the great systems, the concentrations of political and economic power, seem to be out of control. Apocalyptic can lead, as it has done in the past, to passive inactivity, or on the other hand to violent action in the hope of forcing God's hand and speeding up the processes of history. In either case it is unrealistic.

The value of apocalyptic is that it shares with prophecy the conviction that God is in control of his world and that in the end his purposes cannot be frustrated. The correction of it is to be found in Jesus' teaching, which takes account of our activity as important even though only God can establish his Reign. It is sometimes said that the message of Jesus is eschatological but not apocalyptic; he discouraged the nervous attempt to find out when and how God's Reign comes, for that is in God's hands alone. But our attitude and our activity must be in the realization that the crisis and the moment of decision for us is always *today*. "Today this scripture is fulfilled in your hearing"; or, as Paul said, "Now is the acceptable time, now is the day of salvation" (II Cor. 6:2). We are to continue to hear God's Word and to speak to him, and to take an active and constructive part in the social order. Whatever we do to further justice and mercy is of consequence in God's sight.

The Sundays
of Advent

·6

The best way to prepare for Advent preaching is first to study each
of the four Sundays in the three-year cycle, so as to see what the main
emphasis is on the first, second, and so on. After this, one should look
at the sequence of the four in whatever year, A, B or C, the homilist is
working. It is important to bring out the themes in such a way that the
sermons lead worshippers naturally toward the Nativity. Fortunately
the lectionaries are devised with sensitivity to the actual situation in our
culture, for most of the month of December is occupied with holiday
preparations. The Advent Sundays afford an opportunity to deal with
stories and ideas that cannot be given much time on Christmas Eve and
Christmas Day.

We should also be aware that in December our Jewish neighbors
celebrate the festival of Hanukkah or Rededication (of the Temple in the
second century B.C.). Because of the Jewish lunar calendar the date may
fluctuate from early to quite late in the month, but there are contacts
between Christmas and Hanukkah. Both are solar festivals that among
other things praise God for the new light that comes at the solstice and
so correspond to something deep in the rhythms of human life. Another
connection is not immediately obvious. The Book of Daniel speaks of
the Rededication, whereas chapter 7 of the same book furnished Christians with one element in their interpretation of Jesus as Son of Man.

Hanukkah is very important to religious Jews because it is a historical
reminiscence of their national life and they see a counterpart to it in the

establishment of the modern state of Israel. The ancient cry of hope in the Passover Haggadah ("This year here, next year in Jerusalem") has partly been fulfilled, but the Jewish people are not completely secure. Christians can see in Dan. 7 the hope of a true reign of God, but Jews also expect such a Kingdom, in whatever form. Christians cannot have the same perspective as Jews, since they see the purpose of history in a different light, but they can have sympathy with their Jewish neighbors and realize that they, like we, look and pray for a better day on earth. The preacher will have to decide whether and how to relate Hanukkah to Advent, but it is well for him or her at least to meditate on the connections.

Advent 1A. The reading from Isa. 2:1–5 proclaims that in "the latter days" all the nations will be drawn to Mount Zion to hear the law, and war will come to an end. This passage, found also in Mic. 4:1–4, may be the oracle of an unknown prophet, but it fits with the general point of view of Isaiah, who believed in the covenant with David and the southern kingdom. Like such passages as Isa. 60:1–14, it assumes that all nations will be converted to Judaism. Christians tend to reinterpret this as the promise of a universal faith in which all nations are equal. For them, Mount Zion is not merely the Jewish homeland, but also the place sacred to Christians and Moslems, and by extension it is wherever the Father is worshipped "in spirit and in truth" (John 4:23, where the rival claims of Jerusalem and Gerizim are put in a Christian perspective). But we do acknowledge to our Jewish neighbors with gratitude that the Torah has come to us from Jerusalem.

In this spirit we use Ps. 122, which accompanies it. This is a pilgrimage song. Christians who can actually use it as *hadjis* (pilgrims) to Jerusalem will have special feelings about it, but whenever we come into the Lord's house we are obedient to the Isaianic prophecy and believe that in us, at least, it is being fulfilled.

But what is the law that comes forth from Zion? The epistle reading, Rom. 13:11–14, understands this as love for neighbor (Paul can assume that love toward God is included). But the Apostle goes on to say that the night is far spent and the day is at hand. This passage, which St. Augustine read in the garden when a child said "Take up and read," was the occasion of his conversion. Paul expressed the tension that he and other early Christians felt, but history did not end when he thought it would. Augustine had his own understanding of God's Commonwealth

(*The City of God*) and the process of history, but on this occasion he settled on the essential point made by St. Paul, love of neighbor and with it the demand to "put on the Lord Jesus Christ" and to cease making provision for the demands of our lower nature.

When one reads Paul in this light, every moment is a time for decision and expectation (cf. II Cor. 6:2). This is how one should understand the gospel reading, Matt. 24:36–44. This passage, which has parallels in Luke 17:26–30, is a warning that most people lead their usual lives and are not prepared either for judgment or for the joyful return of their Lord. The passage is also a good warning against listening to the extravagant claims of false prophets and those who claim to be liberators. The homilist should, however, make the warnings subsidiary to the good news that the law has come out from Jerusalem and that a better day is already here.

Advent 1B. The readings for this Sunday concentrate on the themes of expectation, watching and readiness. Isa. 63:16—64:8 may respond to a mood that worshippers push into their subconscious and are not willing to acknowledge. This is an oracle spoken by a prophet usually called the Third Isaiah. We have noted previously that after the joyful hope of return from exile expressed in chapters 40–55 (Second Isaiah) there came a time of disillusionment. This pericope reflects discouragement and a deep sense of sin. The Jews who have returned to the Holy Land have not measured up to their calling, and the prophecy is an example of the OT prayer of complaint and yearning for redemption.

Can the homilist help the people to apply this to the problems before them? Somehow all Christians need to be led beyond sole concentration on their personal sin, which is real enough, to a realization of the corporate sin of all humanity that has led to all the massacres and disruptions of populations that we call genocide. This occurred in biblical times and often since, but the plight of refugees in many parts of the world makes us sensitive to them now. We hoped for better times after World War II, and people streamed into the churches in hope and thanksgiving, but we may now be disheartened.

The NT pericopes for this day give us no plan of action in this situation, but they do provide a ground for hope. As God's People wait for the revealing of the Lord Jesus Christ, they must know that God is faithful and that he will sustain them to the end so that they will be guiltless on the day of Christ (I Cor. 1:1–9). This is one of the thanksgivings that Paul characteristically puts at the beginning of his letters. The gospel pericope (Mark 13:32-37) reminds Christians that they are like slaves whom the master has left in charge of the household, and their work must be such that at all times they are ready for his return. This is a passage that was later worked over in Matt. 24 and in Luke 21:5-36.

The theme has two applications. (*a*) Every person who believes and prays goes through periods, sometimes distressingly long, when God seems absent and the spiritual life is dry. This is often expressed in the Psalms (such as Pss. 42 and 63:1) and in the prophetic writings and Job. The answer is that one must hang on and wait; times of dryness can be the means of spiritual growth. But the Scriptures never concern themselves merely with individual need; the symbol of the absentee master applies also to our discouragement about the state of the Church, the nation, and the world. (*b*) The slaves who wait for their Lord are watchful but not idle; they are faithfully at their tasks. This has to do not merely with our ordinary pursuits; it can apply also to our participation in ecclesiastical and national life.

Advent 1C. The gospel reading from Luke 21:25-36 is traditional for this season. One lectionary omits verses 29-33, which is an important part of the message in the parallel passage, Mark 13:18-20. Luke's specific contribution is in verses 34-36. This warning not to be involved in dissipation and the cares of this life was spoken to a church of the late first century which had temptations like our own. I Thess. 3:9—4:2 strikes a more positive note; I Thess. 5:1-6, in the Presbyterian lectionary, closely matches the gospel reading.

Five of the lectionaries prescribe Jer. 33:14-16, which connects the future hope with a "righteous branch" that will spring forth "for David," i.e., a coming king of the Davidic dynasty. This symbol becomes more prominent in the succeeding Sundays.

Advent 2A. The famous passage Isa. 11:1-10 is the first reading. A "shoot from the stump of Jesse" will come forth, and in contrast to other monarchs of the Davidic line he will rule with justice. He will slay the wicked with the breath of his mouth, and a time of miraculous peace will come when the wolf will dwell with the lamb. This oracle comes from the post-exilic period when prophecy began to take on apocalyptic features. The messianic Ps. 72, which also portrays the ideal ruler, is appropriately used with it.

The epistolary reading, Rom. 15:4-13, harmonizes with this. By quoting Isa. 11:10 from the Greek version, Paul emphasizes the mission to the Gentiles as well as to the Jews: the root of Jesse will rule the nations, and Gentiles and Jews are to accept one another, to the glory of God.

The gospel pericope, Matt. 3:1-12, summarizes the preaching of John the Baptist. Here John announces the Kingdom of the heavens, in contrast to the parallels in Mark and Luke, where Jesus is the first to make this proclamation. The tendency of the later gospels is to portray John as the forerunner of Jesus in every respect. John was, however, an apocalyptic prophet who called for repentance and baptized those who came to him in order to purify the nation in preparation for the coming judgment. Ezek. 36:24-28, which is read at the Easter Vigil, had predicted such a divine purification, and possibly John had such a passage in mind.

Advent 2B. Mark 1:1-8 represents the earlier tradition. Here John does not identify the coming one, and the implication is that it is God himself who is to come, as in Isa. 40:3, which is quoted along with Mal. 3:1.

The OT pericope is appropriately Isa. 40:1-11, which has always been dear to Christians and furnishes the opening part of Handel's *Messiah.* The exiles will return to Zion, and God himself will feed his flock like a shepherd. The Second Isaiah has his own perspective on the future and promises not a Davidic king but a nation restored by God.

II Pet. 3:8-15a reinterprets the future hope as the return of Christ and the new heavens and new earth. Since with the Lord "a thousand years are as one day," one should wait patiently. The entire second epistle conventionally ascribed to Peter was written primarily to deal with the problem of the delay of the Parousia (i.e. the return of Christ), and thus is in contrast to the near expectation of Christ's return in Paul's letters and in much of the gospel tradition. Scripture thus has many forms of the future hope, depending on the situation. It is not for us to know times and seasons (Acts. 1:7).

Advent 2C. The theme of this day is essentially the proclamation of good news. Baruch 5:1-9 (Roman, Episcopal, NA) is a beautiful hymn, much in the spirit of Second Isaiah, promising the restoration of Jerusalem. The Presbyterian and Methodist lectionaries use Isa. 9:2, 6-7, the familiar Davidic-messianic prophecy; and Mal. 3:1-4, the promise of God's messenger, is the Lutheran selection. The second reading is Phil. 1:1-11, one of Paul's most beautiful thanksgivings. God, who has begun a good work among the Philippians, will complete it at the day of Jesus Christ. Thus the prophecies are applied to the new life of Christians.

In the gospel reading, Luke 3:1-6, the evangelist begins the gospel story proper by giving the date when John the Baptist first appeared in the desert. Like the Hellenistic historians he fixes this by the years of emperors and princes and by priesthoods. Thus the event is anchored in world history in solemn and elegant fashion, and Luke goes on to give a full quotation of Isa. 40:3-5, which he sees as fulfilled in John and Jesus.

Advent 3A. As in the lectionaries prior to Vatican II, the third Sunday focuses more definitely on the Baptist. The gospel pericopes for the three years are quite different in emphasis. The reading for A, Matt. 11:2-11, is in two parts. John asks whether Jesus is the coming one; by way of answer, Jesus merely points to what is happening, in words reminiscent of Isa. 35:5f.; 42:18; 61:1. Here the gospel tradition is at an early stage; John's religious movement is independent of that of Jesus. The part that follows (verses 7-11) gives Jesus' estimate of John. In contrast to the petty rulers of this world, he is a real man, the greatest that has ever lived till now, and a true prophet. Yet one who is least in the Kingdom is greater than he. To be a disciple of John is not enough; perhaps this mysterious saying suggests that to belong to the new age is a far greater distinction than being the greatest of the prophets. In this connection it is interesting to study other sayings in the tradition regarding those who are greater and lesser.

The OT reading, Isa. 35:1-10, fits well with the gospel pericope. The evangelists probably had these promises in mind as they recorded several of the miracle stories; see especially Mark 7:31-37; 8:22-26. Jas. 5:7-10, with its exhortation to wait patiently for the Parousia, resumes a theme found in the previous Sundays of Advent.

Advent 3B. Parts of Isa. 61:1-11 are prescribed by the several lectionaries; the scripture on which Jesus commented in the synagogue at Nazareth was drawn from this passage (Luke 4:18f.). It is appropriate to this season and to Epiphany. I Thess. 5:12-28 is an ethical admonition whose context is expectation of the return of Christ.

The gospel pericope (John 1:6-8, 19-28), in contrast to the reading for Year A, gives a fully developed Christian interpretation of the Baptist. He is no longer an independent prophet but simply a voice announcing the Messiah (cf. John 3:22-30). The eloquent verses 19-28, formerly read on the fourth Sunday in some lectionaries, were set to great music by Orlando Gibbons.

Advent 3C. A still different picture of John is given by Luke 3:7–18. The Baptist's announcement of judgment is combined with directions for behavior in view of the coming crisis. The time is too short for the peform of society demanded by the eighth century prophets; all that can be done is for people to share their goods generously, for tax-collectors to be honest, and for soldiers to stop oppressing the population and to be content with their wages. This is very little, but it is something possible for everyone, and it is a sign of genuine repentance.

Zeph. 3:14–20 is another of the post-exilic promises of the restoration of Jerusalem, in this case appended to the doom announced by the seventh century prophet. Phil. 4:4–13 is Paul's call to rejoice, since the Lord is at hand. Some lectionaries add verses 8–9, which express the Apostle's ethical ideal; the language is reminiscent of the finest ideas of the Stoic philosophy, which was popular at the time and which praised truth, honor, justice, purity, and deeds that are lovely and gracious (see p. 248).

Advent 4A. The new lectionaries make the fourth Sunday a celebration of the Annunciation. Since the feast of the Annunciation, March 25, is never observed on a Sunday, this ensures that the story will be heard, and it also permits a more thorough treatment of the Nativity than may be possible on Christmas itself.

The first reading is the Immanuel prophecy of Isa. 7:10–16, which is to be quoted in the gospel pericope. Isaiah's oracle was originally spoken in a specific historical situation. King Ahaz of Judah was rightly terrified by the prospect of an invasion from Ephraim (Israel) and Syria, but he piously refused to ask Yahweh for a sign. The response of the prophet is that God himself will give a sign: a young woman will conceive and bear a son. Shortly after he is born, the two kings whom Ahaz dreads will be deposed by Egypt and Assyria, and in thankfulness the girl will name the child Immanuel (God with us). Nevertheless the land will be devastated to such an extent that people will eat curds and honey, not bread and wine (Isa. 7:15–25). The lesson is that Ahaz must trust in God, not in military and political means.

The gospel pericope is an example of Matthew's understanding of the fulfilment of prophecy (Matt. 1:18–25) and it is introduced by a special formula that he uses elsewhere. The word translated "young woman" (*almah*) can include the meaning "virgin" but is not confined to it. For reasons that we do not know, the Septuagint rendered it as *parthenos*, virgin. Matthew and his tradition already believed in the virginal conception of our Lord, and this verse seemed to be a scriptural confirmation of that faith. For us, the truth that lies behind both pericopes is that God himself is in ultimate control of history, that he is indeed with us. The name Jesus, which is the Greek form of Joshua, means "O Yahweh, save," or perhaps "Yahweh will save."

The reading from Rom. 1:1–7 contains one of the most important Christological proclamations of the NT. God's Son "was born from the descendants of David as to the flesh," i.e. so far as his human nature is concerned, and "was designated [marked out as] Son of God in power as to his spirit of holiness by resurrection from the dead." This is put in the context of Paul's universal mission. Ps. 24, which was originally to celebrate the enthronement of Yahweh as king, fits very well with the epistle reading.

Advent 4B. Readings for this day increase the emphasis on the tradition that Jesus was descended from David. The gospel reading, Luke 1:26–38, is also an example of Luke's interest in Mary. It is highly pictorial, as much of his gospel is, and it has inspired countless examples of painting, sculpture, music and poetry.

Luke more than any other evangelist includes in his gospel traditions about Mary—her visit to Elizabeth, the *Magnificat,* her appearance in the Temple, her words to the twelve-year-old Jesus, and her pondering (perhaps interpreting) the events narrated in the first two chapters. After the Ascension she is in the upper room with her family and the Eleven (Acts 1:12–14). Luke portrays her attitude as willing and intelligent obedience; for him she is the first and ideal disciple. When an enthusiastic woman pronounces a blessing on his mother and Jesus replies, "Blessed, rather, are those who hear the word of God and keep it" (Luke 11:27f.), the implication is that she is not excluded from that beatitude.

The theology of Mary that developed from the second century on is very important in the worship and piety of the Roman Catholic and Orthodox churches. The NT puts its emphasis on Christology, but Mariology would scarcely have come into being without the interest in Mary shown by Luke, and to a lesser extent by the other evangelists.

In first century Judaism the status of women was probably higher than anywhere else in the Mediterranean world, but they were nevertheless in an inferior position. Mary is the supreme example of the particular concern for women of Luke the evangelist. We have him to thank for the stories of Martha and Mary, of Mary Magdalene and the others who followed Jesus from Galilee, and of Tabitha (Dorcas) and Lydia in Acts. He was not alone in this trait; women were prominent in the churches founded by Paul, and the Apostle speaks of several of them with affection and appreciation. If Christianity has enhanced the dignity of women, it is partly due to the traditions regarding Mary.

Mary is so much the central figure in Luke's account of the Annunciation that one might not be conscious of the full force of verses 32f.: "He will be great and will be called the Son of the Most High, and the Lord God will give him the throne of his father David; and he will reign over the house of Jacob forever, and of his kingdom there will be no end." The angelic words contain echoes of Judg. 13:3 (the promise to Manoah's wife), II Sam. 7:12f., 16, and perhaps other passages. Nothing could express the messianic hope of Isa. 9:2–7, 11:1–9 and Pss. 89 and 132 better than this passage.

Luke has a sense of historical perspective. He knows that Jesus transcends the OT hope, but in his incomparable first two chapters he catches the emotional tone of simple, pious Galilean Jews who await the Messiah and the redemption of Israel, and do not yet know the fullness of Christian faith.

II Sam. 7:1–16 is the first reading. This is Nathan's prophecy that David will have a son to rule over Israel, and it includes God's promise, "I will be his father, and he shall be my son." This passage is closely related in thought to Ps. 89. In both places the "son" is not Solomon or any other identifiable king, but a symbol of the Davidic monarchy, which will be punished when it disobeys but will never be rejected entirely. Rom. 16:25–27 is an eloquent doxology attached to the epistle. What is relevant here is that the proclamation of Jesus Christ is a mystery expressed in the prophetic writings and now disclosed.

Advent 4C. The pericopes for this day enrich the Advent messages with other symbols. The future ruler will come, like David, from Bethlehem Ephrathah, which is small among the clans of Judah (Mic. 5:1–5a). Here it is interesting to see that Matt. 2:6 revises the prophecy in midrashic fashion; since the coming of Christ, Bethlehem is no longer the least. Heb. 10:5–10 uses a different part of the Bible, Ps. 40:6–8, to express another aspect of the Incarnation: Jesus came to do the will of

God in his perfect offering of himself. The gospel reading (Luke 1:39–55) comprises the visit of Mary to Elizabeth, which links together the tradition cycles of Jesus and John the Baptist.

Some of the lectionaries add at least part of the *Magnificat*. Curiously, some Old Latin MSS. and Church Fathers ascribe this canticle to Elizabeth, not Mary; the point, however, is not important. The *Magnificat* is based on Hannah's song (I Sam. 2:1–10), and like the *Benedictus* and *Nunc dimittis* is a piece of messianic psalmody that expresses very well the hope of devout Jews just before and after the birth of Jesus. The so-called Psalms of Solomon belong to the same species of literature.

The words of the *Magnificat* are so familiar to us that we may forget how revolutionary they are, even though it is only God himself who is to bring the revolution. In Longfellow's poem *King Robert of Sicily* the king exclaims:

> 'Tis better such seditious words were sung
> Only by priests and in the Latin tongue.

The early Christians in general transferred the messianic hope to a point beyond history, whereas in the OT it always had political implications. But so did Jesus' message of the coming Reign of God. At a later point we shall discuss this and the questions that it raises for a Christian citizen in a modern nation.

Son of God and Son of David

When one prepares to preach in the seasons of Advent, Christmas and Epiphany, which are so closely interrelated, it is not sufficient to look at the individual pericopes, for the themes should be seen in a wider biblical and theological context. Thus the gospel reading for Advent 1C is related to the rest of Matt. 1, which as a whole is the "book of Genesis" (genealogy and birth) "of Jesus Christ, son of David, son of Abraham." The genealogy itself is artificially constructed, as any good commentary will explain, and is designed to show that Jesus inherited his messiahship (in part) through his adoptive father Joseph. It serves a theological rather than a historical purpose. Matthew had no difficulty in reconciling the genealogy with the virginal conception, for in kingship it was the legal descent that counted.

History, furthermore, is under the overruling of God. Thus the harlots Tamar and Rahab, Ruth the foreigner, Bathsheba, and good and bad kings alike were ancestors of Jesus. Chaps. 1 and 2 of Matthew play on OT types—Joseph the dreamer who went down into Egypt, Joshua coming into the Promised Land, Rachel, and the Nazirite prophecy (Judg. 13:7)—but the primary theme is Davidic messiahship.

Jesus is, however, more than son of David. When Christians from the earliest times hailed him as Messiah, they completely reinterpreted the concept of the future anointed king. Instead of being a triumphant earthly monarch he was crucified; therefore he must have been Messiah in a different sense, namely that he was and is uniquely the Son of God.

"Son of God," as used in the OT, can mean several things. Angels and divine beings are sons of God (Gen. 6:2, 4; Job 1:6), and so are faithful Israelites (Deut. 14:1; Hos. 1:10). One who is father to the orphans will be like a son of the Most High (Sir. 4:10; cf. Luke 6:35), and Israel corporately is God's son (Exod. 4:22f.; Hos. 11:1; cf. Matt. 2:15). But in Nathan's prophecy regarding one of David's descendants (II Sam. 7:14) the phrase denotes a more specific relationship. In one of the coronation psalms the "decree of Yahweh" is announced, "You are my son, today I have begotten you" (Ps. 2:7), and this is echoed at the Baptism and the Transfiguration (Mark 1:11; 9:7) and quoted in Heb. 1:5 (read on Christmas Day) along with II Sam. 7:14.

Another coronation psalm is fundamental to the early Christian theology of the Resurrection and the person of Christ. Ps. 110:1, "The Lord says to my Lord, 'Sit at my right hand, till I make your enemies your footstool,' " appears again and again. It is quoted in Acts. 2:34f. as a prophecy of the Ascension, and in Heb. 5:5; 10:13, and it underlies Rom. 1:4, Phil. 2:5–11 and probably Mark 14:62.

This famous verse is given a different turn in Mark 12: 35–37, where Jesus is quoted as saying, "David himself calls him Lord, so how can he be his son?" The words might be taken as denial of Davidic descent, or as a challenge to think of the nature of Christ as infinitely more. It is an example of how the gospels reflect perplexities and debates within the Church. John 7:40–44 is another example of this.

All of the above helps to explain the theology of Matt. 1. That evangelist's community understood Jesus as the son of David promised in the OT but also as Son of God, as no other human being is. At some point Christians must have asked when it was that Jesus became God's Son. From some NT passages it might have been guessed that this was at the Resurrection or perhaps at the Baptism. Later on, such speculations were rejected as an "adoptionist" heresy, but when the gospels were written theology was not yet fixed, and the terms "orthodoxy" and "heresy" are not appropriate.

Thus Matthew and Luke perhaps thought of Jesus as being Son of God from the moment of his conception. John was logically consistent in his concept of the intimate relation of Father and Son, and he declared that he who became incarnate was with God from the beginning. The idea that the Son existed before the world and was the agent of creation is found also in Col. 1:15–17 and Heb. 1:1–4.

·7

Christmas and Epiphany

The Christmas and Epiphany seasons disclose various ways in which early Christians contemplated the mystery of the Incarnation, and the pericopes are rich in theological insights.

At Christmas time it may seem sufficient to worship and adore but behind the story are the theological ponderings of the early Church. Neither the people of the first century nor we can separate the spiritual life from our God-given reason. Theology is simply the process of making sense out of the whole of human existence in relation to God, and it is not that existence itself, but it is one aspect of the Church's response to God's action.

As we have said, the function of liturgy is to restore the People of God by bringing them into God's true time and space. Priest and people make liturgy together; first, because it is good in itself to do so; and second, so that vision and hearing may sustain them in the days ahead. Except for Holy Week and Easter, there is no season that brings us into the sacred time more vividly than Christmas. Liturgy can transcend the cheapness and commercialism of so much that goes on during December in our culture. This is the first point to be borne in mind.

Advent, Christmas and Epiphany operate through proclamation (Greek, *kerygma*) that is sometimes expressed in joyful shout ("Unto us a child is born!" "Glory to God in the highest, and on earth peace to men of good will!") but also by story. The story recalls to us the history that has made us what we truly are. It is not so much that we are projected into the past; rather the past and the future are brought into the experience of today and made contemporaneous with us.

Christmas Day

The liturgy and well-chosen music are almost sufficient to proclaim the message. On Christmas itself, the homily is necessary and can be effective, but it should be brief because the attention span of the congregation may be short. It is best to select one important theological point or one feature of the story in such a way that the event of the Incarnation is expressed joyfully. In Advent, particularly on the fourth Sunday, there has already been an opportunity to expound the readings rather fully, and this is also the case on the one or two Sundays that follow.

The first celebration, traditionally at midnight, is the most pictorial in that it gives Luke's account of the Nativity. This passage is used by Roman Catholics, Lutherans and Episcopalians in all three years, and is prescribed by the Presbyterian and Methodist lectionaries for all celebrations in Year A. The first lesson consists of various parts of Isa. 9:1-7; this passage is pure proclamation. What was hoped for in a Hebrew king becomes a universal hope for Christians.

In discussing Luke 2:1-14 (15-20), the homilist may wish to make the scene concrete. Perhaps the inn was, as in the Turkish days of Palestine, a courtyard surrounded by rooms and stables; or, as the ancient tradition has it, the manger was in a cave, such as one may still see near Bethlehem. The dating of the census, which was for purposes of taxation, raises problems of chronology, but the fact that it is mentioned reminds one that Jesus was born in an occupied country always in danger of revolt. We contemplate the scene in awe and love.

The reading from Tit. 2:11-14 gives a theological interpretation of the event. First, *the saving grace of God has been manifested to all human beings.* This refers not only to the Nativity but also to all the consequences of the Incarnation. Then comes the ethical note: Christians are taught by this grace to live with self-control, justly and religiously in this present age. This admonition, wholesome, appropriate and eloquent as it is, is in the language of the Pastoral Epistles; Paul might have spoken of the love that builds up the Church, or the new standing of the believer who is justified by faith. Yet this is more than ordinary morality; the Christian lives in expectation of the appearing of Christ, who gave himself to redeem us and to purify God's People to be his own. Thus the Nativity is in the context of the Cross and Advent.

For years B and C, the Presbyterian and Methodist lectionaries provide other lessons. In Year B, Isa. 62:6-12 is a typical post-exilic prophecy of the restoration of Jerusalem, which begins by speaking of watchmen, a theme that has inspired a great German chorale. Here God appears as the victorious warrior. Col. 1:15-20 (Presbyterian) is a comprehensive proclamation that places the Incarnation in the context of creation, reconciliation, resurrection and the Church. Tit. 3:4-7 (Methodist, NA), which is used in the Roman and Episcopal proper for the second (early morning) celebration, echoes the previous reading from that epistle, with the added note that we are not saved by any deeds of our own but by God's kindness and mercy. This is accomplished through the "washing of rebirth and renewal by the Holy Spirit." The language reflects a development in the doctrine of Baptism, and a deep sense of the purpose of all liturgical action: a return to origins, a new beginning.

Isa. 52:6-10 is read in Year C in the Presbyterian and Methodist systems, and the Lutheran lectionary uses it as the second proper. There are two themes: the watchmen, and "How beautiful on the mountains are the feet of one who brings good news!" Eph. 1:3-10 (Presbyterian) is a rhapsody on salvation through Christ, somewhat similar to Col. 1:15-20. The other readings prescribed in these two lectionaries are discussed later.

Two lessons in the second proper, Isa. 62:6-7, 10-12 (Roman, Episcopal) and Tit. 3:4-7, were discussed above. Luke 2:15-20 continues the Nativity story, telling of the shepherds and the child in the manger. The Lutheran lectionary substitutes John 1:1-14.

The climax comes in the third set of readings, which are the most theologically complete. Isa. 52:7-10 opens with the shout of joy at the presence of the messenger of Good News. "Yahweh has bared his holy arm in the sight of all the nations." In Christian retrospect, the birth of the child is a historical event that can be typified by the return from exile. The eloquent second reading, Heb. 1:1-12, proclaims the history of God's Word, spoken in time past to patriarchs and prophets and in the last days by his preexistent Son, through whom the worlds were made. This passage is rich in typological quotations from II Sam. 7:14 and several Psalms, especially 2:7 and 110:1, which deeply influenced NT Christology. It is a fitting prelude to the gospel, John 1:1-18, the high point of Incarnation doctrine in Scripture.

There are several theories as to the origin of this hymn. The position taken here is that it uses language as close as possible to the Gnosticism that was then developing, but in such a way as to refute that type of theology. He who revealed truth and redeemed the world was also the agent of creation; this contradicts the notion that the world was made by an inferior god. The Word (*logos*) became flesh and dwelt among us, as no Gnostic redeemer could do. This puts an end to all "spiritual" religion which would divest our earthly life of its significance. Note, too, that the Incarnation is anchored in sacred history. As in all the gospel tradition, John the Baptist is the forerunner who announces the Coming One.

It is especially important for liturgical preaching that the hymn alludes so clearly to Gen. 1:1, "In the beginning." That which is hoped for in the future and guaranteed as reality in the here and now is the true time and space recreated by worship.

The First Sunday after Christmas

There may be one or two Sundays between Christmas and Epiphany. If, however, Christmas falls on a Sunday, January 1 is observed as the feast of the Holy Name of Jesus in the Episcopal calendar. It is also to be noted that Roman Catholic churches in the United States and Canada observe the Epiphany on any Sunday that falls between January 2 and 8.

The Episcopal lectionary stands alone in choosing John 1:1-18 as the gospel for the day, except that the Methodist lectionary uses it in Year A. This has two advantages: it permits those who attended a midnight or early celebration on Christmas to hear this supreme Christological passage read and expounded; and it includes the entire prologue to the gospel, which is a theological unity. Other churches read narratives of the childhood of Jesus: the flight into Egypt and return to Palestine (Matt. 2:13-15, 19-23, A); the presentation in the Temple and the establishment of the home in Nazareth (Luke 2:22-40, B); and Jesus in the Temple at the age of twelve (Luke 2:41-52, C). In Luke-Acts the Temple is the scene of Jesus' last teaching before the Crucifixion and of the preaching of the earliest apostles.

The OT readings have considerable variety. Some express the theme of rejoicing and promise (Isa. 61:10—62:3, Episcopal, NA; and Isa. 63:7-9, Lutheran, NA, which adds the theme that God suffered in all the afflictions of his People); the Roman, Presbyterian, and NA schemes read Sir. 3:3-7, 14:17a (Greek 3:2-6, 12-14), and NA, I Samuel 2:18-20, 26, which recall Jesus' obedience to his parents.

Choices for the epistle reading also vary widely. Gal. 3:23-25; 4:4-7 is used in the Episcopal lectionary and 4:4-7 in the Lutheran, Methodist, and NA. This affirms that Jesus was born of a woman, born under the law, so that we might receive adoption as sons. Heb. 2:10-18 (NA) makes a similar point. Col. 3:12-17 (18-21) appears in various places; it is a passage expressing the quality of life that belongs to those who have been made new through the Incarnation.

The Second Sunday after Christmas

Four of the lectionaries read the prologue to John (1:1-18) or parts of it, and the Methodist lectionary prescribes it for Year B. The Book of Common Prayer chooses Matt. 2:13-15, 19-23 (with two other options), and the Methodist lectionary prescribes it for Years A and C.

Eph. 1:3-6, 15-23, or parts of it, is read in all lectionaries as the second lesson (in two cases only in Year A). This is not only a proclamation of the mystery of salvation but also an eloquent prayer for the Church. The Episcopal and NA lectionaries choose Jer. 31:7-14 for the first lesson (the Methodist does so in Year B); it is a passage of great joy from a book that is seldom used in the lectionary. Sir. 24:1-4, 12-16 (Roman, NA alternative) is Wisdom's self-revelation, which is related to John 1:1-18.

Although there are great variations in the way the Sundays after Christmas are treated, all of the lectionaries contain much the same themes: the OT hope and promise, the meaning of the Incarnation, the childhood of Jesus, and the joy and moral obligation of those who hear the message.

January 1

The octave of Christmas was formerly observed in some of the churches as the festival of the Circumcision of Christ, and thus it commemorated his birth under the law. In the Episcopal and Lutheran churches the day is now dedicated to the Holy Name of Jesus. The Roman lectionary observes the day as the Solemnity of Mary, the Mother of God.

The gospel reading (Luke 2:15-21), which is essentially the same in all lectionaries except the Presbyterian, reminds us that in biblical thinking the name characterizes the person and in a sense is that person. A change of name results in a new and heightened identity; hence Jacob is given the name Israel (Gen. 32:28) and Simon that of Peter (Matt. 16:18). The name of Jesus, which speaks of salvation from Yahweh, never changes, but the Cross and Resurrection invest it with its full meaning.

In this connection, special attention should be called to the OT reading in the Episcopal lectionary, Exod. 34:1-8 (read also on Trinity Sunday), a vivid self-revelation of God in his judgment and steadfast love, with the repetition of his name "The LORD, the LORD." It is now believed that "Yahweh" originally meant "he who causes to be;" thus the name Jesus affirms that he who causes to be also saves his People. The Roman, Lutheran, Methodist and NA lectionaries prescribe instead the threefold blessing of Aaron (Num. 6:22-27) which puts God's name upon the people of Israel.

Rom. 1:1-7 (read also on Advent 4) is the second reading in the Episcopal, Lutheran and Methodist lectionaries, and this continues the Christological emphasis of the day. The Roman lectionary uses Gal. 4:4-7, appointed in three others for the first Sunday after Christmas. This, together with the gospel reading, makes the day an appropriate occasion for the Roman Catholic festival of Mary, particularly because it is said in the gospel that she preserved, i.e. remembered, all these things and pondered them in her heart. We have already remarked that "pondering" may mean thoughtful, intelligent consideration.

The Presbyterian lectionary makes January 1 a celebration of the New Year, and NA provides an alternative set of lessons for this purpose. We note especially Eccl. 3:1-13 (B: "for everything there is a season"); Isa. 49:1-10 (C: "a day of salvation"); and Rev. 21:1-7 (A: "Behold, I make all things new").

Proclamation

Kerygma or proclamation has been mentioned as a constant theme in Advent, Christmas and Epiphany. The passage from Exod. 34 is particularly interesting because it is an announcement from God himself, as distinct from those which speak of a future hope or a messianic king. It is no disparagement of the unique glory of Jesus Christ when we remind ourselves that Christology depends ultimately upon theism— theology in its strictest sense, the doctrine of God.

Only occasionally do the lectionaries provide OT readings that express the basis of that faith. Psalms such as 8, 24, 29 and 104, celebrating Yahweh as the creator of nature, are used now and then, but the great creation story of Gen. 1:1—2:3 is read in the Roman *Ordo* only at the Great Vigil of Easter, and in the Episcopal and Methodist lectionaries only on Trinity Sunday in Year A (the Episcopal includes it also in the Easter Vigil). The concluding chapters of Job (38:1—42:6) appear hardly at all (parts of chapter 38 on Y12B), and no lectionary uses the three great liturgical passages in Amos 4:13; 5:8-9; 9:5-6 ("Yahweh is his name").

The working preacher should take what opportunities he or she can to assure people that the living God is not merely a projection of our needs and desires. We have a responsibility to inquirers as well as to those who already accept the Faith. Our situation is not unlike that of Christians in the first century who had to proclaim monotheism to the pagan world. Many are now waiting for this. Some of the scientists who are pushing the boundaries of physics and biology further and further out are more drawn to faith than, for example, many sociologists. One sees what can only be called a religious attitude to life in the great naturalist writers such as Loren Eiseley, Henry Beston, Rachel Carson, and Joseph Wood Krutch.

Christian preaching can build on this. If, following the spirit of the Hebrew Bible, we reflect on the wonders of the created world, its inconceivable hugeness and minuteness, from the farthest galaxies to the tiniest particles within the atom, and the marvel of the human mind and what it has constructed, this carries us some distance toward finding God—or, as the writers of Scripture usually prefer to say, *being found* by him.

Kergymatic passages in the OT, which were originally oral composi-tions and only later put in writing, had specific forms that corresponded to their use. Warnings and encouragements spoken by the prophets are often introduced by the formula "thus says Yahweh" or "oracle of Yahweh." Exod. 34:6f. is believed to have been a creed or confession of faith used in worship; just how we do not know. In its present context it is connected with the giving of the Torah on Mount Sinai, and certain-ly it is part of the covenant tradition. The words translated "steadfast love" and "faithfulness" in the RSV ("kindness" and "fidelity," NAB) are *ḥesed* and *emeth*. *Ḥesed* is the grace and mercy that are inseparably connected with the covenant. *Emeth* can mean "truth" and "reliability"; *amen* is a word derived from the same Hebrew root, and Paul is faithful to the original meaning when he speaks of Christ as the Yes through whom the *Amen* comes (II Cor. 1:20). This creed is the answer of Mosaic religion to the continual temptation to worship false gods.

Two other self-revelations of God are read in Lent and will be considered in connection with that season, but they should be mentioned here. They are Exod. 3:1–6 and Deut. 26:5–9. One may add the story of Jacob at Bethel (Gen. 28:10–17), used in Lent 2B by the Lutheran lectionary and as an alternative in the Methodist.

Many OT proclamations celebrate God in history. Deut. 26:5–9, Josh. 24:2–15, and Pss. 78 and 105 are among these. One of the most beautiful (Exod. 19:4–6) tells how God carried his People on eagles' wings, like a mother bird, and promises that if they will keep his covenant they will be a kingdom of priests and a holy nation for him (I Pet. 2:9 is a NT adaptation of this theme). Such passages could have been appropriately used in worship if there was a ceremony in which the covenant was solemnly renewed (II Kings 23:1–23; Neh. 9). The great kerygmatic oracles in Isa. 40–66 were primarily to encourage the returning exiles and to teach that there is and can be no god other than Yahweh.

Several NT proclamations, all of which are Christological, have already been mentioned. Others will be considered in the context of the succeeding seasons of the liturgical year.

Epiphany

Epiphany was originally, as it still is in the eastern churches, a celebration of the baptism of Jesus, his first "manifestation." The western church has connected this festival more closely with Christmas, and the gospel reading for all three years is the story of the Magi (Matt. 2:1–12). Thus it has often been used to symbolize the announcement of the gospel to the Gentiles.

That Herod the Great was suspicious and brutal was well known, and in this narrative he acts in character. Attempts have been made to identify the star that was seen; they are interesting but not quite persuasive. Magi and even holy men from India came to the west from time to time. But the point of the story is not historical at all, but symbolic; we are to enjoy its beauty and learn its lessons. Apart from the Bethlehem prophecy, there are references to the Joseph story in the OT with its dream-revelations, and the star in the Balaam narrative that symbolized Israelite royalty (Num. 24:17). Balaam came from the east, and after the vision departed to his own home (Num. 23:7; 24:25). Thus Herod corresponded to the wicked king Balak.

The theme of the Gentiles is prominent in the OT reading (Isa. 60:1–6). Jerusalem is called to arise and shine, for its light has come. Not only will her children return; the wealth of the nations will flow into the city, and camels from Midian, Ephah, and Sheba (south Arabia) will bring gold and frankincense. Just so in the messianic Ps. 72, used on Epiphany, the kings of Tarshish and the isles will render tribute, the kings of Sheba and Seba bring gifts.

There has always been a temptation on the part of the Church's leaders to apply this ancient Jewish hope to a triumph that they wish the Church to enjoy. The true hope of Christians is not for the wealth and power of the institution but for the working out of God's plan. The second reading, Eph. 3:1-12, sets forth the purpose of Paul's ministry to the Gentiles. What was not known, when Isa. 60 was written, is the mystery of the unity of Jews and Gentiles, in which we all have *parrhesia,* the freedom of speech that citizens enjoy, and access to God in Christ through faith.

The Baptism of the Lord

The lectionaries are so arranged that Sundays after Epiphany, like those after Pentecost, are among the Sundays "of the Year," sometimes called "ordinary time." In calendars other than the Roman, these next Sundays are numbered from the Epiphany, and in some of them the other Sundays "of the year" are numbered from Pentecost. The Book of Common Prayer has numbered propers to be used on the Sunday nearest a given date, but in all cases the Sundays "of the Year" correspond rather well.

The first Sunday after the Epiphany is, however, a special celebration of Jesus' baptism, except that in the Roman Catholic Church this can sometimes fall on a weekday. In accordance with the general policy of the lectionaries, Matthew's account of the event (3:13-17) is read in Year A, Mark 1:4-11 in B, and Luke 3:15-17, 21-22 in C. The oldest form of the story preserved to us is that of Mark, but traces of a parallel tradition are to be found in the others. The Marcan account has already undergone some Christian theological interpretation. Although John was a prophet whose movement continued independently for many years, the Church was interested in him mainly as a forerunner of Jesus. In contrast to Matthew, Mark does not try to explain why Jesus accepted a baptism of repentance or speculate on when he became Son of God. Mark recounts the events accompanying the baptism as something that *Jesus* saw and heard. He evidently understands these as the act of God in inaugurating Jesus' ministry as Messiah, and also as the prototype of Christian baptism, for Jesus is the Stronger One who will baptize with the Holy Spirit.

Matthew deals with a question which by his time had arisen in Christian minds. Since Jesus did not need to repent, why did he go to John?
The answer is that, as representative of his People, he performs every
righteous deed, and associates himself with all others in the corporate
repentance. In Luke, the epiphany is visible to everyone, for the dove
comes down in bodily form.

The Roman *Ordo* uses parts of Ps. 29 as the responsorial psalm,
evidently because the phrase "the voice of Yahweh is upon the waters"
suggests God's voice at the baptism. This vivid nature psalm, which is
a proclamation, is used in Proper 11A in the Episcopal lectionary.

The OT reading from Isa. 42:1-9 speaks of the Servant of Yahweh,
whose full significance will be disclosed in 52:13—53:12, a pericope read
on Good Friday. The Servant is God's Chosen One (a phrase echoed in
Mark 1:11 and its parallels) who will establish justice but do it gently and
quietly. He will be a covenant to the people and a light to the nations,
he will open blind eyes and bring prisoners out of the dungeon. NA
prescribes Isa. 61:1-4, which makes a similar point, for Year C; for Year
B, Gen. 1:1-5 (the Spirit at creation).

The second reading is Peter's explanation of why he transcended
Jewish tradition by baptizing the Gentile Cornelius (Acts. 10:34-43).
Actually, this pericope is a summary of the entire Gospel of Luke and
a classic example of the *kerygma* of early Christianity. The three readings
for the day are artistically and theologically harmonious. NA provides
other readings for Year B (Acts 19:1-7) and C (Acts 8:14-17), which tell
of the gifts of the Spirit on unusual occasions.

The Next Sundays "of the Year"

As we have noted, the Sundays between Epiphany and Lent are
Sundays "of the Year." The lectionaries use modified course readings
from the NT on such Sundays; accordingly, First Corinthians is begun
on the second Sunday and the story of Jesus' ministry from the Synoptic
Gospels on the third. Most of the gospel pericopes will be discussed in
Part Three of this book.

Epiphany themes are, however, carried on to some extent in these
days, partly because of the nature of the events recorded in the early
chapters of the gospels, and four of the lectionaries make the last Sunday
before Lent a celebration of the Transfiguration.

On the second Sunday of the Year (Y2), passages from John are read.
In Year A, the proclamation of the Lamb of God (1:29-41) is matched

by the second Servant song (Isa. 49:1–7). The calling of Philip and Nathanael (1:43–51) is prescribed for Year B by the Episcopal and Lutheran lectionaries, that of Andrew and Peter (1:35–42) by the Roman and Presbyterian, while the Methodist includes both. The theme of calling disciples is continued in the gospel readings for Y3 in Years A and B. This is prefigured by the call of the child Samuel (I Sam. 3:1–20, Y2B), and one may note the call of Jeremiah (Jer. 1:4–10, Y4C). Five lectionaries read the story of Jonah's preaching to the Ninevites (Jonah 3:1–5, 10, Y3B). This of course is the point of the Book of Jonah, rather than the episode of the great fish (cf. Luke 11:29–32).

The marriage at Cana is definitely an epiphany (John 2:1–12, Y2C). It is the first of the great Johannine "signs" and is read with Isa. 62:1–5, which prophesies that the Holy Land will no longer be called Desolate, for its name will be Married. The Cana story symbolizes a renewal; though purification, represented by the jars of water, was necessary, it has been replaced by joy and the new wine of the gospel.

The theme of renewal and the contrast between the new and the old can also be seen in the readings for Y3C, when Ezra's reading of the Torah (various parts of Neh. 8:1–10) is coupled with Jesus' first sermon at Nazareth (Luke 4:14–21). The reading of NA (I Cor. 7:29–35) adds to this the warning that, since the time is short, one should sit loosely to the world (cf. p. 224).

Other passages that should especially be noted are Mic. 6:1–8 (Y4A, four lectionaries); Jer. 17:5–10 (Y6C); and the gospel message of Hos. 2:14–23 (Y8B), in which God promises that he will woo back ("allure") his wayward bride. The gospel passage read with this (Mark 2:18–22) suggests that these are the days of wedding celebration.

The Last Sunday before Lent

All lectionaries except the Roman and Presbyterian provide for a last Sunday after Epiphany which is a festival of the Transfiguration of our Lord. The story of this theophany occurs in the three Synoptic Gospels shortly after Peter's confession, and the accounts are read in successive years (Matt. 17:1–9, A; Mark 9:2–9, B; Luke 9:28–36, C).

Mark's account, the earliest, is filled with symbols drawn from the OT and Jewish tradition. Moses and Elijah were believed to have been taken into heaven without suffering death. There are echoes of the narratives of Moses on Mount Sinai (Exod. 24:1, 16; 34:29–35). The booths suggest the Feast of Tabernacles which figures in Jewish eschatology as a sign of the new age when all nations will observe it (Zech. 14:16-19). Possibly the theology of the passage has connections with II Cor. 3:12—4:4, where Paul teaches that Christians see the glory of Christ and are metamorphosed (the verb is used in Mark 9:3) into his likeness. NA recognizes this by prescribing II Cor. 4:3-6 for Year B and II Cor. 3:12—4:2 for Year C. Finally, in II Pet. 1:16-21 (Lutheran, NA, Year A; Episcopal, Year B) the Transfiguration is explained as proclaiming "the power and coming of our Lord Jesus Christ." This last perhaps is a true understanding of the function of the story in Mark's gospel; it is a foreshadowing of the Parousia of the Son of Man.

The only place where four lectionaries agree is on the OT lesson for Year A, Exod. 24:12-28 (Moses on the Mountain). They do, however, select various themes that have been mentioned above: Elijah at Mount Horeb (I Kings 19:9-18, Episcopal, Year B); the translation of Elijah (II Kings 1:1-12a, Lutheran, Methodist, NA, Year B); the shining of Moses' face (Exod. 34:29-35, Episcopal, Year C); Moses on Mount Pisgah (Deut. 34:1-12, Lutheran, Methodist, Year C); II Cor. 3:12—4:2 (Lutheran, Methodist, Year B).

It has often been conjectured that the Transfiguration story was originally a resurrection appearance that has been transferred to the body of Mark's gospel. Whether this is so, or it represents an experience of the disciples interpreted theologically, does not matter. What is important is that it is a proclamation of Christ's divine nature which links him with Moses and the covenant on Sinai, the work of the prophet Elijah, and his future coming in glory. As such, it is a symbol of the whole gospel message, sums up much of the message of Advent, Christmas and Epiphany, and is a good preparation for Lent.

·8

Lent

The liturgical year as a whole, with its readings and homilies, can serve as a comprehensive catechesis on Christian faith and life. Lent, Holy Week and Easter lie at the heart of this. The origins of Lent go as far back as the second century, when fasting, self-discipline and instruction were preparations for the Christian Passover. Catechumens were specifically prepared for Baptism at the Vigil of Easter, after which they received their first Holy Communion. By the fourth century such a practice was firmly established, and the Catechetical Lectures of St. Cyril of Jerusalem show how candidates were taught in that city. The length of the pre-Easter period differed in various regions, and the forty-day Lent which we have in the west developed in the sixth century.

The seasons from Advent to Ash Wednesday set forth many aspects of Christian proclamation and teaching, and there are allusions to the Cross, Resurrection and the gift of the Holy Spirit, but they are essentially preparatory, a heralding of the new life that comes to God's People together with the hope of the Last Things. Lent, Easter and Pentecost are necessary to complete the cycle and explain God's plan of redemption and restoration.

In what follows, as elsewhere in this book, not every pericope will be discussed. The purpose is to treat the principal themes in their broad biblical and theological context, relating them so far as possible to the readings for specific days.

Ash Wednesday
The new lectionaries follow in general the traditional pattern for Ash Wednesday and set the tone for a season of self-discipline. Joel 2:12–19

is an example of an OT communal fast in time of a national famine. The gospel reading (Matt. 6:1–6, 16–21) concentrates on the inner spirit that is essential in fasting; the act is directed toward God and not a way of exhibiting one's piety in public. The second reading (II Cor. 5:20b— 6:10) sets the whole of the religious life in the context of identification with Christ and reconciliation to God; hence Paul's catalogue of his toils, sufferings and triumphant joy. The Episcopal lectionary provides Isa. 58:3–12, with its description of the good works to be done during a true fast, as an alternative to the Joel pericope; the Presbyterian and Methodist books prescribe this passage for Year B, and parts of the pericope are read on Y5A.

The Human Condition

Lent 1. Lent is a time to assess realistically where we actually are. As Bishop Angus Dun once said, "Penitence is calling things by their right names." On the first Sunday of Lent the gospel readings call attention to one universal aspect of the human condition, that of being tempted (or tested, which is nearer the meaning of the corresponding Greek verb).

Jesus in his humanity was not exempt from this, and two of the pericopes (Matt. 4:1–11, Year A; Luke 4:1–13, Year C) are an example of how his followers may stand the test. The story is highly stylized; in response to the tempter's quotation of Scripture, Jesus answers with quotations that express God's true purpose. Matthew evidently regards the desire to dominate the earth by political and military power as the climactic temptation—as contrasted with the true sense in which authority in heaven and earth is given to Christ (Matt. 28:18)—but Luke may reflect an earlier order of the passage, in which the most subtle and dangerous temptation is for Jesus to test the validity of his own vocation. That would indeed be a lack of faith. Ps. 91, which was quoted by the tempter, is used in Year C.

The temptation takes place in the wilderness. This in fact is the principal emphasis in Mark 1:9–15 (Year B). In the Exodus story the wilderness was where the tribes met Yahweh, were given the covenant, and put to severe tests. It was a place to be dreaded, and there the Hebrews had none of the resources of agriculture and settled life. They had to depend entirely on God and came to learn that he could not be represented by any form from the world of sense experience; hence the prohibition of images. When in the time of the monarchy they went astray, Hosea predicted that Israel would be forced to return to the desert, for only there would the people respond to God's wooing (Hos. 2:14f.; 13:4-8; cf. Jer. 2:2). The wilderness testing is thus a symbol of Jesus' confrontation with ultimate reality; so also is Lent.

The disobedience of Adam and Eve (Gen. 2:4b-9, 15-17, 25—3:7) is recounted in Year A. St. Augustine used this passage with others in developing his doctrine of original sin, but this was not the meaning intended by the J source or the compiler of Genesis. The story is a symbolic one, like other parts of chapters 2 and 3, that can be under-stood in more than one way.

Scholars are not agreed on the function served by the story of the tabu against the tree of knowledge of good and evil. The snake is a sexual symbol in many cultures, but nothing in the text demands inter-preting this "knowledge" as sexual. In the OT, sexual life is a good gift of God, but dangerous, and its abuse is heinous. The story certainly teaches that human beings are responsible when in their presumption and pride they disobey God's commands. Adam is not excused by blaming Eve, nor Eve by blaming the serpent.

How can it be wrong to know good and evil? Paul says that but for the law he would not have known sin, yet the commandment itself is holy and just and good (Rom. 7:7-12). Perhaps the pericope is a com-ment on the ambiguity of human existence: *Homo sapiens* can never have the innocence of the other animals.

The OT is realistic in its doctrine of man, which has many aspects. Men and women are mortal creatures, children are born in pain, and they get a living only by the sweat of the brow. They are tempted and prone to sin; rabbinic Judaism explains that the good impulse and the evil impulse are both present in them. Yet they are creatures of dignity, capable of virtue and heroism, made only a little less than God (Ps. 8:5). Yahweh himself formed Adam (a word meaning "human being") out of the earth (*adamah*), breathed his own breath of life into him, and gave him the dignity of tilling the ground and mastering nature. The final author of Genesis, in putting the priestly account at the beginning of the book, affirms that *adam* was made in the image and likeness of God and created male and female (Gen. 1:26f.).

The second reading for Year A (Rom. 5:12-19) is closely linked to the OT pericope. As Paul understands it, from Adam's time sin has been universal. He does not say that all sinned *in* Adam, only that everyone sinned. The process that began with the first man has been reversed through the grace of God in Christ, specifically through the obedience of one man. Sin can now be overcome, and with it death and (as he says elsewhere) the Torah, with its condemnation.

Exodus and the Covenants

During Lent, the lectionaries provide a number of readings whose theme is the remedy for the evil in the human condition. What God has done is of supreme importance and is the precondition for humanity's response in penitence and conversion.

The act of God is seen in two aspects: the events connected with the covenants, and the work of Christ. In both cases this is for the community and for the individual, but in the covenants the emphasis on the community is relatively greater while in the NT there is more emphasis on the individual.

Those who are not familiar with the Scripture may find the idea of a covenant with God strange and quaint. They are accustomed to agreements and contracts, but these words do not fit the Hebrew word *b^{e}rith* precisely, for when applied to God it can never be a contract between equals. Recent studies have shown that there is a close analogy between the biblical covenants and ancient Near Eastern treaties made by a great king and his vassals. Such treaties are not negotiated but *given* by the stronger party.

There are two kinds of these. The first is an act of grace because it does not stipulate conditions that are imposed on the vassal, and it is usually a reward for loyal service. The second type may have as many as six features: (1) a preamble; (2) a historical prologue; (3) requirements made of the vassal; (4) provision for the document to be preserved and read in public; (5) witnesses to the treaty, which include the gods and natural forces; (6) blessings on the weaker party if he fulfills the conditions and curses in case of disobedience. All these features can be found in the OT with respect to the Mosaic covenant.

There is also the interesting concept of a "lawsuit" which God brings against his People for violating the covenant, in which the mountains and hills are witnesses (Mic. 6:1-8; cf. Deut. 4:26; Hos. 4:1-10).

The covenant with Noah (Gen. 9:8-17, Lent 1B) is unconditional. Here God promises that there will never again be a flood to destroy all life. This story also discloses the vast difference between faith in Yahweh and the primitive religion of Syrian Baalism, with its anxiety over the sun's decline during the second half of the year and the magical techniques to insure fertility. Nature is reliable because of the promise that God has made. "While the earth remains, seedtime and harvest, cold and heat, summer and winter, day and night, shall never cease" (Gen. 8:22).

Lent 2. Readings for the second Sunday in Lent tell of the covenant given to Abraham, which is another example of pure grace. The patri-arch is bidden to leave his ancestral home in Babylonia and go to a new land where his descendants will become a great nation (Gen. 12:1-8, Year A). The encounter with God is seen in both the OT and the New as an adventure into the unknown, fraught with peril and blessing.

NA prescribes Gen. 17:1-10, 15-19, in which the covenant with Abra-ham includes the promise of Isaac, and this is coupled with Rom. 4:16-25, where Paul speaks of Abraham's faith in the promise. The covenant is also the theme of Gen. 15:1-12, 17-18 (Year C), in which Abraham's descendants are promised an empire reaching from the river Euphrates to the present frontier of Egypt. If this is taken literally and out of context it can be the warrant for a single nation to dominate this large region politically, and the history of Israel shows how in the eighth and seventh centuries B.C. this dream led to futility and tragedy. The lectionaries bracket with this Phil. 3:17—4:1, where Paul affirms that the true *politeia* (commonwealth) of God's People is in heaven.

Lent 3. The third Sunday centers in the covenant established through Moses. Exod. 3:1-15 (Year C) should be considered first. In this story of the Burning Bush, God introduces himself as Yahweh, and Moses is ordered to tell the people of Israel, " 'Yahweh, the God of your fathers, the God of Abraham, the God of Isaac, and the God of Jacob, has sent me to you': this is my name for ever, and thus I am to be remembered throughout all generations." This proclamation formula reminds the holy People of their origins and identity and the uniqueness of their God.

Although the name Yahweh is frequently used in the J source of the Pentateuch from Gen. 2:4 on, this pericope and Exod. 6:2f. represent an old tradition according to which God's uniqueness and the name (which evidently means "he will cause to be") were first disclosed in the time of Moses.

Another passage, Deut. 26:1-11, read on the first Sunday in Year C, has a bearing on the theme of the Mosaic covenant. Many critics regard this as one of the earliest formulas that set forth God's saving acts in history. Moses, speaking as the supreme prophet, teaches the Israelites a confession of faith that they are to recite at the harvest festival when they come into the Promised Land. It recites how Yahweh brought his People out of Egypt, but the most poignant part is the opening clause which cuts away all chauvinism and complacency. "A wandering Aramaean [Jacob] was my father." It was only the act of God in making covenant that gathered the Hebrew tribes and gave them their identity.

The biblical tradition does not idealize the Israelite people of the Exodus period. As they wander in the wilderness, they complain of thirst, and at Yahweh's command Moses strikes the rock to bring out water; he is gracious even when they put him to the test (Exod. 17:3-7). This passage is read on the third Sunday in Year A, along with the story of the woman of Samaria to whom Jesus promises the living water (John 4:5-42). Another passage that matches Exod. 17 more closely is I Cor. 10:1-13 (Year C), where the manna and the water from the rock are evidently types of Baptism and the Eucharist, and Paul gives warnings against the sins committed by the ancient Israelites. The gospel reading for Lent 3C (Luke 13:1-19) deals with judgment on the unrepentant, but it includes another idea, that not every calamity is a direct punishment from God.

The Mosaic covenant contained sanctions in the form of laws, and the Ten Commandments (Exod. 20:1-17) are the OT reading for the third Sunday in Year B.

God's Action and the Believer's Response

The covenants can be considered the background of the NT answer to the human condition. Humanity is restored to its true destiny by the act of God in Christ.

Portions of the story of Abraham's sacrifice of Isaac (Gen. 22:1-18) are read in four lectionaries on Lent 2B. Perhaps this was originally to explain how God abolished the pagan custom of human sacrifice, but the biblical account as it stands makes it an example of faith in God, who will himself provide the offering. Christian tradition has of course seen this as a type of the sacrifice of Christ, and Rom. 8:31-39, coupled with the OT reading, proclaims that God gave his Son so that we might be righteous, and that Christ intercedes for us continually. We have been reconciled to God by the death of his Son (Rom. 5:1-11, Lent 3A). The message of Christ crucified is a stumbling block to Jews and nonsense to Gentiles, but it is the power and wisdom of God (I Cor. 1:22-25, Lent 3B, Roman, Presbyterian, and Methodist). NA prescribes Gen. 17:1-10,

15-19 and Rom. 4:16-25 (covenant with Abraham and promises to him) for Lent 2B.

Paul says more than once (as in Rom. 1:16) that the Good News, the Word itself, is a power of God that saves. Thus in Rom. 10:8-13 (Lent 1C) he gives his exposition of Deut. 30:11-13. The latter passage, one of the most beautiful in Deuteronomy, tells the Israelites that God's commandment is not something far off and difficult to find, but very near them, in their hearts (i.e. minds). Paul applies this boldly to the gospel and the corresponding confession of faith in Jesus as Lord. *This is the response of the believer that makes possible his or her acceptance of what God has done and offered.*

We can see, then, that the first three Sundays of Lent provide, often by narratives read symbolically, a rich body of teaching to prepare catechumens for baptism at the Vigil of Easter and also to lead the faithful to renewal of their covenant with God. Baptism is in fact the initiatory rite by which individuals enter the covenant, just as in Judaism the word *b^e rith* means not only covenant but also circumcision.

The Fourth Sunday of Lent

The fourth Sunday, in the Roman calendar, was previously called *Laetare* (from the first word of the Introit, "Rejoice") and in Anglican tradition Refreshment Sunday, because the feeding of the Five Thousand was the gospel (John 6:4-15, still read in the Episcopal lectionary in Year B). A note of joy was thus introduced into what was otherwise a penitential season. This principle is still maintained in that the theme appears to be the Good News and the response to it in conversion.

The three gospel readings in most lectionaries are the healing of the man born blind (John 9:1-41, Year A), which illustrates Jesus as the light of the world (9:5) and is also an example of conversion (9:35-38); the conclusion of Jesus' speech to Nicodemus and part of the evangelist's comment, which includes John's summary of the gospel (John 3:14-21, Year B); and the parable of the Prodigal Son (Luke 15:11-32, Year C).

The second reading for Year A (Eph. 5:8-14) speaks of the moral conduct appropriate for children of the light. Eph. 2:4-10, with its theme of grace and faith, harmonizes with the gospel for Year B (the Lutheran lectionary uses this on Lent 3A), and the great passage II Cor. 5:16-21 is particularly happy as a companion to the parable of the Prodigal Son, emphasizing as it does the message of reconciliation and the fact that in Christ we are a new creation. The Lucan parable has another aspect, the contrast between the father and the elder brother, but it is the love of the father that is principally suggested by the lectionary.

The lectionaries do not agree on OT readings for A and B, but attention should be called to Josh. 5:9–12 (Year C), which tells of the keeping of the Passover on the plains of Jericho just before the people enter the Promised Land.

Jesus Christ as Lord and Savior

We have seen that several readings for the Sundays in Lent portray conversion and the believing response of the individual to the Good News. The verse John 3:16 is often regarded as a summary of the gospel. Because Lent can be a particularly good time for the orientation of inquirers, it is well to look at the process of conversion and to ask what initiation into the People of God ought to mean.

Conversion, the deliberate choice of the individual, is characteristic of many religions. There are examples of it in Jesus' time. Apuleius tells how the worship of Isis redeemed him; potentates and poor people alike were initiated into the mystery religions; when one embraced Stoicism or Gnosticism it was a species of conversion; and many thoughtful persons who yearned for intellectual and moral direction became Jews.

There are deeply religious people who grow up normally in a religious fellowship without any consciousness of having previously been alienated from God or of a moment or process of conversion. William James long ago made a distinction between the "once born" and the "twice born." Some systems of religious education emphasize nurture, others conversion, and sometimes they promote both. But human beings frequently tend to think that there must be *one* way, some formula that will apply to everyone. In certain mainline Protestant churches in the past two centuries it has been thought that every child must experience a crisis of conversion, an emotional experience leading to a firm decision, before proceeding to baptism, or confirmation, or communion and adult membership. If catechetical instruction is the principal test, the initiation is somewhat like graduating from the sixth grade or junior high school.

A religious community must have regular procedures, but the notion that everyone must come out of the same mold causes many to fall by the wayside. Some are bored by the whole process, others disillusioned, many are anxious because they feel that they have not met the test of their own standards or those of the Church.

Trends in American Christianity vary somewhat with the emotional and sociological climate of the nation. Immediately after 1945, nearly all the churches, conservative and liberal, traditional and innovating, experienced a large growth in membership. But beginning with the Vietnam war, many Americans became anxious and alienated from the prevailing culture; not only the socially and economically deprived, but also many of the affluent; not just radicals, but also conservatives who saw their traditional values in danger. There was a widespread feeling of spiritual starvation with which the mainline churches could not quite cope. The beneficiaries were the radical and conservative denomina-tions and new cults, some with Christian roots and others based on oriental religions and philosophies.

From the Christian point of view, certain features of the new religions are destructive to the mental health of society and the individuals in it, but they bear witness to widespread feelings of lostness and alienation and a need for identity, support by a group, and guidance in life. The only hopeful response that the churches can make is to show what true conversion is and what kind of leader one should follow. The examples of Jesus and Paul, when rightly understood, disclose wholesome leader-ship as distinguished from spiritual tyranny.

Jesus as Savior

"Jesus Christ is Lord and Savior" is the most ecumenical formula that we have in Christendom today. Many denominations and congregations that reject creeds on conscientious grounds can use these words without hesitation.

The formula makes no sense, however, unless Jesus is truly the incar-nation of God; otherwise we are giving improper allegiance to a man, and then he is Lord only in the sense of leader, and a savior comparable to medical doctors, psychologists, and teachers, necessary though all of these are. On the other hand, to make him only a god, and to divest his humanity of any real significance, makes him alien to our everyday life. He becomes a divinity masquerading as flesh and blood, like those Greek gods who occasionally came to earth for their own amusement. What is perhaps worse is that it makes the OT irrelevant. Marcion in the second century A.D. was consistent in following this line; he re-garded Yahweh as an inferior god of justice and wrath, and for him the true God was the "stranger," Jesus Christ, who loves and redeems.

We have to hold together the affirmations that Christ is true God and true man, however difficult this is to imagine. Then we can see the authentic character of God as he is known in the OT and distinguish this from partial and mistaken conceptions of him that are also found in the Hebrew Bible. Without the OT we may easily forget the social message of the prophets, the realization that God is always active in history, and the communal side of human life that is expressed in the covenants and in Hebrew-Jewish worship. It is important to read the OT pericopes in church.

Systematic theologians deal with the doctrine of the God-man. In the fourth and fifth centuries the Church tried to settle disagreements by means of the creeds and doctrines of the ecumenical councils, but the language used was based on Greek philosophical concepts that now are foreign to all but experts. The struggle to express NT faith in terms that speak directly to us still goes on. All creeds and theologies give only an approximation of what we believe. They are attempts to take a vital, dynamic faith and experience that can be expressed fully only in meta-phor, poem, picture and worship and to put them into prosaic and rational terms. Such efforts are never to be despised, because questions inevitably arise in our minds, and we have to love God with our reason as well as with our hearts and hands. But theology is not, in itself, faith.

The main problem of affirming NT faith is psychological. It is a question of what pictures we put in our minds; it is these which give substance to our meditation and worship. When I was a child, I thought of God as a gentleman with white hair and grey eyes and a benevolent expression, peering over a white cloud. We outgrow such imaginings, and some theologians say we must think of him as "the ground of all being" or "all reality." This is more difficult, but if we try we can conceive of him as the power upholding the universe and also as the living God of the OT. There is no harm in anthropomorphism, if we do not push it too far.

God, as we think of him, will not be different from Jesus. But whenev-er we think of Jesus we should also think of the Father and remember that Jesus prayed to God. Sometimes we pray to Jesus, but the character-istic prayer of Christians in the early centuries was *to* God the Father, *through* the Son, and *in* the Holy Spirit.

Jesus as Lord

To accept Jesus Christ, or rather to accept God through him, means to accept the prophetic message of the OT of the God of justice and mercy, who acts in history and in our individual lives. We agree to a covenant as members of a community that potentially embraces the whole world. Being a Christian means to participate in God's care for all creation, and to perceive the congregation to which we belong as part of an ecumenical Church with a universal mission.

The Christ to whom we give allegiance is the one who walked and taught and suffered in Galilee and Judaea. This unconventional man, so independent of any human authority, was marked by openness and candor. If we really hear him, all our values are reoriented. It seems at first presumptuous to think that anyone should see his or her life and the world from God's perspective, but this is what the prophets and Jesus did, and we approximate this when we turn in the right direction. From time to time we will forget, but we can always turn again.

It is painful to realize that the way of the gospel is not precisely that of the culture around us or even what is conventionally regarded as Christianity. There is a lot of good in the best of American life, as there was in the Judaism of Jesus' day, but what he said at that time still applies: "If you love those who love you, what credit is it to you? Don't even tax collectors do the same?" (Matt. 5:46; cf. Luke 6:33f.). It is in the radical, paradoxical sayings of Jesus that we come to know him best and discern the character of God, whose thoughts are not our thoughts and whose ways are not our ways. It is the perspective that makes the difference.

Conversion has been defined as a change of taste. It is the substitution of higher values for those that are only conventionally acceptable. A change of taste means that we like the new taste better. The parable of the Pearl of Great Price (Matt. 13:45f.) makes this clear: to accept Jesus' message of the Kingdom is to find what the heart's desire really is and to rejoice. Conversion is not just a resolution of the will; it is also a release of the emotions in love. If we do not actually want the new life, we are like the person who gives up alcohol but cannot get the thought of a drink out of the mind. That is a negative situation, like that of the house that is swept and put in order and ready for the demons to come back in (Matt. 12:43–45; Luke 11:24–26). Tastes do not usually change overnight; therefore, though conversion may begin at a definite hour, it may also be a process. The four disciples followed Jesus without delay, but the gospels indicate that they still had a way to go before they were mature.

To accept Jesus as Lord is to turn in his direction; to accept him as

Savior is to receive what he offers, what the Father offers, what the Holy Spirit offers. Evangelical religion often emphasizes salvation from sin, pardon of past sins and power not to sin again. Paul spoke of liberation from law, from sin, and from death. These concepts are paradoxical and have to be defined further. They make sense only in terms of the new life: we live only if we die in union with Christ; we go on sinning but the future is open, not closed, if we live by faith; we are free from law if our love and desire are set in a new direction.

The Fifth Sunday of Lent

Readings for the fourth Sunday celebrated the newness of Christian existence, and the OT lesson for Year C foreshadowed Holy Week and Easter by speaking of the Passover. The fifth Sunday (formerly called Passion Sunday, a term now applied to the sixth) is a more direct preparation for the message of the Cross and Resurrection.

Ezekiel's vision of the Valley of Dry Bones revived by God's Spirit (Ezek. 37:1–14) is the first reading for Year A. This was a promise that the Israelite nation would be restored; Christians have, however, naturally used it as a type of the Resurrection. Ps. 130 is used with it because it echoes Ezekiel's word of hopeful waiting for redemption. The psalm strikes a note of penitence, but it is essentially a poem of quiet confidence.

Rom. 8:6–11, the second reading in lectionaries other than the Episcopal, announces that the Spirit will give life to our mortal bodies. The gospel reading tells of the raising of Lazarus (John 11:1–45), a rich and many-sided pericope which the Fourth Evangelist sees as the event which aroused extreme hostility and led to the plot to put Jesus to death. It is also a parable of conversion.

Year B is more directly related to Holy Week. In John 12:20–33, when the Greeks come to see Jesus, that is the signal for him to say that the hour has come for the Son of Man to be glorified and lifted up by his Passion and by the Resurrection and Ascension; this is to draw all people to himself. Heb. 5:1–10 looks at the work of Christ from another angle: he learned obedience from what he suffered, and having been perfected he becomes the cause of eternal salvation, called by God to be high priest in the order of Melchizedek.

Readings for Year C at first seem to be more miscellaneous. Isa. 43:16–21, however, is placed here to show that God is doing something new (the symbol is that he makes a way in the wilderness and rivers in the desert). The newness of the age inaugurated by Jesus is indicated by the other readings. Paul makes a brief, eloquent statement of his Christian experience (Phil. 3:8–14): the loss he has suffered in order to gain Christ and to have a "righteousness not his own," his hope of resurrection, and his continual striving toward the goal.

The story of the woman taken in adultery (John 8:1–11, Roman and Methodist only) does not belong to the Fourth Gospel, though it is part of the canon of Scripture. Its language and style are like those of the Synoptics, and several early manuscripts omit it or place it after Luke 21:28 or in other places. The pericope perhaps had difficulty in being accepted because it seemed to offer forgiveness too easily, but it fits with other actions attributed to Jesus and it does not condone sin. The concluding words are "Go, and sin no more."

Othe lectionaries instead prescribe Luke 20:9–19 (parable of the Wicked Husbandmen) or Luke 22:14–30 (the Last Supper). NA provides John 12:1–8 (the anointing at Bethany) as the reading for Year C.

·9

The Way of the Cross

The speech at the Areopagus attributed to St. Paul (Acts 17:16–34) portrays the Apostle as trying to meet the intellectuals of Athens on their own ground by using arguments for monotheism similar to those employed in popular philosophy. When at the end he spoke of Jesus, the Resurrection, and the judgment, his words fell on deaf ears. The style of this speech is more like Luke than that of the Paul whom we read in the epistles, yet it is significant that when the Apostle came to Corinth, as he told the Christians in that city, he "decided not to know anything among you except Jesus Christ and him crucified" (I Cor. 2:2).

It is the hard parts of the Scriptures, those that demand the most faith and allegiance—words of the prophets and Jesus and the story of the Cross—that form us into Christians and give strength and the peace and joy that surpass all understanding. They may strike home, now or later, or they may not; to some they are a stumbling block, to others foolishness; but that is the risk we take, and to paraphrase Paul, it is the risk that God in his wisdom has taken.

The Passion Narratives in the four gospels tell the story directly, and one may well ask whether much more is needed. The lectionaries follow the traditional custom of reading the Passion on Palm Sunday and Good Friday and parts of it on other days of the week. Many parishes use several readers to recite the parts of the *dramatis personae* and the congregation speaks as the crowd. This custom, which arose in the Middle Ages, has given us Bach's Passions of St. Matthew and St. John.

It is now generally agreed that the earliest theological reflection and preaching of the early Church was kerygmatic; that is, its subject was the Cross and Resurrection, which disclosed the nature of Jesus as Messiah and Lord. The other parts of the gospel tradition, the incidents of his earthly ministry and his teaching, were made subservient to the main message. This can be illustrated from the earliest gospel, that of Mark, which is Christological in purpose and leads up to the suffering of the Son of Man, the news of his Resurrection, and the hope of his return.

The original disciples not only knew the whole story of the Lord's ministry but also participated in its events. But as time went on the second generation of Christians might not have known what Jesus was like as he walked in Galilee and Jerusalem, and the unique features of his teaching would have been lost if the rest of the Jesus tradition had not been collected and included in the gospels of Matthew and Luke.

To put it another way: if the gospels had not been written, the kerygma could have become only another myth of a revealer and redeemer. That is exactly what happened in Gnosticism, as we can see from the recently discovered Gospel of Truth and other Coptic books written by Christian Gnostics. These writings exhibit an aberrant form of Christianity in which Jesus is taken out of history, and the whole context of his life and ministry within Judaism and the OT tradition is lost.

The framers of the lectionaries were right when they followed what has been liturgical practice since the early centuries, in putting the principal emphasis on the proclamation of Christ's Incarnation, Cross and Resurrection, and the coming of the Spirit. These are the most important parts of the Christian year, for without the faith expressed in them Jesus would appear only as a supremely great prophet and teacher.

Yet Christians believe that the Incarnation of Christ is also a revelation of God's nature and purpose which illuminates the prior history of God's People. What is unique about the Incarnation? Certainly the death of Christ and his Resurrection. But what Jesus did and said before he went to the Cross is also a specific revelation of God in action that enables us to find a guide through the OT, affirming certain features of it, revising others, and putting all of it in a new light.

The Sundays "of the Year" or "ordinary time", with their modified course reading of the gospels and epistles, are indispensable if we are to understand the purpose of our Lord and the events that led historical-ly to the Cross. The homilist who prepares to preach in Holy Week and Eastertide should be conscious of the parts of the gospel tradition that put the Cross in its larger context. Recent study of the gospels has sharpened our understanding of the uniqueness of Jesus' teaching and activity, and several of the later chapters of this book attempt to bring this out.

The Sunday of the Passion (Palm Sunday)

Palm Sunday has traditionally been associated with the triumphal entry of Jesus into Jerusalem because it is possible to read chapters 11–15 of Mark in such a way that this event seems to fall on a Sunday. Mark's narrative framework is not, however, coherent enough to de-mand this interpretation. The pericopes in these chapters originally circulated separately, and the evangelist put them together for theologi-cal rather than historical purposes.

The custom of a procession with palms began in Jerusalem in the fourth century, so far as we know, and it is still observed there, with great throngs marching from some point on the Mount of Olives to the Holy Sepulchre. By the sixth century such a procession had been adopted in Rome and is part of the liturgy prefaced to the Eucharist in the Roman rite and in many Lutheran and Episcopal churches.

The three Synoptic accounts of the triumphal entry are read as part of the liturgy of the palms (Matt. 21:1–11, A; Mark 11:1–11, B; Luke 19:28–40, C). Ps. 118:19–29 is the psalm that was used in the procession in the fourth century. At the Eucharist, however, the lectionaries pre-scribe the accounts of the Crucifixion and the events leading up to it, so that the day is now properly called the Sunday of the Passion. This traditional plan is useful because some worshippers attend the liturgy only on Sundays.

The Triumphal Entry

Matthew and Luke basically follow Mark's account of the triumphal entry. In John 12:12–16 a somewhat similar pericope (used as an alterna-tive in the Methodist and Roman lectionaries), the only one that men-tions palms, comes between the plot against Lazarus and the visit of the Greeks to see Jesus.

Mark's story suggests that Jesus entered the Holy City as a peaceful king, as in Zech. 9:9. Matthew makes this an explicit fulfilment of that prophecy, even to the point of mentioning two animals, the ass and the colt. It is quite possible that Jesus had friends in the city who gladly provided him with an animal to ride.

This is a scene of festival pilgrimage. We know that at Tabernacles in the autumn and Hanukkah in December the worshippers carried leafy branches and lemons and sang Ps. 118, in which the Hebrew word meaning 'Save now" is transliterated as *Hosanna* (verse 25). Jewish tradition in fact calls these branches "hosannas." There is no evidence that these customs were followed at Passover time, and it has been conjectured that the triumphal entry occurred some months previously. The Gospel of John tells us that on other occasions Jesus was in Jerusalem for the great festivals. If he already had a following there, this would help to explain the great success of the gospel after the Resurrection (Acts. 2:41).

Jesus' purpose in entering Jerusalem, riding in dignity, must have been to continue proclaiming the Reign of God as he had done in Galilee, even though he knew that he would face opposition in the Holy City. He came as a prophet and teacher, surrounded by his disciples, but his well-wishers in Jerusalem already regarded him as the Messiah. They not only sang parts of the psalm, but also added a shout, "Blessed is the coming Kingdom of our father David!" and spread their garments on the road to acclaim him as King, just as Jehu's soldiers had done (II Kings 9:13).

If the authorities heard of this incident they would have been greatly disturbed. Their alarm would have been heightened by the next episode, the cleansing of the Temple, which curiously appears in the lectionaries only in the highly theological form of John 2:13–25 (Lent 3B) and as an alternative in the Book of Common Prayer for Tuesday in Holy Week (Mark 11:15–19). Mark's story tells of the symbolic act of a prophet rather than a king, but it was nonetheless a challenge to the high priest and his Sadducean friends. Now they were certain to plan to arrest Jesus and have him put to death. On this occasion he proclaimed that the Temple must be a house of prayer for all nations (Isa. 56:7) but that it has been made a cave of bandits (Jer. 7:11). The rabbinic tradition itself charged the priests of that time with profiteering in the sale of sacrificial animals.

Jesus, like Jeremiah before him, did not hesitate to prophecy against the corruption of religion and society, and for both of them the duty was painful, for the institutions reflected cherished values. Jesus was not interested in kingship for himself but only in the sovereignty of God. Judaea at this time was an occupied country with a Roman prefect as governor, and the Sadducees, to whose party the high priest belonged, were Pilate's collaborators. The Jewish people had suffered many miseries from high taxation and especially in the revolt of A.D. 6, which the Romans put down savagely, and worse was yet to come. The message of Jesus brought hope to the poor and a warning to all that justice and mercy were the only remedy for the nation's ills.

The triumphal entry, like the Passion Narrative and the Passover haggadah of Jewish worship, is a story that enables worshippers to identify themselves with a supremely important event in sacred history; in this case to make themselves contemporary with the disciples and the people who welcomed Jesus.

Sometimes a preacher is tempted to say that the same throngs who welcomed our Lord at his triumphal entry were the hostile crowd present at the Crucifixion. There is no reason to assume this. Those who received him into the city with such joy would later have heard of Jesus' arrest and the events at Golgotha; perhaps they kept to their homes in terror and discouragement. The mob that cried "Crucify him!" was made up of friends and supporters of the high priest.

The cleansing of the Temple does not actually teach us much about the difficult moral and political problems of the use of force. Such force as Jesus used was a symbolic, prophetic act that did little or no damage to anyone. But it was dangerous and courageous and is an example of the indignation that Jesus also expressed on other occasions during his ministry.

The Proclamation of Passion Sunday

The lectionaries, except for the Episcopal, provide part of the third Servant Song (Isa. 50:4-9a) as the first reading for Passion Sunday. The words "I gave my back to the smiters . . . I hid not my face from shame and spitting . . . I have set my face like a flint" inevitably evoked the thought of the Crucifixion in Christian minds.

The second reading, Phil. 2:5-11, is one of the most important Christological proclamations in the NT. It is interesting in itself and also for the way in which Paul uses it. Verses 1-4 spell out his reason for quoting the hymn, which we believe to be pre-Pauline and originally written in Aramaic. Behind these verses there may lie a myth which told of the descent of a divine being, equal to God, who took the form of a slave and was afterward exalted. The Gnostics used similar patterns. But as employed in Christian praise it is much more because it expresses Jesus' great love and because it also sets the story in history that actually occurred. The language is dramatic: he regarded equality with God as not something to be grasped and held onto; he emptied himself or divested himself of his glory; he was obedient even to death, and death on the Cross at that. Nothing is said about his ministry, but Paul implies Jesus' true humanity by the way in which he uses the hymn: "let this mind be in you which was in Christ Jesus" or "which you have in Christ Jesus."

We may compare this pericope with II Cor. 8:9, "You know the grace of our Lord Jesus, that although he was rich, yet for your sake he became poor, that you through his poverty might be rich," and with Luke 9:58, "The foxes have lairs, and the birds of the sky nests, but the Son of Man has nowhere to lay his head." The gospel writers thought of this as a paradox: the heavenly Son of Man, the future judge, homeless on earth!

How could anyone know such things? The great proclamation in Philippians can only have been a revelation to a believing Christian, whether that person was Paul or someone else. The truth could have come only from an experience analogous to those of the Hebrew prophets and Jesus himself. The majority of Jews believed that prophecy had ceased some time before the first century, and that further understanding of God's will could come only through interpretation of the written and oral Torah by the rabbis. John the Baptist was a prophet, but only a few recognized him as such. Jesus was also a prophet, and the early Church had many prophets, who are mentioned in Acts and even in the gospel tradition (Luke 11:49), and Paul speaks of prophets who receive gifts of the Spirit along with apostles and teachers (I Cor. 12:28f.; cf. 11:5; 13:2; 14:4, 29). Phil. 2:5-11 does not have the form of such prophecies as we find in chapters 1-3 of the Apocalypse, but it must have come from someone like a prophet who composed the hymn after prayer and meditation. The hymn gives us a theological interpretation of the Passion and the Ascension.

The Story of the Passion

All lectionaries except the Presbyterian, which observes the day as Palm Sunday only, provide for the recital of the Passion story or some part of it on this last Sunday in Lent. In Year A the reading is from Matt.

26:14—27:66 or part of this. The narrative begins with the betrayal by Judas and ends with the death of Jesus and the guard on the tomb. The whole of Mark's narrative (chapters 14–15 or parts therof) is the lesson for Year B, and the reading for Year C (Luke 22:14—23:56 or parts therof) begins with the Last Supper and ends with the burial.

Mark's account is the principal source for the others, but Luke also makes use of one or more separate sources. Scholars used to believe that most of Mark's Passion Narrative (except for 14:3–9, 32–42) came from a single connected source that contained little theological interpretation. Careful studies by redaction critics have now concluded that this story is not completely unified and that one can see Mark's editing in it as well as theological motifs drawn from the OT that existed in the pre-Marcan tradition.

At the same time, the outline of the story was well known and there was no doubt about the order of events, as we can see from John's Passion Narrative, which apparently comes from an independent tradition. The sequence is: the Last Supper, the betrayal and arrest of Jesus, a hearing before the high priest, Peter's denial, the trial before Pilate, the Crucifixion, and the death and burial. It is in the details and in the interpretations that the gospels diverge from one another.

Certain things that actually occurred in the Crucifixion inevitably reminded the disciples of the OT psalms. Jesus must surely have spoken the words of Ps. 22:1 in his native Aramaic, not the Hebrew, and this cry from the Cross aroused such theological questions that it could scarcely have been invented. It is also very likely that the executioners divided his garments among them (cf. Ps. 22:18), that he was offered wine to slake his thirst (Ps. 69:21), and that his enemies mocked him (Ps. 22:7). From this point on the tradition could easily grow because of the belief that the OT prophesied the events of Jesus' life. Thus Matthew speaks of wine mingled with gall (27:34) and quotes Ps. 22:8 (Matt. 27:43). Other examples are found in John 19:36f., where OT quotations are applied to the narrative.

The homilist should be familiar with standard commentaries on the gospels, but at this point it must be noted that some episodes in Matthew seem to be legendary, whereas the narrative in Mark is almost completely lacking in miracle. The dream of Pilate's wife (27:19) has a curious resemblance to the premonition of Calpurnia before Julius Caesar was assassinated. Another legend that is historically dubious is that of the guard on the tomb (27:62–66; 28:11–14). There was also a tradition that Judas Iscariot came to a bad end and was buried in the field (or place) of blood, but the two accounts of it, Acts. 1:18f. and Matt. 27:3–10, cannot be reconciled. The latter story is much influenced by OT passages.

What is more serious is the scene in which Pilate washes his hands and the people say, "let his blood be on us and on our children" (27:24f.), because for centuries this passage has been an excuse for persecution of the Jewish people.

Nothing can exonerate Pilate from the guilt of the judicial murder of Jesus. Had he wished, he could have resisted the will of the high-priestly gang. It is also unlikely that a Jewish crowd would have invoked a curse on the nation; and even if some individuals in a hostile mob uttered such words, it is a question how many they were. The God and Father of Jesus Christ would not accept such a curse.

The NT, taken in its totality, is not an anti-Jewish book. The Gospel of John does indeed contain several passages in which "the Jews" are the enemies of Jesus, but there "the Jews" (or perhaps Judaeans as distinct from Galileans) serve only as a symbol of opponents of the gospel message. Paul at times says bitter things about Jewish opponents, but he believed firmly in the destiny of his own people (Rom. 9:1–5). Israel is the old olive tree and the Gentiles are only branches of wild olive grafted into it (Rom. 11:13–24).

The Betrayal and the Last Supper

The gospels tell of Pharisees who were hostile to Jesus, and it is certain that he differed sharply from them on points of interpretation of the Torah. He also denounced Pharisees for conduct and attitudes that the rabbinic tradition itself condemns. We do, however, read of friendly discussions between Jesus and the scribes (Mark 12:28–34; Luke 10:25–28), and the occasion when Pharisees warned him against Herod Antipas (Luke 13:31) is a sign that relations with members of that party were not always unfriendly.

There is no evidence that Pharisees had anything to do with the events that led to the Crucifixion. Some Pharisees were members of the Sanhedrin, but it was the high priest Caiaphas, his father-in-law Annas, who had previously held that office, and their followers, who denounced Jesus to Pilate. These people belonged to the Sudducees, a conservative party in which much of the landed wealth of the country was concentrated, and it was to their interest to collaborate with the Roman government.

These were the ones who suborned Judas Iscariot. We can only guess at his motives, since money alone does not sufficiently explain why one who had been specially chosen by Jesus, or at least had closely attached himself to him, would betray his Lord. What he evidently agreed to do was to lead the Temple police to where Jesus was likely to be and to identify the man whom they sought.

The Last Supper will be discussed in connection with Thursday in Passion Week, but since the gospel for that day is from John, except for three lectionaries in Years B and C and Luke 22:14-30 as an alternative in the Episcopal, a few comments on the place of that story in Mark and Luke are appropriate here. Matthew adds little to Mark's account.

The tradition in the Synoptics is that this supper was a Passover meal, whereas in John the Passover does not occur until after Jesus' death. Various theories try to explain the discrepancy, but for our purposes it is important only to remember that it occurred in close relation to that festival. According to Mark, Jesus had made secret preparations for the feast. At the supper, as the host, he probably said the traditional thanks-givings over the bread and wine that are used in Jewish households to this day. But he added, "Take this; this is my Body . . . This is my Blood of the covenant . . . " Thus he indicated that his approaching death was to be for the benefit of God's People. This was by no means strange in Judaism, for many believed that the deaths of martyrs in Maccabean days had saved the nation.

Luke has an account of the Supper that differs from that of Mark but supplements that gospel in important respects. (1) Jesus first gives the disciples the cup, then the bread, saying that he will not eat the Passover or drink the fruit of the vine until that festival is "fulfilled in the Kingdom of God" (22:15-19a). (2) Some important MSS. omit verses 19b-20, but the text read by most authorities adds "which is given for you; do this in remembrance of me" and also a second giving of the cup after the Supper, with the words, "This cup is the new covenant in my blood, which is shed for you." These words are very similar to Paul's tradition as found in I Cor. 11:23-25. (3) Jesus puts the Supper into the context of lowly service by teaching that he is in their midst as one who serves, and that this must be the pattern for "the one who is greatest among you" (22:24-27). He then announces a covenant with his disciples; they will eat and drink at his table in his kingdom and sit on thrones judging the tribes of Israel (22:28-30). Finally there are two brief pericopes: the command to Simon Peter to strengthen his brothers after Satan has sifted him, and the enigmatic dialogue about the two swords.

The gospel writers obviously have in mind both the Christian Pass-over and the Eucharist; the latter was probably celebrated each week, as it certainly was by the second century. Like Paul, they connect its institution with the Last Supper. Mark and Luke show that it is also an anticipation of the future Messianic Banquet, which was a feature of Jewish eschatology. It should be remembered, too, that the metaphor of eating and drinking as a symbol of the reception of spiritual gifts appears in the gospels more frequently than any other. The feedings of the Five Thousand and the Four Thousand are examples of this. It seems possible that the Lord's Supper is a continuation of Jesus' many joyful meals with his disciples and with outcasts and sinners, and that these were signs of the presence of the Reign of God. This explains why it was necessary for Paul to remind the Corinthians that in celebrating the Supper they were proclaiming the death of the Lord "until he comes."

Luke's account, with its emphasis on humility, has similarities to the story of the Last Supper in John 13, but scholars are not agreed on how the traditions are related. This will be discussed further in connection with Maundy Thursday.

The Arrest and the Trials

When one compares the account of the arrest of Jesus in Mark 14:43–52 with the corresponding sections in the other gospels, it is easy to see how the tradition grew. The earliest form is straightforward. Judas has led the Temple police to the place where Jesus could be found and has pointed him out in the gloom of the olive orchard. Jesus asks ironically why they did not seize him in the Temple and have now come to find him as though he were a bandit. The incident of the young man with a linen cloth about him is mysterious. Some have thought that this was the evangelist Mark himself; more probably he is the same as the young man at the empty tomb (Mark 16:8).

The essential part of the hearing before the high priest (Mark 14:53–65), historically speaking, is the charge that Jesus had threatened to destroy the Temple. The gospels themselves give evidence that he had prophesied against it, but witnesses could not agree on the charge. From all that we can learn about Jewish law, this was not a legal trial; it was only an attempt to find evidence against Jesus. The high priest then asked Jesus if he were the Messiah. His answer, as it stands (14:62) is formulated from the point of view of Christian theology: he is Messiah, but only in the sense of the coming Son of Man. The opponents made up their minds that he must die, but they could achieve this only by denouncing him to Pilate as one who claimed to be King of the Jews. Either they twisted whatever words he said or relied on the fact that other people had called him the Messiah.

This hearing provides the framework for Peter's denial of his Lord. The early Church found an important lesson here, and Mark probably wrote his gospel after the martyrdom of Peter. Like all other Christians, Mark knew that Peter was the most prominent of the disciples. His denial was an example of the temptation faced by all, and Peter's objection at Caesarea Philippi had already foreshadowed the denial. Yet even such a person could be restored; in the future he was to strengthen his brethren (Luke 22:31f.) and become a courageous herald of the gospel.

There are historical problems in the accounts of the trial before Pilate but some points are clear. Only Pilate had the power to order an execution. As governor of a Roman province he was not bound by the rules of jurisprudence that applied to trials in Rome. He could conduct the hearing as he chose, and his responsibility was to keep order in what was essentially an occupied country. Jesus offered no defense, yet Pilate was convinced that he was innocent and harmless. The charge was high treason; that is, that Jesus claimed to be King of the Jews. It was evidently for the purpose of preserving public order that Pilate gave in to the shouts of the angry mob and ordered his crucifixion.

Mark tells us that Simon, from Cyrene in North Africa, was compelled to carry the heavy cross beam that was to be nailed to the tree or pole at the place of crucifixion. This man was evidently known to the first readers of the gospel, for he is identified as the father of Alexander and Rufus. The place of execution was outside the city. A tradition of the fourth century, which may be much older, locates this within the Church of the Holy Sepulchre, and most archaeologists think that in the first century this spot was outside the walls.

According to Mark, Jesus suffered on the Cross for only six hours. This was a merciful release, for such an execution was essentially a death by torture, and condemned men sometimes hung on the cross for days. We should not exaggerate the extent of Jesus' sufferings, although they were undoubtedly horrible. The Romans had learned this barbarous practice from the Carthaginians and inflicted it on rebels and slaves.

The traditions in the four gospels suggest that Jesus meditated on verses from the Psalms. Mark tells us that at the end our Lord gave a great shout. The pagan centurion may have understood this as a cry of triumph, or perhaps he was impressed by the way in which Jesus met his sufferings, for he said, "Certainly this man was a son of God." Only the faithful women who had followed Jesus from Galilee stayed at the Cross.

Maundy Thursday (Holy Thursday)

Although some lectionaries provide readings for every day of Holy Week, we shall discuss only the days that are celebrated in the majority of churches. Holy Thursday commemorates the institution of the Eucharist; in the Lutheran and Episcopal service books it is called "Maundy Thursday" because of the words in John 13:34, "I give you a new commandment" (*mandatum novum do vobis*).

The Roman and Episcopal lectionaries use the same readings for all three years, and the other lectionaries provide them for Year A. These are the institution of the Passover (Exod. 12:1-14) and the accounts of the Last Supper given by Paul (I Cor. 11:23-32) and the Fourth Gospel (John 13:1-15).

The pericopes prescribed by other lectionaries for Years B and C include other stories of the origin of the Passover, the ratification of the Mosaic covenant (Exod. 24:3-11), Jeremiah's prophecy of the New Covenant (31:31-34), a passage from First Corinthians speaking of participation in the Body and Blood of Christ and of Christ as the Paschal Lamb (10:16-17), accounts of the Last Supper from the Synoptic Gospels and a pericope from Heb. 10:15-39 bearing on the high priesthood of Christ and the New Covenant.

The Pauline narrative in I Cor. 11 is necessary as a counterpart to the reading in John 13, for the latter does not include the words of institution that are a part of all eucharistic liturgies. There have been various conjectures to account for this omission. One theory is that by the time the Fourth Gospel was written, these sacred words were not disclosed to outsiders. John's theological method may provide a better explanation. He continually reinterprets the older gospel tradition and his sequence of events is independent of the outlines of the Synoptic Gospels. The Feeding of the Five Thousand, which has eucharistic features in Mark 6:30-44, is probably John's model for the Eucharist (John 6:1-15) and it is combined with a long discourse in which the Bread of Life is a principal theme (6:22-59).

When the Fourth Evangelist comes to the Last Supper, he is therefore able to put that event in a larger theological and moral context. He affirms the Incarnation, Jesus' return to the Father, his knowledge of what would happen, and his enduring love for his own (13:1-3). The washing of feet, like so many other elements in this gospel, has more than one meaning. It is a dramatic example of humble service (cf. Luke 22:24-27) and also a symbol of that forgiveness of sins which is one of God's gifts in the Eucharist. Peter, conscious of his sin, would like to be baptized again, but he needs only to have washed away the dust and mire that cleave to the feet during our walk through life (13:6-10).

The pericope read on Holy Thursday also contains the prophecy of Judas's betrayal, and this is significant for our understanding of John's doctrine of the Eucharist and the Church. Judas is still one of the Twelve although he has planned to betray Jesus, but it is only after he receives the morsel of bread from the Lord's hands that Satan enters into him (cf. I Cor. 11:27-30). He immediately goes out *into the night* (13:26-30).

Just after this, Jesus discloses the final mystery of the Supper, the commandment of love, which for John is the key to understanding God's action in the Eucharist and the sum of all moral teaching. The Eucharist begins in the love of God through Christ, it creates the fellowship of the Church, and it leads to reciprocal loving-kindness.

Good Friday

The Roman *Ordo* is followed in the main by other lectionaries in the reading of Isa. 52:13—53:12, Heb. 4:14-16; 5:7-9, and John 18:1—19:42 or parts thereof. The differences are that the Presbyterian book has other pericopes for Years B and C that carry on similar themes, and the Book of Common Prayer uses Heb. 10:1-25 (the Methodist as an alternative) as the second reading in all three years. The psalm in most lectionaries is 22, which our Lord quoted as he hung on the Cross.

The Isaiah passage is the climax of the four Servant Songs in Second Isaiah. These oracles, which bring a new element into Hebrew prophecy, speak of the Servant of Yahweh as though he were an individual who has announced God's Word to the people and has suffered on their behalf. One is tempted to think of Jeremiah or some other prophet, but Christians immediately related this figure to Jesus, and the gospel tradition contains sayings of Jesus which suggest that he himself made this identification.

Other parts of the Servant Songs, however, show that the Second Isaiah understood the Servant to be Israel, which will establish justice in the earth and be a light to the nations (Isa. 42:5-7; 43:10; 49:6). This exemplifies the idea of corporate personality; the word Israel is the surname of the patriarch Jacob, and the nation is sometimes addressed as Jacob.

In the fourth song the Servant is despised and rejected, but "he was wounded for our transgressions . . .with his stripes we are healed," he was cut off from the land of the living, was an offering for sin, bore the sin of many, made intercession for transgressors, and will cause many to be vindicated or accounted righteous. These aspects of the song seem to have been neglected in the rabbinic tradition, perhaps because it was difficult to fit them into the prevailing Jewish theology. It has been left to Christians to see a unique significance in this passage.

The Johannine account of the Crucifixion contains an independent tradition that throws some historical light on the trial before Pilate. The story as a whole, however, is interpreted in terms of the evangelist's theology. The Synoptic accounts are more closely related to history, while John's story enables the homilist to perceive a more explicitly theological meaning in the events.

Much of the Gospel of John understands Jesus as Prophet and King. He is the prophet like Moses who is to come and announce the truth. In the Passion Narrative he is seen primarily in his aspect as King, and his Kingdom is not of this world (18:36). At the same time, he is a witness to the truth (18:37) and as such is the model for Christian witness and martyrdom.

John's typological use of Scripture (19:24, 33-37) is similar to that in the other gospels. There are, however, other theological features. Jesus commits his Mother and the Beloved Disciple to one another (19:26f.), and since in 2:1-11 (the marriage at Cana) Jesus' Mother is probably a symbol of the true Israel, this part of the story may be a symbol of the Church. The word "I thirst" and the spear thrust serve to teach Jesus' true humanity (cf. 4:6f.), for the divine Word truly became flesh. Jesus' last word is *tetelestai* (19:30). The verb means "to finish," "to complete," and the perfect tense denotes an action in the past whose results abide in the present. This word sums up the teaching of 16:25-33 ("Rejoice, I have overcome the world"), and the Vulgate renders it admirably, *consummatum est.*

The Meaning of the Cross

One who undertakes the awesome responsibility of preaching and teaching about the Cross should have wrestled with its theological meaning.

Why did Jesus die? A secular historian might say that he was an innocent man whose ways and teaching were so disturbing, and his influence with the people so great, that the high-priestly gang and Pilate thought it prudent to do away with him, just as Herod Antipas had put John the Baptist to death. If it had been rumored that some of Jesus' disciples called him the Messiah, it would have been possible to persuade the prefect that he was a pretender to the Jewish throne. The account in John 19:12–16 fits the historical situation. Pilate knew, on the one hand, that the emperor Tiberius disapproved of mistreatment of people in his provinces—in fact, Pilate was removed from office a few years later because of his savagery—but on the other hand, Tiberius was merciless when he suspected treason. As soon as Caiaphas and his associates hinted that they would accuse Pilate to Tiberius of having released a man accused of treason, he gave in and pronounced the sentence. Now he was able to insult the accusers by insisting that the inscription should read "The King of the Jews." According to all accounts, it was not the Jewish people, or any significant part of them, who committed the judicial murder, but the personal representative of the of the emperor.

Most historians would reconstruct the events in some such way. But history itself does not answer the theological question of why this happened. Why did Jesus put himself in this position? Has his Cross brought salvation to human beings in a unique way, as nothing else could do? How has it accomplished this?

The attempt to answer these questions has gone on since the beginning. Only with the greatest intellectual and spiritual humility can a Christian dare to approach them. St. Anselm of Canterbury put his reasonings in the form of a prayerful meditation. Whatever is said in this part of the chapter represents the attempt of just one person to explain the Cross to himself.

Since Christianity, like Judaism, is a historical religion, we begin with history as far as we can know it. The Christian faith affirms that God became man in Jesus. If this is our conviction, what he said and did is the revelation of God that tests all else that claims to reveal him. He went to Jerusalem in prayer and obedience. As a vigorous young person who loved life and rejoiced in the created world, he had no desire to die; but he was ready to die rather than disobey. He is the example of all men and women who have stood fast in defense of what is right and true. In this he was like Amos, Jeremiah, and Socrates.

The agony in Gethsemane (Mark 14:32-42) is told in highly stylized fashion, but it discloses Jesus in his true humanity, appalled and shuddering at what lay ahead. The objection that the disciples were asleep and could not have heard Jesus in prayer is not important; people who are half asleep can often hear. The story serves Mark's purpose of declaring that a Christian must keep awake and watchful, facing reality with his Lord.

Whether the Cross saves mankind, and how, are the most important questions. One of the earliest solutions offered to the Church is that it marks God's triumph over the powers of evil. We find this in Col. 2:13-15, which can be paraphrased as follows: Christ gave life to those who were dead in their sins, uniting them with himself, forgiving their trespasses; he annulled that document, the Law, that held them in bondage as slaves, and nailed it to the Cross, thus cancelling it; he stripped the rulers and authorities of their power, publicly exposed them for what they were, and triumphed over them by the Cross.

This reasoning involves the power of the Resurrrection. Behind it lies also the concept that the world as it now exists is ruled by spiritual forces that are enemies of God. Pilate was under the control of this personified evil and the Crucifixion showed this, but he could not defeat Jesus. Even the Law, because its purpose was misunderstood, served the evil purpose of making slaves of human beings.

Such an approach was followed by several early Church fathers, and sometimes in the form of a myth according to which Satan tricked himself. He tried to swallow up Jesus by putting him to death, but he could not subdue the divine nature which defeated him. Certainly the gospel tradition contains the idea of triumph over demonic forces. When the disciples return to Jesus, telling of the casting out of demons, he exclaims, "I was seeing Satan fallen from heaven like lightning!" (Luke 10:17-20; cf. Rev. 12:7-12).

This is worth pondering. It must have seemed certain to Jesus' enemies and even to the disciples that the Cross was the final defeat of his mission. Yet, even if we leave aside for the moment faith in the Resurrection and Jesus' divine nature, it was a historical victory. The Good News spread throughout the world. Surely it was a human triumph also; the unjust death of a good man may be only a stage in the success of his ultimate purpose, just as the "forlorn hope" of the Greeks at Thermopylae had much to do with the victory over Persia.

Another theory of the Atonement that has been influential down to our own day, that of St. Anselm, is based on a picture that is just as mythical as the idea that Satan was tricked. It rests on medieval ideas of sovereignty and justice. If defiance to a lord goes unpunished, the whole structure of feudal society will collapse. God is the infinite King, and humanity's sin against him is an infinite affront. No human being can pay the price of this, and yet only man can satisfy the divine justice. But God in his love and mercy does not will the destructon of his People, and therfore only one who is truly God and truly man can make the sacrifice.

One can only respect the faith and sensitivity that led Anselm to this conclusion. His doctrine combines faith with scholastic logic and is an attempt to reconcile reason and revelation, as every theologian must try to do. Yet, as it is too often presented, it tends to divide the Father and the Son and to contrast the justice and anger of the one with the love and obedience of the other. Jesus accordingly becomes the real God of the Christians, and it is very easy to have feelings of resistance toward the God of the OT.

We believe that there is and can be only one God. Therefore, if we respect the Christian tradition as a whole, we can never separate God and Jesus in our thinking and prayer. We will not make this mistake if we remember Paul's interpretation: "God was in Christ reconciling the world to himself . . . and he has placed in us the message of reconciliation" (II Cor. 5:19).

The OT reconciles God's justice and mercy but never tries to do this theoretically. It puts them side by side or uses the frankly anthropomorphic expression "Yahweh repented himself of the evil that he had planned to do"; in other words he changed his mind because of someone's repentance. The biblical writers used symbolic language and did not trouble themselves with the problem of a God who might change his plans.

God does not change, but history does. The NT proclaims everywhere that the Incarnation, mission, Cross and Resurrection of Jesus Christ created a totally new situation in human history. What is new about it? Not that God is just, good and loving, and forgives the repentant. Yet this man's life inaugurated a New Covenant, a new relationship between humanity and God. Paul understood this to mean that the relation does not come from obedience to a law, written or oral, however good in itself, but that obedience and the good life result from a relationship to God in faith and love that comes through Jesus Christ. This is open to everyone, Jews and Gentiles alike.

Such a way of thinking depends on the Incarnation, the faith that at a specific time and in a specific place God entered uniquely into human life and shared all the experience of mortals. Men, women and children undergo some of the miseries of other animals: sickness, pain and rejection. But the misery and fear that belong to humanity alone come to us because we can project ourselves into the past and the future and we know that we are going to die. It is this that led Albert Camus to regard life as absurd, and Martin Heidegger to say that we are "thrown" into our existence. Various religions and philosophies try to deal with this, and one way is to say that both life and death are mere illusions. Or "let us eat and drink, for tomorrow we die." There is also the attitude of the Stoic, who lives by a strict moral code, is just in his dealings, tries to despise pleasure and pain, power and slavery alike, and proudly defies fate, relying on his own moral integrity.

Many religions promise some kind of life after death, and so does Christianity. Paul believed this to be guaranteed by the Resurrection of Christ, and believers find an assurance here. The Apostle's conviction does not rest on this as an isolated event; behind it is faith that God is not just any kind of god, but rather that his character and purpose are supremely revealed in the human life of Jesus. Thus, despite all appearances, despite the dark miseries and questionings of Job or the skepticism of Ecclesiastes, despite the demonic forces that slaughtered millions of innocent Jews in gas chambers and the many other massacres that make history hideous, despite the Cross of Christ, senseless though all of this is, the universe in which God acts is ultimately to be trusted. Nothing in life or death can separate us from the love of God which is in Christ Jesus our Lord (Rom. 8:38f.).

But how does the Cross make a difference in the universe and in human history? It is not quite enough to say that it *reveals* the character of God and the way of the Cross that is to be imitated in our lives, though it does that. Socrates willingly suffered an unjust death though he could have avoided it (as Jesus also might have done), and many of Socrates's philosophic successors tried to follow his teaching that it is better to suffer than to do wrong. He and Plato believed that anyone who really learns what "the good" is will do it, but either this is a mistake or very few ever "learn." Revelation is essential, but it is not enough. Paul found that the Cross gives *power*. He made explicit what is implicit in the gospels, that in union with God through Jesus Christ we find the power to do what we cannot do by ourselves. The grace of God is more than pardon, it is power.

Paul never pretended that relying on this force is easy. He pictures the *results* of grace eloquently in the eighth chapter of Romans; else-where he describes the *process* as carrying in our bodies the death of the Lord Jesus so that the life of Jesus may also be manifested in them (II Cor. 5:6–18). Even this bears with it a sense of triumph—"cast down but not destroyed"; "sorrowful yet always rejoicing, poor but making many rich, having nothing and yet possessing all things" (II Cor. 6:10).

As we look at ourselves, we do not find our union with the crucified and risen Christ to be perfect. Paul's letters show that he was continually engaged in conflict, and he claimed no more than that he was straining forward like an athlete to receive the prize (Phil. 3:14). The greatest of saints regularly describe themselves as sinners; but that does not matter. God accepts us even when we are slow to accept ourselves.

It is not easy to answer the objection of an inquirer who still asks, "But how does this message of the Cross change matters in the universe as a whole?" Paul and other Christians believed that it does, and this is a matter of faith. The only answer I can give is faith in the triumph of Jesus' way. The earth is inconceivably old, and humanity as a distinct species has existed for many millennia. Despite the danger of nuclear war and other possible calamities, life may go on for a very long time. We may not be the late Christians, but the early ones; with God a thousand years are as a day.

Easter
and Eastertide

Easter Day provides problems as well as great opportunities for the preacher. The Easter parade temporarily leaves bunnies and eggs to one side and goes to church. In some churches at least, one must try to reach both the faithful—who have been through the events of Holy Week and are ready for an important message—and others who will not be present again until Mother's Day and then not until Christmastide. Unfortunately, some people have been so well vaccinated by pseudo-Christianity that they are all but immune to the real thing.

Is this a result of the old rule that in order to stay in good standing one must make one's communion at least three times a year? Or is it deep in human nature? In OT times only a few festivals were obligatory, and perhaps this is all that can be expected from the mass of humanity. The three-times-a-year people do not realize what they are missing, and this baffles the clergy, but it will do no good to scold the Easter worshippers for their laxity.

Another possible factor is that many experience Christmas and Good Friday as realities, because we know about birth and death, but life after death is a hope rather than an experience. The happy ending of Easter can seem to be a fairy tale. Too many Americans know Jesus not as the risen Lord but only a great teacher who lived long ago.

Northrop Frye, the literary critic, finds elements of romance, tragedy, comedy, and even irony in the gospel story. From one point of view, Jesus' ministry is a heroic quest, fraught with deadly danger, in which he is victorious; this is the essence of romance. But it is also a comedy which contains a tragedy within itself: that is, "comedy" in the sense of Dante's great poem, but not a farce. Christianity, says Frye, "sees trage-dy as an episode in the divine comedy, the larger scheme of redemption and resurrection. The sense of tragedy as a prelude to comedy seems almost inseparable from anything explicitly Christian" (*Anatomy of Criticism,* p. 215).

Perhaps modern people can accept tragedy and irony as more true to life than comedy, and much of our contemporary literature illustrates this. Comedy seems either naive or trivial; it is all right for popular amusement but not as an interpretation of our existence. But is this an accurate judgment? There are more happy endings in life than one might suppose, otherwise so many would not plan and strive; but it is also true that the hoped-for happiness often comes after one has been down into the valley of death.

Our purpose, then, is to expound the divine comedy in such a way that it can become real. The Resurrection is the essence of this; Paul went so far as to say that without it our preaching and our hope are in vain (I Cor. 15:17).

The Great Vigil of Easter

Recent liturgical reforms have restored the Great Vigil of Easter to its proper place, and it should be the greatest experience of the whole Christian year. As we have said, this was originally the climax of the process whereby catechumens were initiated into the People of God through baptism and first communion. In those churches where the vigil is celebrated the worshippers are likely to be the solid core of the faithful.

The vigil consists of four parts. The first is the lighting of the paschal candle, and this is followed immediately by the *praeconium* or Easter proclamation (*Exsultet*). The typology that was so dear to the early Church comes to its highest poetic expression in this song or solemn declamation which evidently was influenced by the still more ancient Jewish Passover liturgy. Then follows the liturgy of the word, consisting of seven or nine OT lessons interspersed with psalms. The cumulative effect is tremendous. The third part is the liturgy of baptism, and the fourth is the Eucharist itself.

Only three of the lectionaries, Roman, Episcopal, and Methodist, provide the powerful OT "prophecies." At five points they coincide completely, though not in order, and in two other cases two of the lectionaries agree. All three have the same epistle and gospel lessons for Year A for the Eucharist that is to follow; the Roman and Methodist schemes agree in Years B and C.

Four of the OT readings call for special attention. The series begins with the creation story from the Priestly source (Gen. 1:1—2:2). The third or fourth (Exod. 14:10—15:1) tells of the crossing of the Red Sea, which typologically is related to redemption and particularly to baptism. Isa. 55:1-11, the fifth or sixth reading, is God's invitation to banquet "without money and without price" and offers an everlasting covenant. It concludes with an announcement of God's ways which are not our ways, and of the power of his word. Ezek. 36:16-28 promises that God will "sprinkle clean water" upon his People and put a new heart of flesh in them in place of the heart of stone.

Equally appropriate to the occasion is the epistle reading (Rom. 6:3-11), which teaches that the Christian is buried with Christ in baptism and is dead to sin. It is characteristic of Paul's teaching and of much of the NT that this statement of a fact (the all-important indicative) which expresses the possibility of the new humanity, is joined in verses 12-14 (not read at this time) with the imperative: "Therefore do not let sin reign in your mortal body."

The gospel pericopes (Matt. 28:1-10, A; Mark 16:1-8, B; Luke 24:1-12, C) appointed in the Roman *Ordo* for the vigil will be discussed in connection with Easter Day.

The psalms that are interspersed with the readings add to the power and beauty of the vigil liturgy. The three lectionaries do not agree altogether in the choice of these, but it is worth noting that all include Isa. 12:2-6 and Psalm 42. The former is a song of trust and joy proclaiming that God's People will draw water from the springs of salvation. In the latter, as in many songs of lament, the worshipper feels himself oppressed by enemies who taunt him, but it is more than this. He is far from God's house, evidently in the far north, and longs for God's presence, yet he is able to trust and pray. Here it fits with the mood of the congregation, which has identified itself with Christ in the loneliness of the Passion and now looks forward to the joy of Easter.

Easter Day

The three lessons in the Roman *Ordo* are Acts 10:34a, 37-43; Col. 3:1-4 (or I Cor. 5:6b-8); and John 20:1-9. The responsorial psalm consists of parts of Ps. 118. These should be considered first, since all other lectionaries use the three lessons for the principal service in Year A, expanding the first reading to include all of verses 34–43, and in some cases providing alternatives. NA thus employs Jer. 31:1–6 (the restora-tion of Israel).

Acts. 10:34–43 is one of the most remarkable examples of the early Church's proclamation that have come down to us. It is represented as Peter's joyful speech before he had baptized the Gentile centurion Cor-nelius. Luke, like other Hellenistic historians, provides speeches suitable to the occasion for his characters. This pericope admirably sums up the Gospel of Luke and places the Resurrection in the context of Jesus' whole ministry, the expectation that he will return as judge, and the witness of the OT.

Col. 3:1–4 affirms the basic meaning of the Resurrection for believing Christians. They have died with Christ and in principle are raised with him; therefore they are to seek that which is above. As we can see elsewhere in Paul's letters, the imperative is joined with the indicative. I Cor. 5:6b–8 was formerly the epistle in the Roman missal and also that of Sarum. It connects the Easter celebration with the Passover and Unleavened Bread.

John 20:1–9 is traditional for the day. Mary Magdalene is the first to come to the tomb and find it empty; and she summons Peter and the Beloved Disciple. The latter, who symbolizes the ideal follower of Jesus, outruns Peter, but he does not enter the tomb; he leaves this honor to the chief of the disciples.

John's account is independent of the other gospels and has features that are found elsewhere in the Fourth Gospel. It preserves the tradition, found also in Mark, that Mary Magdalene was the first to visit the grave, and it fits with the tradition in First Corinthians and Luke that Peter was the first actual witness of the Resurrection.

The Episcopal, Lutheran, and NA lectionaries provide Matt. 28:1–10 as an alternative for Year A, and all except the Roman have Mark 16:1–8 for Year B. Luke 24:1–11 is the Episcopal and Lutheran reading for Year C. The Roman rite uses these readings at the vigil and permits their use on Easter Day. These three pericopes should be considered together.

Mark's account of the empty tomb is the oldest. Here Mary Magda-lene and the other women are the first to have news of the Resurrection. The young man at the tomb directs the disciples to meet Jesus in Galilee; many scholars think that, according to Mark, what is expected there is not a resurrection appearance but the Parousia of the Son of Man. Whether or not this is so, the pericope is Mark's sole account of the Resurrection, for 16:9-20 is not from Mark's hand but a later summary of the traditions in the other three gospels and Acts with some additions.

The corresponding pericopes in Matthew and Luke seem to be developed out of the brief narrative in Mark. In Mark 16:8 the women say nothing to anyone because of their fear, but in the other gospels they report their experience to the disciples. The young man is interpreted by Matthew as the angel of the Lord, while Luke speaks of two men in dazzling clothing.

The story of the two disciples who met the risen Lord on the way to Emmaus (Luke 24:13-35) is included in the readings of the Presbyterian and Methodist lectionaries for Year C and for the third (evening) celebration in the Book of Common Prayer. The Roman *Ordo* appoints this pericope for optional use at afternoon Eucharists. The Lutheran order and NA add verses 36-49 for an evening Eucharist or one on Easter Monday. This beautiful story is a recognition scene, like the one in which Jesus appears to Mary Magdalene (John 20:11-18) and thus belongs to a genre found frequently in Hellenistic literature. But its most important feature is that the risen Lord is made known to the disciples in the "breaking of the bread," Luke's term for the Lord's Supper (Acts 2:42). It is composed in harmony with Luke's theology of the fulfilment of Scripture (24:27; cf. 24:44-47; Acts 8:30-38); note that prior to the common meal Jesus expounds the OT.

Alongside the narratives of the Resurrection in the four gospels, there is the earlier statement in I Cor. 15:1-11, which is read on Easter Day only in the Lutheran, Methodist, and NA lectionaries in Year C, and appears in three lectionaries in the season after Epiphany. Paul tells us that this is the tradition as he received it and passed it on to the Corinthians; thus it might be considered the "official" formulation of the Church's faith about the Year A.D. 50. Peter was the first to have seen the risen Lord, and it is noteworthy that Paul speaks of two appearances of Christ not mentioned in the gospels, to five hundred Christians, some of whom were still alive, and also to James, evidently the "brother of the Lord."

Thus there are great variations in the tradition of the empty tomb and in the stories that tell of seeing the risen Lord and hearing him speak. The first readers of the gospels, and most Christians since, have not been concerned about the discrepancies, for all parts of the NT testify to the tradition that after the Resurrection the disciples encountered Christ as living and powerful.

Ps. 118 or parts of it are prescribed in the lectionaries for Easter Day and for two of the Sundays in the season. The psalm was evidently used in Jewish worship at the Feast of Tabernacles. Verses 19–20, 27 suggest that it was sung in procession, and verses 25–26 welcomed pilgrims on that occasion. The *Hosanna* (Heb. *Hoshiana,* "Save now") greeted Jesus on his triumphal entry, as though he were coming to this festival of hope for national deliverance, and it has always been a feature of Christian liturgy. "The stone which the builders rejected" (verses 22–23) referred originally to a king, actual or ideal, who had escaped death and won victory; Christians applied it to Jesus from the earliest times (Mark 12:11–12; Acts 4:11). Parts of the psalm (verses 10–18) are almost an incantation. This feature, characteristic of some other psalms, is an example of faith in the power of the word to protect and redeem, bless or curse (Luke 10:5f; Rom. 1:16). Although incantation can degenerate into magic, in itself it is a form of faith and prayer.

Ps. 114, provided by the Episcopal lectionary for the first and third celebrations, is another psalm traditional for Easter. The Resurrection, like the Exodus from Egypt and the crossing of the Jordan, is God's mighty act to redeem his People.

Proclamation of the Risen Christ

The pericopes from Acts 10:34–43 and I Cor. 15:1–11 are kerygmatic, and in this connection we should mention certain other proclamations of the Resurrection.

The NT contains two kinds of announcement, namely Jesus' proclamation of the Reign of God, which is closely related to the message of the Hebrew prophets, and the Church's gospel of salvation and new life through Jesus Christ. It is the second that we are now discussing. This faith begins with the gospel account of the Resurrection and goes on to interpret the work of Christ, and especially his Passion.

Some of these have been mentioned in previous chapters. Rom. 1:1–4, which is read on Advent 4A, teaches that Jesus Christ was marked out (or designated) as Son of God *in power* by his Resurrection from the dead. Since Paul believed in the preexistence of Christ, this is a more precise theological statement than the primitive acclamation in Acts 2:36, "Therefore let all the house of Israel know with certainty that God has made him both Lord and Messiah, this Jesus whom you crucified."

The lectionaries prescribe parts of the great speech at Pentecost attributed to Peter, of which this verse is the climax (Easter 4A or 3A), but they do not include the quotation of Ps. 110:1 (Acts 2:34f.) that it is intended to interpret. The psalm was probably composed for the enthronement of a Hebrew king, but its first verse must have been applied to Jesus soon after the Crucifixion, and it is one of the most important foundations of NT Christology. The concept of the Son seated at God's right hand lies behind I Cor. 15:25, is an element in the complex of ideas about Jesus as Son of Man (Mark 14:62; cf. also 12:35–37), and is used also in Heb. 1:1–13. Verse 4 of the same psalm is used in Heb. 5:6 to show that Jesus is high priest after the order of Melchizedek.

Another proclamation (Acts. 3:19–26) is also very early. This recalls the prophecy of Deut. 18:15–20 that a prophet like Moses will arise, but the part of the pericope that contains this is read only in the Episcopal lectionary (Easter 2B).

Two other passages that interpret the Incarnation and Ascension have already been discussed, John 1:1–18 (Christmas Day) and Phil. 2:5–11 (Passion Sunday). A third, Col. 1:12–20, is the second reading in Year C on the Sunday before Advent, the festival of Christ the King. The German scholar Ernst Käsemann has argued that this passage is a Gnostic hymn that has been adapted as a confession of faith made at baptism, but we do not know that this type of Gnosticism can be so early. The passages from John and Philippians can perhaps be understood as based on Gnostic patterns of thought that have been purified and corrected by Christian faith.

This may seem shocking until we realize that Paul was dealing with a destructive error in Colossae that threatened to undermine the Christian faith by inserting a series of mediators betwen mankind and God. Elsewhere in his letters Paul uses Gnostic language in a decidedly non-Gnostic way. Why? Because this type of thinking was in the air. What the old hymn in Colossians might have said about a Gnostic redeemer (the primal or archetypal Man) could be said better of Christ—the sole mediator—but with a decisive difference. For the Christian confession of faith adds that God "has delivered us from the power of darkness and transferred us into the kingdom of the Son of *his love,* in whom we have redemption, the *forgiveness of our sins.*" This is the essential meaning of baptism. "The body" is now explained as being the Church, and peace is made through the blood of Jesus' Cross. The Christian answer to many high-flown philosophical speculations is in these simple affirmations: (1) We need no mediator in addition to Christ; (2) The loving God forgives sins, and in a mysterious way the Cross has made peace between God and mankind.

The Resurrection Faith

Faith in the Resurrection of Jesus Christ was universal in the Christian community. It is only in Matt. 28:17 that we are told that some doubted, though they also had apparently seen the Lord. The doubts of Thomas were soon dispelled (John 20:24-29).

The Church was also convinced that the Risen Lord had commissioned it. The terms of the commission take different forms that reflect or perhaps determine the theology of each evangelist. Matt. 28:18-20; Luke 24:46-47; and Acts 1:1-5 are read on Ascension Day, the first of these also on Trinity Sunday. The commission in John 20:21-23 relates to discipline in the Church, and appears in all lectionaries as part of the gospel reading for the second Sunday of Easter.

The first purpose of Easter preaching is proclamation of the Resurrection and its consequences for faith and life, rather than the details of the narratives. The stories themselves, and the symbolic language of the proclamation, are ways of pointing to the truth.

In the nature of things, the evidence in the NT does not add up to historical *proof* of the Resurrection, for there is no independent way to verify it. What it does prove is the firmness of the conviction of the early Christians. This was the faith of men and women who acted in no hysterical fashion but went out resolutely to spread the news, found a community of love, accept persecution and death, and turn the world upside down (Acts 17:6).

To many modern theologians the story of the empty tomb has been a difficulty. Do we have to believe, they ask, that God revivified the body that was laid in the grave and that Jesus ascended bodily into heaven? Many are able to affirm this, and the Gospels of Luke and John emphasize the physical nature of the Lord's risen body.

Others say that if the disciples saw Christ risen, in whatever form, this is sufficient, and they point to Paul's language in First Corinthians. The seed that is sown in the ground cannot be compared with the green wheat that rises from it; in the case of Christ and the Christians, what is sown in corruption is raised in incorruption, as a spiritual body (I Cor. 15:35-44). Flesh and blood cannot inherit the Kingdom of God; we shall be changed and clothed with immortality (15:45-53). We do not know how Paul conceived of the spiritual body, but the foundation of his thought is the Creator God of the OT. Perhaps it is enough for us to affirm that Jesus Christ truly rose from the dead and is the living Lord, and to add that any person of faith may think of this mystery as he or she is able.

Another aspect of Paul's thought, and perhaps the most important, is his conviction that here and now we are already risen with Christ. We were buried with him in baptism, and this act, which involves conversion, assures our resurrection. Even now we are dead so far as sin's power is concerned, and we can walk in newness of life (Rom. 6:1-11).

To be sure, this is an *anticipation* of life after death, and we have the *obligation* to live the new life (6:12-14). Yet chapter 8 of Romans expresses triumph throughout. We are children of God, no longer in the flesh (in the bad sense of that word) but in the Spirit (8:8-17). For centuries theologians have debated the relation between chapters 7 and 8. Is 7:21-25 a description of Paul before his conversion, or does it express the ambiguity of life even now that we are Christians? Perhaps the solution is that sometimes we are one thing and sometimes the other, but that when we are most truly ourselves we live in the freedom described in chapter 8. We may slip back from time to time, but we can always return to the true life that is guaranteed to us once for all because we are risen with Christ. The liturgy is a constant sign of the possibility of restoration.

The Sundays of Eastertide

The octave of Easter, formerly called the first Sunday after Easter, is now known as the second Sunday *of* Easter. This change is for no trivial reason; the purpose is to restore the great fifty days, Easter to Pentecost inclusive, to the importance that they had at one time. The Easter Vigil is conceived of as the great celebration, and Easter Day is the first of a sequence of Sundays celebrating the consequences of the Resurrection.

On the six Sundays following Easter Day, selections from the Book of Acts that portray life and preaching in the earliest Church are used as the first reading. The Episcopal and Methodist lectionaries, and often the Lutheran, diverge from the others. The North American Committee on Calendar and Lectionary is now making recommendations to the churches which it hopes will result in a unified scheme in place of the present discrepancies. The second lessons in Year A are drawn from First Peter, mainly in sequence, and in Years B and C there are selections from First John and the Book of Revelation respectively.

The Methodist and Episcopal lectionaries provide OT readings as alternatives to the first lesson, and one may hope that this will continue in future revisions. When the OT lesson is chosen, the pericope from Acts may be used as the second reading.

The gospel readings for Easter 2 and 3 are narratives of resurrection appearances. Parts of the Good Shepherd discourse in John 10 are read on the fourth Sunday and on Easter 5 and 6 selections from the Upper Room discourse in John 13–16. The seventh Sunday, which comes after Ascension Day, completes that discourse by using the three parts of chapter 17.

Easter 2A. Acts 2:14a, 22–32, which is read in all except the Roman and Presbyterian lectionaries, is part of Peter's great address at Pentecost. This speech contains a Christology of a very early type, expressed in verses 33–36, which the lectionaries omit (but see Easter 4A or 3A). It is an example of the Church's missionary preaching as the author knew it.

In Acts 2:42–47, read in the other churches, Luke tends to idealize the primitive Church, as he does the devout Judaism of the families of Jesus and John in Chapters 1–2 of his gospel. It is probable, however, that the earliest days of the Jerusalem church were marked by enthusiasm and the generous sharing of goods. At a later time, Paul brought a collection from Greece and Macedonia to aid that church in time of famine. NA employs this pericope on Easter 4A.

I Pet. 1:3–9 is a blessing or thanksgiving, similar to those which begin nearly all of Paul's letters, and this proclaims the joy of the new life brought by the Resurrection and looks forward to the "revelation of Jesus Christ" in the last times.

The words of this epistle, "Though not having seen him, you love him," fit well with the gospel reading, John 20:19–31. This pericope consists of two scenes. The first is on the evening of the day of Resurrection, when the disciples assemble in fear in a closed room. This will be discussed in connection with Pentecost (p. 138).

The second scene is one week later, when Thomas is present and is able to believe that the risen Lord is indeed God, because he can touch Jesus' hands and side. Yet there is a higher stage of faith than this: "Blessed are those who have not seen and yet believe." The early Church insisted on the physical reality of Christ's risen body here and in Luke 24:39–40, to guard against the notion that his body, before and after the Resurrection, was only a semblance. This error, known as Docetism, was a danger to the Church in the late first century and for some time thereafter.

Easter 2B. Three of the lectionaries prescribe Acts 3:12a, 13–15, 17–26 as the first lesson. (The Roman and Presbyterian books and NA instead read Acts 4:32–35, which speaks again of the sharing of wealth, but use a form of the pericope from chapter 3 on 3B.) In 3:22, Jesus is identified with the prophet like Moses promised in Deuteronomy, and this is important in the theology of both Luke and John. The second lesson, I John 5:1–6, proclaims that it is our faith that overcomes the world (cf. John 16:33). Verse 6 of the pericope, with its reference to the water and the blood, is related to the gospel reading; there is also a reference to the witness of the Spirit. NA substitutes the great proclamation of I John 1:1—2:2, now in some lectionaries at Easter 3B. First John was evidently written in the community that edited the gospel and added the conclusion to John 21. It emphasized the apostolic witness and has two themes that are interwoven throughout, the reality of Christ's Incarnation and the commandment of love. Thus it is a happy choice for the Easter season.

Easter 2C. The Methodist lectionary reads Acts 5:12–42, and the other schemes choose parts of this. The latter part of this passage will be discussed in connecton with Easter 3C.

Rev. 1:4–19 is the letter to all seven churches of Asia Minor, which is followed by separate letters to each of them. The risen Christ is also the one who will come again ("one like a son of man," verse 13), and he is seen in the Advent glory. The themes of this pericope are roughly parallel to those in the selection from First Peter, read in Year A.

The Book of Revelation

The Christian prophet who wrote the Apocalypse was named John. Ecclesiastical tradition has often identified him with the author of the Fourth Gospel and John the son of Zebedee; hence he is called "the divine," i.e. the theologian. Dionysius of Alexandria in the third century, however, denied that the book could have been written by the author of the gospel (Eusebius, *Ecclesiastical History,* vii. 24), and Eusebius noted that some people rejected it as uncanonical. The Church ultimately included it in the canon because it was found to be useful, though at times it has led people to wild speculations.

The Revelation to John should be considered in relation to the apocalyptic movement as a whole. It accords with the hope and conviction expressed in many parts of the NT, as well as the Creeds, that God's will must ultimately prevail. A constant symbol of this is the promise that Christ will return as judge.

Certainly most Christians seem to have expected the Parousia to occur within a generation. Paul proclaimed it twenty years or so after the Resurrection and believed that the time was short (I Cor. 15:22-28; 7:29). Words attributed to Jesus in Mark 13 that reflect such a faith are balanced by other statements that no one can know the day or the hour. The other evangelists edit this tradition freely. Matthew seeks to explain the delay of Christ's coming (Matt. 24:14), while chapter 21 of Luke is a rewriting of Mark 13 that applies the predictions primarily to the fall of Jerusalem. Both Luke and John expect a rather long delay of the Parousia. The Fourth Gospel does not deny the primitive faith but teaches that in the truest sense Christ has returned in the Spirit. Watching and waiting and the crises of life therefore take on a different aspect.

The principal purpose of Second Peter, the latest book in the NT, is to reaffirm the earlier forms of the apocalyptic hope against "scoffers" who object that a long time has already elapsed. The Book of Revelation, however, shows that late in the first century the hope was as vivid as ever in some parts of the Church.

Just as Daniel is the classic example of a Jewish apocalypse, so is the Revelation to John in early Christianity. Both of these books are "tracts for the times," written to give encouragement in days of persecution. Unlike the author of Daniel, the prophet John of Asia Minor, exiled to the island of Patmos, writes in his own name. This was probably late in the reign of Domitian (A.D. 81-96).

John's concern is for the People of God, who are represented by the seven small churches of Asia Minor. They are persecuted by the Roman empire (2:10, 13; 12:13-17) and are under pressure to worship the emperor (chapter 13). The emperors are symbolized by beasts and Rome by Babylon, the great harlot. The empire in its commercial greed oppresses the people of Asia and other provinces and sells human beings as slaves (chapters 17-18).

There are other dangers. "Those who say that they are Jews and are not" have made trouble for the churches of Smyrna (2:9) and Philadelphia (3:9). We do not know whether these were non-Christian Jews or Jewish Christians. But the greatest menaces are within the churches: the

Nicolaitans have compromised with idolatry and sexual immorality (2:14f., 20-23), the Christians of Ephesus have lost their first zealous love (2:4), the church in Sardis is almost dead (3:1f.), and Laodicea is rich, complacent, blind, and lukewarm (3:14-21).

Paul Minear, in his book *I Saw a New Earth*,[1] interprets the "dwellers on earth," who are mentioned several times (6:10; 8:13, 13:8, 12; 17:2), as a symbol for any people, Christian or not, who live on a purely worldly plane. If he is correct, it is not merely the empire that is the problem, but worldliness, in the Church and out of it. In this respect John preserves the true spirit of the Hebrew prophets, and this is one of the great positive values of the Apocalypse.

The book as a whole is framed by the letter to the seven churches (1:4-19) and the proclamation that Jesus is coming soon (22:12-20). The poignant cry of early Christianity, "Come, Lord Jesus," must often have been uttered in Aramaic. It is the *Maranatha* of I Cor. 16:22.

The visions of the Apocalypse are filled with quotations and echoes of Ezekiel, Isaiah, Zechariah, and other OT books. The language is so Semitic that one would almost suppose that the prophet is thinking in Hebrew or Aramaic. He reflects apocalpytic and other theological ideas that are found in other parts of the NT. Portions of the book seem to have been written a generation earlier and are adapted to the new situation. Apocalyptic, like prophecy, is a tradition that builds on earlier writings. This Apocalypse is so rich and complicated that not all of its problems can be solved. But the tradition has passed through the prophet's mind, and he believes that he saw all the visions and heard the voices.

A sensitive reader may feel that the Book of Revelation shares the weaknesses of OT apocalyptic. The prediction of the end of history was not fulfilled in John's time, or in A.D. 1000, or at any time since when fearful and hopeful souls have looked for redemption. What is even more troubling is that the prophet seems to have no feeling for the millions of ordinary people, the relatively innocent farmers, laborers, and merchants who are to be slain in the final conflict. These limitations have to be acknowledged.

We do, however, have to realize that John perceived the Mediterra-nean world as dominated by a *system*. The empire, though it brought many material and cultural advantages, had a demonic character, and it deified itself through the cults of Rome and the emperor. It was

[1]Washington: Corpus Books, 1968.

based on conquest, greed and slavery, and like all such empires it finally broke to pieces, though the end was long delayed. In this process, as in the Jewish revolt, the innocent suffered with the guilty. Perhaps, too, the Apocalypse achieved its original purpose of strengthening the Christians of Asia Minor against hostile forces outside and temptations within.

The lectionaries omit those parts of the book that have fascinated the alienated and the merely curious. They include several passages that have sustained faith and enriched art and worship: visions of heaven (4:1–11), the slain and victorious lamb (5:11–14), the Hallelujah choruses of heaven (7:9–17; 19:1–8), the new heaven and the new earth (21:1–4), the new Jerusalem that is to be the Bride, the city with the water of life flowing through it (21:9—22:5).

It is natural to ask, in what way does the apocalyptic tradition contain the Word of God? Perhaps one should formulate this differently: in what way does it speak the Word of God to us? We will hear it in one way in our generation, and perhaps another age will hear something else to which we are deaf.

Apocalyptic shares with Hebrew prophecy the conviction that God is in control of the world and that his purposes cannot be frustrated. This is necessary in an age when the great systems, the concentrations of political and economic power, seem to be out of human control. The weakness of apocalyptic is that it ignores the essential part of human beings in shaping the destiny of the community. It can lead to passive inactivity, or on the other hand to violent action in the hope of forcing God's hand and speeding up the process of victory. In either case it is unrealistic.

Yet the book of Revelation reinforces the faith of Jesus and of the whole NT that God's Reign will be established on earth. We do not know how or when that will be, but the Hebrew prophets and Jesus remind us of our proper stance. We are to continue to hear God's Word and to speak to him, and to take an active and constructive part in the social order. Anything that we do to further justice and mercy is of consequence in God's sight.

The NT Apocalypse also shows us that we should examine ourselves and ask whether some of the evil is in our own communities and our own minds, and not solely in the systems that we regard as our enemies. The seven churches of Asia are symbols of all the churches.

Sundays 3 through 6

Easter 3A. Here the lectionaries read parts of Peter's speech at Pentecost as the first lesson. In the Roman and Presbyterian schemes the pericope is Acts 2:14, 22-28, which argues that in Ps. 16 David had predicted the Resurrection. The other lectionaries employ Acts 2:14a, 36-47, which proclaims Jesus as Lord and Messiah (cf. notes on Easter 2A).

I Pet. 1:17-23 is read as the second lesson. Although First Peter in its present form is a catholic epistle, it is quite possibly based on a discourse first addressed to the newly baptized and also to other members of a specific congregation. Here they are reminded of what it cost (verses 18-19) for them to be born again (verse 23). Because of this they can call God Father (verse 17) and they are under obligation to fear him and to live in brotherly love. The gospel is Luke 24:13-35, discussed on p. 116.

Easter 3B. Selections from Acts continue to reveal the variety of early Christian use of the OT to explain Jesus' ministry, Cross and Resurrection. The Episcopal, Lutheran and Methodist lectionaries read Acts 4:5-12, the first part of Peter's defense after the healing of the lame man at the Beautiful Gate. This includes the quotation of the "stone rejected by the builders" (Ps. 118:22), used in Mark 12:10f.; Matt. 21:42; Luke 20:17; the Gospel of Thomas 66; and I Pet. 2:7. Sometimes it is combined with other "rock" or "stone" passages; cf. pp. 37, 129, 166.

The other lectionaries prescribe Acts 3:12-19 (or parts thereof). Here the titles used to refer to Jesus, God's *pais* (servant), reminiscent of Second Isaiah, and *archegos* (pioneer or founder) of life, are unusual. As Servant, Jesus proclaimed justice and Good News; and, like the founder of a Greek colony, he led his People to their new city. I John 2:1-6 corresponds to one of the functions of the Servant; he is the expiation for the sins of the whole world. NA has rearranged the readings from First John, and here uses 3:1-7. Luke 24:36-49 was discussed in connection with Easter Day.

Easter 3C. Four of the lectionaries prescribe Acts 9:1-20, the conversion of Saul of Tarsus. The others have Acts 5:27-32, 40b-41. Here the Sanhedrin orders the apostles to cease preaching in the name of Jesus, and the story also tells of the wise counsel of Gamaliel I ("the Elder"), grandson of the great rabbi Hillel, not to interfere with them. The most striking feature of this pericope are Peter's statements that "one must obey God rather than men," and that "we are witnesses (*martyres*) of all these things. The question of civil disobedience will be discussed on pp. 183–185.

Rev. 5:11–14 contains hymns in honor of the Lamb who was slain; he was the "faithful martyr" (1:5), the model for all the others. These pericopes lead naturally to the gospel reading, John 21:1–19, the scene in which the risen Lord bids Peter to feed his sheep and predicts his martyrdom.

Easter 4A. Acts. 6:1–9; 7:2a, 51–60 is the first reading in the Episcopal, Lutheran and Methodist lectionaries. This tells of the choice of the Seven and the martyrdom of Stephen. 6:1–7 is chosen by the other lectionaries for Easter 5A. The pericope as it stands pictures the Seven as prototypes of the diaconate. The phrase translated "to serve tables" can refer to management of finances, in which deacons assisted the bishop. In the sequel, however, Stephen and Philip also preach and make converts, and the story therefore may have originally told of their appointment to work among Greeks or Greek-speaking Jews.

The first reading in the other lectionaries, Acts. 2:14a, 36–41, contains the conclusion of Peter's great speech at Pentecost. The theology of verse 36 is based on Ps. 110:1, quoted in verses 34–35. NA substitutes Acts. 2:42–47. I Pet. 2:19–25 is an exhortation to follow in Christ's steps of non-resistance in the face of persecution; thus it is appropriately addressed to the newly baptized, who have formerly been sheep going astray and have now returned to the shepherd and overseer of their souls. This leads naturally to the gospel reading.

Beginning with the fourth Sunday, the gospel pericopes are from parts of the Fourth Gospel prior to the Passion Narrative. In the Roman missal before Vatican II and in the mediaeval Sarum missal, from which the Book of Common Prayer took its pericopes, the second Sunday after Easter was Good Shepherd Sunday. Readings from John 10 are now assigned to the fourth Sunday, along with Ps. 23, which will be discussed in Chap. 20 in notes on Y28A. In John 10:1–10 the true shepherd is contrasted with the hirelings, thieves and bandits; in this we can see echoes of Ezek. 34 and Zech. 11 and 13. "*All* who came before me are thieves and bandits" is an extreme statement; it most naturally refers to false prophets and false Messiahs, but it may include Jewish teachers hostile to Christianity.

This choice of gospel lessons can be understood if we realize that the Fourth Gospel as a whole is a reinterpretation of the gospel tradition in the light of the risen Christ and the Church's experiences of his presence through faith, worship and Christian prophecy. The parts of the gospel read in this season purport to be spoken by Jesus before the Crucifixion, but he speaks as revealing through the Holy Spirit the meaning of his life and ministry. It is the glorified Christ who is portrayed in John's gospel.

The mosaics and frescoes of Byzantine art, and the Greek Christian iconic tradition to this day, have been deeply influenced by the Gospel of John and illustrate its point of view. *There is no perspective,* spatial or temporal. Everything is seen under the aspect of eternity. The patriarchs and prophets, the saints and martyrs, all appear on the same plane. The Christ, powerful yet compassionate, is always the central figure. His mother, the *Theotokos,* and John the Baptist are most closely associated with him; then the apostles and other saints of the old and new dispensations.

Easter 4B. Part of Acts 4:23-37 (Episcopal, Lutheran, Methodist) is read in the Roman and Presbyterian lectionaries on Easter 2B. Verses 23-31 include an interesting prayer in which Jesus is called God's *pais* ("servant" or "child") as in the second century Didache (Teaching of the Twelve Apostles). Acts 4:8-12, used by the other lectionaries, is part of Peter's speech in a confrontation with the high-priestly group, similar to the one in 5:27-42, and contains one of the reminiscences of Ps. 118, "the stone rejected by the builders"; cf. the remarks on Easter 3B. In the second reading, I John 3:1-8 (Easter 3B, NA), the most striking part is verse 2, which promises that when Christ appears we shall be like him, for we shall see him as he is. This reminds one of II Cor. 3:18; true seeing is not only believing, it is transformation (cf. p. 211f.). John 10:11-18 continues the discourse begun in Year A; the Good Shepherd in protecting his sheep lays down his life for them.

Easter 4C. Acts 13:15-16, 26-39 (Episcopal, Lutheran, Methodist) gives part of Paul's speech in the synagogue at Pisidian Antioch. Here the argument is much like that of Peter in 2:14, 22-28 (Easter 3A). The Roman and Presbyterian reading, Acts 13:14, 43-52, tells of Paul's rejection by the Jews of that city and his acceptance by the Gentiles. This is matched by Rev. 7:9-17, in which unnumbered multitudes from all nations stand as witnesses before the throne and the Lamb. John 10:22-30 concludes the theme of the Good Shepherd in Jesus' controversy with the "Jews" at the Feast of Dedication (Hanukkah). When he proclaims,

"I and the Father are one," this is good news to his followers but a challenge to unbelievers. The Fourth Gospel uses the term *Ioudaioi* ("Jews" or "Judaeans") as a symbol of all in the world who resist the gospel.

Easter 5A. We have discussed the Roman and Presbyterian reading (Acts 6:1–7) in connection with 4A. The other lectionaries tell of Paul's work in Thessalonica (Acts 17:1–15, "These men who have turned the world upside down have come here also") or of the martyrdom of Stephen (Acts 7:55–60).

I Pet. 2:1–10 proclaims to the newly baptized the great dignity that is now theirs. They still have to be nourished by milk but will grow up to be a chosen race, a royal priesthood, a holy nation that offers spiritual sacrifices. This concept brings to completion thoughts implicit in Jeremiah and in Isa. 40–66. With it is interwoven the elaborate midrash on stones. Christ is the living stone, and so are his People who are to be built into a spiritual house (cf. Eph. 2:19–22).

John 14:1–14 is a passage often used in devotion. As so often in this gospel, there are interwoven themes that are developed elsewhere in different contexts. (1) There is enough room for all in the Father's house. Jesus goes to prepare a way for them and will lead them there. (2) The way is not observance of a law but union with a person, Jesus himself; indeed, he is the Torah, and there is no other way to the Father. This appears to be quite exclusive, but when it is put alongside Paul's teaching one can say that all who have come to God have come through Christ (i.e., by believing and abiding, in personal relationship) whether they know it or not. (3) To have seen Jesus is to have seen the Father; thus those who believe in him will also do God's works. (4) A prayer that is truly in union with Jesus ("thy will be done") cannot fail to be answered.

Easter 5B. The vivid story in Acts 8:26–40 (Episcopal, Lutheran, Methodist, NA) exhibits Luke's theology of prediction from Scripture (cf. the Easter stories, Luke 24:26–27, 32, 44–48). The eunuch, who came from Ethiopia (Nubia) was evidently a Jew, and he was reading aloud, which was the ancient custom. The significance of Acts 9:26–31 (Roman, Presbyterian) in the context of the other readings seems to be that Saul of Tarsus, who had been an enemy of the Good News, is accepted as a brother by the Jerusalem church. I John 3:18–24 (Easter 4B, NA) is an encouragement to a person like Paul, in that God knows our hearts better than do we ourselves (cf. I Cor. 4:3–4). This confidence in God ensures the answer to our prayers; thus a theme from John 14 is resumed. I John 4:7–12 (NA) is another expression of confidence. The gospel reading reinforces these thoughts.

The Episcopal lectionary employs John 14:15–21 at this point; the others read it on Easter 6A. Here Jesus promises to come again to the disciples through the "other Paraclete," the Spirit. The allegory of the true vine (John 15:1–8) is the reading in the other lectionaries and is prescribed by the Book of Common Prayer for 6A.

The symbol of the true vine is more organic than the figure of the building of a house. Branches of this vine are parts of the risen Christ, but they do not lose their individuality. They must bear fruit; otherwise they will be pruned out. This is one of several symbols used by John to express the process of the new life and the obligations incurred thereby. Behind it lie Isaiah's song of the vineyard (Isa. 5:1–7), Ps. 80, and the parable of Mark 12:1–11.

Easter 5C. The first reading in the Episcopal, Lutheran and Methodist lectionaries (Acts 13:44–52) was mentioned briefly under 4C. Acts 14:19–28, prescribed by two other lectionaries, recounts the return of Paul and Barnabas to Antioch from their first journey to Asia Minor, which had resulted in significant success, in spite of their having been frequently rejected and even stoned. "Through many tribulations we have to enter the Kingdom of God" (verse 22). NA prescribes Acts 14:8–18, discussed below under Easter 6C. In contrast, Rev. 21:1–5 looks forward to the final triumph in which the earthly Church is replaced by the new Jerusalem, adorned like a bride for her husband. The tabernacle of God will be with human beings; but this is not merely a future hope, for the Word has already become flesh and tabernacled among us (John 1:14). The moral consequence of this is set forth in the new commandment of the gospel reading, John 13:31–35, which should be considered in the entire context of chapters 13–17.

Easter 6A. Paul's speech at the Areopagus (Acts 17:22–31) is chosen by the Episcopal, Lutheran, Methodist, and NA lectionaries. The arguments addressed to his pagan audience are quite unlike what we find in his letters; most of the speech is a good example of Jewish propaganda on behalf of monotheism, quoting commonplaces of popular philosophy. If there is a secure tradition behind this incident, the Apostle later changed his approach; in any case it is a fine example of early Christian missionary teaching.

The story of Philip at Samaria (Acts 8:4-8, 14-17), chosen by the others, is puzzling, because elsewhere in Acts, as in Paul's letters, it is assumed that all who have been baptized receive the Holy Spirit. Did the story arise because *outward signs* of the Spirit's presence had not been observed? Perhaps the purpose of the pericope is to show that the Jerusalem church accepted the Samaritan mission; it was one more stage in the propagation of the Good News. The Book of Common Prayer no longer uses this pericope in the service of Confirmation.

The other readings are not closely related to this, nor is Paul's speech at the Areopagus. I Pet. 3:13-22 resumes the command to new converts found in 2:19-25 (Easter 4A); they must be ready to suffer in innocence.

Easter 6B. Acts 10:25-26, 34-38, the choice of the Roman and Presbyterian lectionaries, was also read on Easter Day. Perhaps for this reason, three others substitute the story of the founding of the church in Antioch (Acts 11:19-30, and NA reads 10:44-48. Many scholars believe that the account in Chapter 11 is of high historical importance. Not only were the disciples first called Christians here (probably in scorn, "partisans of Christ"); this was the first significant conversion of non-Jews. I John 4:1-11 and 5:1-6 (NA) declare that there are two tests of true discipleship, confessing Christ and loving the brotherhood. The gospel reading, John 15:9-17, concludes the discourse on the true vine. Paul had considered it an honor to be a "slave of Christ"—this Semitic way of speaking is normal in the OT and in Islam—but John transposes discipleship into a higher key: "I no longer call you slaves, but friends." His followers know the entire secret of his purpose.

Easter 6C. The readings essentially continue themes of the previous Sundays. The Holy City that comes down from heaven needs have no temple, for God himself and the Lamb are the temple (Rev. 21:2-4, 10-14, 22-27). Thus the dreams of Ezek. 40:1—47:12 are partly fulfilled but superseded by a grander conception; and there is no night in that city (cf. Zech. 14:7). John 14:23-29 discusses the Paraclete further. What he will teach is a reminder of what Jesus has already said.

Acts 15:1-2, 22-29 (Roman, Presbyterian, NA) is not related to the other pericopes except that it affirms the unity of the Church. The council in Jerusalem accepts the mission to the Gentiles, but the prohibition in verse 29 of foods that are not kosher was perhaps unknown to Paul; at any rate it was one that he would not have accepted.

Acts 14:8–18, substituted by the other lectionaries, is the dramatic account of how Barnabas and Paul were hailed as Zeus and Hermes respectively (Paul, like Hermes, was the speaker and messenger). The story is fascinating because this was the region where the pious Philemon and Baucis were visited by the gods.

The Ascension

It is in the light of the gospels of John and Mark that we should think of the Ascension. The new lectionaries give this festival due honor because it recalls an important clause in the creeds, put in perspective as part of the fifty days of Eastertide.

The earliest Christian preaching probably regarded the Resurrection and the Ascension as a single event. The two OT passages that confirmed the resurrection faith to them are Ps. 110:1, "Sit at my right hand," and Dan. 7:13, in which one like a son of man comes with the clouds of heaven and is presented to the Ancient of Days. Rom. 1:4, Acts 2:32f., and the hymn in Phil. 2:6–11 fit with this. It is Luke who has made two events out of the one (Acts 1:3–11). In this way he accounted for the fact that for some time various people saw the risen Lord, and then the appearances ceased. In Luke-Acts the Ascension is the occasion for Jesus' final commission to his disciples.

Most preachers and congregations in our time seem to have little difficulty adjusting their thinking to what astronomy teaches us about outer space. "Heaven" for Christians is not "up there" or "out there" but where God is. The disappearance of the "three-story universe" is a problem only for the most literal minded. Every cosmology, even that of our astronomers, is a more or less imaginative construct that tries to explain phenomena, and the essence of the Ascension faith has nothing to do with cosmology. It is that Jesus, with all that his earthly existence implied, is inseparably united with God, and that God, as known in Jesus, is Lord of the universe and his will must ultimately prevail.

The basic first reading for all three years is Acts 1:1–11 and the second is Eph. 1:15–23, which is a rhapsody on the riches of salvation and concludes with a proclamation that Christ, at God's right hand, rules the world and the Church. The Book of Common Prayer provides alternatives to the Acts pericope, which can then be substituted for the passage in Ephesians. These are Dan. 7:9–14, (A); Ezek. 1:3–5a, 15–22, 26–28, (B), the vision of the four living creatures and of God in human form; and II Kings 2:1–15, (C), the assumption of Elijah into heaven.

Ps. 47, or parts of it, is prescribed by the Roman and Episcopal lectionaries. This is a hymn of the enthronement of Yahweh as ruler of all nations; he "has gone up with a shout." The Lutheran order substitutes Ps. 110, which the Episcopal book provides as an alternative.

The Roman and Methodist lectionaries furnish separate gospel pericopes for the three years. Matt. 28:16–20 (A), Jesus' final commission to his disciples, is particularly appropriate. Mark 16:15–20 (B) is part of the longer ending of Mark, which has canonical status but is omitted by some of the oldest manuscripts. Luke 24:44–53 (C) tells of Jesus' final farewell to his disciples at Bethany. The words "and was carried up into heaven," omitted by a few Greek and Latin manuscripts, make it explicitly an Ascension story and thus a doublet of the account in Acts. This pericope is chosen as the gospel reading in the lectionaries, except that the Episcopal Prayer Book gives parts of the longer ending of Mark as an alternative. The conclusion of Luke is significant because, like Matt. 28:16–20, it includes a commission of Jesus to his disciples, here stated in characteristically Lucan language.

Easter 7A. This is the Sunday after Ascension Day, and therefore it is appropriate for Acts 1:1–14 or parts of it to be read. I Pet. 4:12–19; 5:6–11 continues the exhortation given to converts on the previous Sunday: if you are to suffer, let the only possible charge against you be that you are a Christian. The gospel pericope, John 17:1–11, is the first part of what is often called the high-priestly prayer. This is the magnificent climax which brings several themes of chapters 13–16 to completion. Christ speaks almost as having risen and ascended to the presence of the Father. He has completed his work in the world by having revealed God's name, i.e., his true nature, to the disciples, and now he prays for them.

Easter 7B. The story of Matthias's election to take the place of Judas (Acts 1:15–26) is chosen because in the gospel reading (John 17:11–19) Jesus says that he has guarded the disciples, and none has perished except the "son of perdition." In verse 9 he had said that he was not praying for the world. "World" is used there in the sense of that which has rejected the plan of salvation, not the cosmos as the object of God's love (3:16). He does not ask that they be taken out of the (hostile) world but only preserved from the Evil One (an echo of the Lord's Prayer), and he prays that they may be made holy, protected as God's own possession and sustained morally and spiritually. Just so he sanctifies himself in view of his Passion, which will soon take place.

The prayer is that they may be made holy *in the truth,* and Jesus is the truth (14:6), the Son whom God has sent into the world (17:3). This is also the theme expressed in the second reading, I John 5:9-13 (or 4:11-21) and throughout that epistle. But knowing the truth involves doing it (John 3:21), and this can be summed up in the commandment of love, which is the other part of the truth.

Easter 7C. The final part of the chapter (John 17:20-26) is a prayer for the future Church, that its members may be one in Christ, as Christ is one with the Father, and that it may be perfected in its unity so that the world may know that God has sent his Son. The story of Stephen, who at his martyrdom sees the Son of Man standing at the right hand of God (Acts 7:55-60), is evidently chosen by the Roman and Presbyterian lectionaries as an example of the fidelity of those who believe in the apostolic witness. The reading of the others (Acts 16:6-10, 16-34 or parts thereof) tells of Paul's call to preach in Macedonia and his imprisonment and release at Philippi. Its only connection with the gospel reading is the general theme of the spread of the Good News.

Rev. 22:12-14, 16-17, 20 looks forward to the Parousia. The risen Lord proclaims that he, the Alpha and Omega, will come soon, and the pericope concludes with the prayer of the earliest Church, "Come, Lord Jesus," which was given in Aramaic in I Cor. 16:22b (*Maranatha*).

·11

Pentecost and Trinity Sunday

"Pentecost" comes from a Greek word meaning "fiftieth." In the NT it refers to the Jewish Feast of Weeks, celebrated on the fiftieth day from Passover (a "week of weeks"), which originally celebrated the ingathering of the grain harvest. In the liturgical calendar, Pentecost is the last day of Eastertide, the great fifty days.

Trinity Sunday is included in this chapter partly for convenience and also because the readings resume in part the themes of Pentecost. It is actually the first of the Sundays "after Pentecost."

In rabbinic tradition Pentecost commemorated the giving of the Torah on Mount Sinai, whereas the narrative in Acts 2:1–11 has made it for Christians the celebration of the descent of the Holy Spirit and thus the conclusion of the saving events connected with the Resurrection. Perhaps Luke regarded the law as a type and the Spirit as its antitype, but we cannot be certain of this.

The OT frequently mentions God's spirit. At creation the breath of God moved on the waters (Gen. 1:2). It came upon charismatic leaders (the "judges"), kings, and prophets, and it inspired men of wisdom and even craftsmen (Exod. 31:2). Like expressions such as God's word or his hand, it is a way to speak of Yahweh's activity in the world. As a gift to specific persons it came and went.

In the NT the Spirit is regarded as the permanent endowment of Christians, and Paul sees this as an essential part of the process by which one comes to faith and is initiated into the People of God by baptism.

Luke does indeed tell of a singular instance in which the gift of the Spirit preceded that rite and was a sign to Peter that it was right to baptize the Gentile centurion Cornelius (Acts 10:44–48). Pentecost has been traditionally regarded as an appropriate time for the administration of baptism.

The Vigil of Pentecost

The Roman, Episcopal, and Lutheran lectionaries provide for a Vigil of Pentecost, which can be a Saturday evening celebration of the Eucharist. The pericope from Acts 2 can be read on this occasion except in the Roman liturgy, but the OT readings harmonize with it. There are four of these. Gen. 11:1–9 tells of the tower of Babel, and Luke understands Pentecost as a reversal of the confusion of languages, for the ecstatic speech of the apostles (which makes unbelievers say that they are full of new wine) enables people from many parts of the world to hear the message in their own tongues. Another reading, Exod. 19:1–9, 16–25, is appropriate because it begins the tradition of Yahweh's revelation on Mount Sinai and includes in verses 4–6 a great credal proclamation that was mentioned in a previous chapter. (The Lutheran service book provides Exod. 19:1–9 as the only OT pericope.) Ezekiel's prophecy of the valley of dry bones (37:1–14) promises that God will raise up his People and put his spirit within them. Finally, Joel 2:28–32, which is quoted in Acts 2:17–21, predicts the outpouring of the Spirit on all humanity.

The second reading is from Rom. 8:14–17, 22–27. Much of the eighth chapter has to do with the Holy Spirit; this selection makes two points: first, that we possess the first fruits of the Spirit, which are the guarantee of our adoption as sons and daughters and of our redemption; second, that the Spirit intercedes for us when we do not know how to pray.

The gospel reading (John 7:37–39) is Jesus' promise of the living water, which the evangelist explains is the gift of the Spirit. The context is Jesus' visit to Jerusalem at the Feast of Tabernacles, one feature of which was the ceremonial pouring out of water.

Ps. 104 adds particular beauty to the Pentecost Vigil. It was chosen because of verse 30, which echoes Gen. 1 ("when you send forth your spirit they are created"), and this applies to all of Yahweh's works, including mankind. The hymn enumerates these vividly and poetically. It is one of the nature psalms and has many parallels to the Hymn to the Aton, which the Pharaoh Ikhnaton composed or at least used to celebrate the sun's disk as the only God. Like Ps. 29, the language of which is Canaanite, Ps. 104 is an example of the genius of Hebrew worship in adapting elements from the surrounding cultures to the worship of Yahweh. The Lutheran lectionary provides the psalm as an alternative for Pentecost.

The Day of Pentecost

The lectionaries vary so widely in their provisions for Pentecost that we can discuss this festival only by selecting a few very important pericopes. The Roman *Ordo* uses a single set of lessons for all three years, while the others have three sets. In addition, the Episcopal and NA provide for two celebrations.

Nevertheless, certain pericopes are always read somewhere: Acts 2:1-21; I Cor. 12:3b-13; and John 20:19-23; others frequently: Joel 2:28-32; Ezek. 37:1-14; Gen. 11:1-9; and parts of John 14-16.

The OT readings were discussed in connection with the Vigil of Pentecost, and all are used typologically. Acts 2:1-11 (NA adds verses 12-21, which quote Joel's prophecy) is the classic passage which has made Pentecost the culmination of Eastertide. Two aspects of it have been of enduring influence on Christian theology and liturgy. Luke regards the gift of the Spirit, as well as the Ascension, as events distinct from the Resurrection that mark the beginning of a new era, that of the Church and the Spirit. This is in contrast to the theology of the Fourth Gospel, in which Resurrection, Ascension and the transmission of the Spirit are closely related. Second, what was perhaps originally the account of a "speaking in tongues" has become a miracle; people from all parts of the earth hear the Good News, each in his native language. This has encouraged translation of the Scripture into many different tongues.

It is now important to reflect on I Cor. 12:3b-13. Here Paul speaks of the diverse gifts (*charismata*) bestowed on members of the one Body. At the bottom of the list of pneumatic endowments come "tongues of a different kind" and the interpretation of tongues. Toward the end of the same chapter the Apostle enumerates apostles, prophets and teachers as those who receive the preeminent gifts; then there are others, with tongues again coming last (12:28-30).

Chapters 13 and 14 of First Corinthians continue an integrated discourse that began at 12:1. The "much better way" is the love (*agapê*) that has concern for others and builds up the community; without it, the greatest gifts and even martyrdom are worth nothing.

In the primitive Church the gift of the Spirit was often accompanied by prophecy and ecstatic speech. Paul now deals extensively with them. He does not in any way despise the gift that the Corinthians prized so highly; in fact he claims to speak in tongues even more than they do, but it is a form of prayer whose principal benefit is only for the speaker. He prefers the more important charisma of prophecy, which strengthens the Church (14:12-20).

The early Church in fact had three sources of authority: the OT, the words and deeds of Jesus, and the Holy Spirit speaking through Christian prophets. Some of these, like Agabus, who foresaw a famine, made specific predictions (Acts 11:28); apparently it was this same man who bound Paul's hands and feet and said that just so the Apostle would be bound and handed over to the Gentiles (Acts 21:10f.). The Book of Revelation comes to us from a prophet. Prophecy continued long in Asia Minor, especially in Philadelphia and in parts of Phrygia. Philip the evangelist had four daughters who were prophetesses (Acts 21:8f.), and according to tradition they later lived in Asia Minor. What Paul called prophecy seems to have been inspired proclamation of the gospel and its consquences; much of what now passes for preaching he would have termed "teaching" (I Cor. 14:26). It is probable that some of the eloquent passages in Paul's letters (e.g., I Cor. 13 and parts of Rom. 8) were originally prophecies that he had delivered. They are carefully constructed and rhetorically effective, and so are many of the oracles of the OT prophets. NA has appropriately included Rom. 8:22-27 (Year B) and 8:14-17 (Year C), which disclose the mystery of the Spirit working in prayer.

The scene of the gospel reading, John 20:19-23, is on the evening following the Resurrection, when the disciples are assembled and in fear of their enemies. Jesus shows them his hands and his sides and utters the word "Peace" (Greek *eirênê,* Heb. *shalôm*), the ancient greeting that confers a blessing and refers to all good gifts, material and spiritual, as it still does in Jewish and Muslim speech (cf. Luke 10:5f.; John 14:27). He now commissions the disciples for their work in terms quite different from Matt. 28:18-20; Acts 1:8. They are his apostles, men sent, as he himself is the Apostle of the Father; and he confers the Holy Spirit on them. Reginald H. Fuller has argued that the forgiving or retaining of sins, which is part of the commission, refers to admittance to the Church through baptism; only later does the tradition apply this to discipline for post-baptismal sin.

NA also provides John 7:37–39 (A); 15:26–27; 16:4b–15 (B); and 14:8–17, 25–27 (C), passages found here and there in other lectionaries. The first of these is the proclamation of the living water, mentioned above as read on the Vigil. The others are on the theme of the Paraclete Spirit, which we shall now discuss in its context.

The Spirit, the Trinity, and the Church in the Fourth Gospel

As the homilist prepares to think about Pentecost and Trinity Sunday, it is important for him or her to consider what is said about the Paraclete Spirit in the Fourth Gospel. This in fact involves the whole of chapters 13–17 and John's doctrine of the Church.

The NT does not contain a formal doctrine of the Trinity; one can say that it is implied, or rather that all the necessary elements for it are to be found in the NT books.

Paul does not make a clear distinction between Christ and the Holy Spirit. He speaks sometimes of the Holy Spirit, the Spirit of God, or just the Spirit; at other times of the spirit of Christ. The effect of God's grace and that of the Spirit are much the same. We do find the Apostle using a trinitarian formula in II Cor. 13:14, but it is the Gospel of John that makes the clearest distinction.

The Father will send another Paraclete (John 14:16); another, because he is like Jesus but distinct from him. The thinking that led to the doctrine of the Trinity apparently grew out of the need of the early Church to understand sacred history. God the Father never ceased to be God; Jesus was surely his unique Son; but after the Resurrection there was an experience of tremendous power, and the Spirit kept bringing new messages; although, as John says, they must always be in harmony with what Jesus taught (14:26; 16:12–15). This is what distinguishes true prophets from false (Matt. 7:15; Mark 13:22).

Much of the Gospel of John must consist of meditations and prophecies committed to the evangelist by the Spirit. The climax of these revelations is in the discourses of the Upper Room (chapters 13–16) and what is often called Jesus' high-priestly prayer (chapter 17). Certainly it is the risen Christ who speaks directly to the situation of the Church in the late first century and therefore to the church in all times.

All the lectionaries provide for reading most parts of 13:31—15:17 on the fifth and sixth Sundays of Easter and all of chapter 17 on the seventh Sunday. Parts of chapter 16 are read on Pentecost. It is now appropriate to go further into chapters 13–17.

The new commandment, that the disciples love one another, follows Jesus' announcement that the Son of Man will be glorified and that God will be glorified in him (13:31-35). It has been observed that John does not need to tell the stories of the Transfiguration and Gethsemane as such, for the entire gospel is recounted in the light of these events. The glorification of Jesus is his "lifting up" on the Cross and his Ascension (12:23-33). For John, the new commandment sums up all the teaching of Jesus, and this supernatural love has its beginning in the Father (17:26).

Several themes are combined in 14:1-14, which was discussed above (Easter 5A p. 129). In 14:15-21 and 14:23-29 the theme of obedience to Jesus' commandments is resumed, together with the assurance that his physical absence is not a separation from him, for the Paraclete is always present.

The Synoptics, of course, maintain the eschatological tension of earliest Christianity. John does not deny a future resurrection and judgment (5:28f.), but for his church there is no fear in this. The judgment has already occurred in this life (3:16-18), and we are already risen (5:24). The raising of Lazarus is the supreme parable of this (11:1-44). This "realized eschatology" runs throughout the Fourth Gospel, in which the risen Christ speaks to those who are risen with him.

Matthew perhaps thought of the Church, the true Israel, as having been founded in two stages, by Peter's confession (Matt. 16:13-20) and the final commission (28:16-20); the counterpart of this in John is in chapters 13-17. John is the most churchly of all the gospels, not in the aspect of an organized institution but that of a theological reality. This is not an "invisible" Church, for one enters it by baptism (3:1-5), and it has discipline (20:23), but the emphasis is on the spiritual reality that holds it together.

The allegory of the true vine (15:1-8, Easter 5B, p. 130) makes all this clear. In this gospel the process that we call "salvation" or "the new life" includes several elements that are inseparable: believing, being born of water and the Spirit, spiritually feeding on the flesh of the Son of Man and drinking his blood, abiding in the true vine, and keeping the commandment of love. In 15:9-17 the theme of love is repeated and connected with "abiding."

The climax of the Easter pericopes comes on the seventh Sunday of Easter, which follows Ascension Day. Here Jesus commits himself in prayer to the Father and asks for his glorification, for the Cross is the supreme "sign" of all the signs that Jesus has performed.

There is nothing in Christian literature quite like these chapters, which take certain themes and repeat them over and over, like motifs in a symphony that are developed in different ways. They are the product of many meditations and they result in a coherent theology. Chapters 13–17 give the gospel its characteristic devotional tone. Here the fellowship of the Church is an important theological theme, but the individual believer and his or her needs are always in mind. The Gospel of John has always sustained the perplexed, the sick, the sorrowful, and the dying.

Trinity Sunday

Trinity Sunday is a day that celebrates a basic doctrine of the Christian faith. As a special festival it arose in the middle ages and was especially popular in northern Europe; hence the former Lutheran and Anglican custom of numbering the remaining Sundays of the year after Trinity.

The lectionaries we have been considering vary greatly in their selection of pericopes for this Sunday. Exod. 34:4–6, 8–9 (Roman, Year A) in its present form tells of the renewal of the covenant on Sinai after the idolatry of the golden calf, but in the J source it was probably the continuation of 24:12–15. It is significant that it contains Yahweh's proclamation of his judgment and grace. By placing it here, the lectionaries remind us that the Trinity is essentially the doctrine of one God who is the God of the covenant. Yahweh is Father, Son, and Holy Spirit.

The Episcopal and Methodist reading for Year A (Gen. 1:1—2:3) can serve a similar purpose. So also Deut. 4:32–34, 39–40 (Lutheran, A; Roman, B) speaks of God's uniqueness in his self-revelation and his dealings with Israel. Ezek. 37:1–4 (Presbyterian) is evidently chosen because this Sunday is the octave of Pentecost.

In Year B, the Episcopal lectionary has the story of the Burning Bush (Exod. 3:1–6), the Lutheran reads the Shema', which affirms God's unity (Deut. 6:4–9), and the Presbyterian Isa. 6:1–8 ("Holy, holy, holy"). The last is the Episcopal reading for Year C, when the Lutheran order has Num. 6:23–27, the threefold Aaronic blessing. Prov. 8:22–31 is the C reading for the other lectionaries. Here it is said that Wisdom was God's first creation, before the world was made. This concept, which is developed further in the deuterocanonical Book of

Wisdom, probably influenced the Christology of Hebrews and the Fourth Gospel.

The second reading for Year A is II Cor. 13:5-14, which contains the oldest trinitarian formulation (used in Year B in the Lutheran scheme), and for Year B, Episcopal, Rom. 8:12-17 (the cry "Abba, Father" is the Spirit's witness that we are God's children; Lutheran, Year A). Three of the lectionaries resume the Pentecost theme in Year C by prescribing Rom. 5:1-5, while the Episcopal and Presbyterian orders have other readings not so obviously related to the day.

In Year A, the gospel reading for all lectionaries except the Roman is the commission of the risen Christ with its command to baptize in the name of the Trinity (Matt. 28:16-20). This is used in the Roman lectionary in Year B. The choice of the Roman *Ordo* for Year A, John 3: 16-18, is interesting because it is the famous Johannine summary of the Good News. All the other gospel readings center in the Holy Spirit: John 3:1-17 or parts thereof, Year B; John 16:12-15, Year C, all lectionaries except the Presbyterian, which prescribes John 20:19-23.

Choice of the psalms varies considerably in the Roman, Episcopal, and Lutheran orders. Ps. 149 (Lutheran, B) and Ps. 150 (Episcopal, A), and the psalm from the Greek version of Dan. 3, *Benedictus es Domine*, (Roman and Episcopal, A) are general songs of praise. The other psalms celebrate God as creator of the universe and the human race. Ps. 8 (Roman and Episcopal, C) express the wonder that God has given mankind dominion over nature. God's power over the created order is the theme of Pss. 29, 33, and 93.

Whichever lectionary is followed, the readings for Trinity Sunday over the three years speak of God in such a way that his being and work are seen as those of Father, Son, and Holy Spirit, always inseparable.

·Part Three

Sundays
of the Year

·12

The Message of Jesus - Year A

The seasons from the first Sunday of Advent to Epiphany, and from Ash Wednesday to Pentecost, set forth and interpret the story of our redemption. The Sundays "of the year" after Epiphany and Pentecost afford additional insights into Christian faith and life, and tell the story of Jesus' ministry as it is found in the Synoptic Gospels.

We note that the NA now provides modified course readings from the OT for Sundays after Pentecost; in Year A from Genesis, Exodus and Ruth, with a passage from Numbers and one from Deuteronomy; in B from First and Second Samuel; and in C from First and Second Kings, with three pericopes each from Jeremiah and Ezekiel. These give episodes in the sacred history of the Hebrews from Abraham's call down to the Exile and thus supplement the other OT readings. In the chapters that follow we shall usually discuss OT pericopes in the other lectionaries. Many changes have been made by NA in readings from the Minor Prophets, but especially toward the end of the year some pericopes stand where they appear in other lectionaries.

The message of Jesus comes to the community of worship in fragmentary form, in more or less isolated pericopes, but that is how the teachings of our Lord and the separate events of his ministry circulated before they were combined in the gospels and such written sources as lay behind them. The difference is that the pericopes now found in the lectionaries are not always "rounded off" and independent, as they were in the oral tradition. They usually include the connective material that was added by the gospel writers which reflects their own interpreta-tion of the materials. Further, the divisions made in the lectionaries do not always coincide with the natural divisions that the structure of the gospels discloses.

Redaction criticism studies the ways in which each of the evangelists adapted the Jesus tradition, and form criticism seeks to trace that tradi-tion through the oral stage. These processes, even though their results are only approximate, enable us to come very close to the actual words of Jesus, but that is not their sole purpose. It is almost as important to understand the purposes of the evangelists and those of the anonymous teachers in the early Church who preceded them. These have much to teach us, and often their interpretation, as distinct from Jesus' message, is also needed by the contemporary Church.

Both the words of Jesus and the interpretation can be said to be the Word of God, even though the latter is subsidiary. If this is so, why is it desirable to isolate Jesus' message from that of the interpreters and bearers of tradition?

One reason is that in historical revelation God's purpose can be seen more clearly if the historical perspective is clear. A more important theological point is that we believe Jesus to be the supreme revelation of God. Therefore the distinctive traits of his message and the way in which he carried out his ministry are the proper standard by which all else is to be interpreted.

These distinctive features are disclosed by using one of the methods of form criticism that is called the criterion of dissimilarity. There are numerous items in the recorded teaching of our Lord that are in sub-stantial agreement with the Judaism of his time. Two obvious examples of this are the call to repentance and the Summary of the Law ("You shall love the Lord your God . . . and your neighbor as yourself "). Just as clearly, there are other teachings that fit the needs and interests of the early Church; for example, denunciations of false prophets (Matt. 7:15–23) and the warning not to reject an outsider who expels demons in Jesus' name (Mark 9:38–40). When we isolate the sayings that do not fit with contemporary Judaism and that have no application to the situation of the early Church—indeed some of them run counter to its tendencies—we have the distinctive elements of Jesus' teaching.

This is not to say that he never taught what the great rabbis taught—of course he sometimes did—both he and they stood on the basis of the OT revelation. He could also have given teachings that were useful to the Church in its task of converting and training Jews and Gentiles. But in the gospel tradition there are words that are startling and new, often spoken in a style that seems peculiar to Jesus, that shocked his hearers and forced them to examine the teaching they had learned from child-hood, and the conventional attitudes that had shaped their existence. These words confront us too. They make us uncomfortable, but they also liberate us.

Although the lectionaries are very valuable, they are not designed to bring out the unique teaching of Jesus. Their purpose is to ensure that large parts of the gospels are read, and with few exceptions they include everything that is important. This chapter, however, is written to aid the homilist in getting the perspective on Jesus' ministry and teaching of which we have spoken, so that he or she can give that specific message its full force.

One way to organize this chapter might have been to deal topically with several themes of Jesus' teaching. But this would necessitate much skipping back and forth; furthermore, the themes are so interrelated that it is all but impossible to separate them. Since our aim is to serve the needs of the preacher, it seems best to go through the readings for Sundays of the year in each of the sequences, A, B, and C, and note the distinctive features as they arise. Not all of the pericopes will be discussed, and the miracles and the accounts of controversies call for separate treatment. There must be some cross-references, since the three gospels often parallel one another. Nevertheless the sequence of Sunday readings will be followed as much as possible.

The New Perspective

The pericopes now to be treated will illustrate the new perspective from which we believe that Jesus regarded God's relation to the world and mankind. The Kingdom (or Reign) of God is central in his parables and sayings. Since God's Reign involves all of his activity, it is many-sided. The phrase has been called a tensive or multivalent symbol; that is to say, it looks in various directions. As a symbol, it is not to be defined but only suggested by story and metaphorical language. Its function is to stimulate imagination and thought.

God's sovereignty, and therefore his loving care, is offered especially to the poor, the sufferers, the outcasts, to all who are in need and too often disregarded by others. God's covenant with his ancient People is never denied, but now his judgment and grace are in principle extended to all nations, as the Church began to learn after the Resurrection. In Judaism, women had more dignity than in most ancient cultures, but Jesus treated them with especial respect and concern.

The OT knew of what theologians call God's prevenient grace—the covenants are striking examples of this—and Jesus emphasized God's prior action even more. He brought a fresh message of God's involvement in human life and, so to speak, acted out what he said God was doing. Jesus spoke words of judgment, particularly on heartlessness, carelessness and hypocrisy, but the dominant note of the gospel was surprise and joy. The OT announcement that God was doing a new thing in the world was given new dimensions.

He took up another theme to be found in Second Isaiah and elsewhere, that God's ways are not man's ways. His purposes sometimes coincide with those of mankind but they also cut across them, and reality is not precisely what theologians of the past and the majority of people even today think it to be. Jesus looked at life realistically and knew that things do not always turn out as in theory they ought to do. Life has both comic and tragic surprises. His attitude toward political power and wealth was not one of angry denunciation; rather he found these things petty and absurd. This is what it means to view the world scene from God's perspective.

Jesus was able to rejoice and enjoy life when at the same time he contemplated the coming crisis and the probability of his own violent death. Such was the measure of his freedom.

The demands that he made on his intimate followers, sometimes stated directly but often obliquely in parables, forced on them a radical reexamination of their existence. The message of God's Reign—that God is truly in charge of events—shattered the conventional opinions that they had learned from the surrounding culture. Jesus did not hesitate to speak of reward, but God's rewards differ in kind from human recompense and in the end are gifts of his grace. They can never be reckoned, and it is wrong above all to guess what God gives or should give to any other person. What counts finally is not reward but relationship to God. This comes first and produces a good life and good works; we cannot achieve it by developing our own virtues and adding them up. One enters God's Kingdom, or comes under his rule, by becoming like a child, open, candid and free, sitting loose to life and death; being responsible, but taking each day as it comes in trust and expectation.

The Message of the Reign of God

When preparing to discuss the teaching of Jesus, the homilist should have a harmony of the gospels before him. Sections in Matthew or Luke that run parallel to Mark ought to be compared with that gospel; where Matthew and Luke are parallel but Mark is wanting, the two gospels should be compared to try to determine the earlier (Q) tradition.

We begin with Matthew in Year A.

Y3A.* Modified course reading begins on the third Sunday "of the year" with the beginning of Jesus' ministry (4:12–23). Matthew is dependent on Mark, but he adds that Jesus actually made his home in Capernaum, a village by the Sea of Galilee that figures in the gospel story many times. The OT reading for the day is Isa. 9:1–4, and Matthew sets the scene with a quotation from 9:1f. which he introduces with a formula that he uses elsewhere in his gospel. Such formula citations may come from a special source and are peculiar to Matthew. The context suggests that Galilee is the land of revelation *par excellence.* The alternative (Amos 3:1–8, Episcopal) sets forth the necessity laid on a prophet.

Here the Good News actually begins: "Repent, for the Kingdom of the heavens has drawn near!" It is only later, especially in the parables, that the full meaning of this announcement will be disclosed. Jesus' first hearers would have understood it to say that the long period of foreign domination would soon end and God's new order would be established.

Narratives of the several incidents of Jesus' ministry circulated separately in the oral tradition, but the next part of the pericope must always have been told as part of the beginning of Jesus' work. The first four disciples are called, and they immediately leave their fishing boat to follow him. Since such narratives stand by themselves, this one neither affirms nor denies that Jesus had previously met the disciples and talked with them. The emphasis is on their immediate response to the call; such is the power of Jesus' word.

---

*In this book the Sundays "of the year" are numbered as in the Roman *Ordo,* which counts the First Sunday after Epiphany as the First Sunday of "ordinary time." See the table of conversion on page ix.

Y4A. The Beatitudes (5:1-12) are the gospel reading. The Reign of God is offered to the poor, the mourners, the meek (or humble), those who hunger and thirst, the merciful, the pure in heart (or single-minded), and the persecuted. These are not separate groups; the Beatitudes describe the same people in all these ways. Matthew (or perhaps the tradition before him) explains that the "poor" are poor "in spirit." The echoes in the Beatitudes of Pss. 37:11; 24:3f.; 34:14, and perhaps other psalms, show that these are not just penniless folk but the oppressed poor who put their trust in God.

Luke 6:20-23, the parallel, is addressed directly to the poor and hungry: "Blessed are you." In Matt. 5:6 these people hunger and thirst "for righteousness" or "justice," i.e. vindication, but the evangelist may also think of them as aspiring to the new way of living, the righteousness of the Kingdom (6:33), the true Torah set forth in the Sermon on the Mount.

The OT reading, Zeph. 2:3; 3:12-13, which speaks of God's care for the humble and lowly, is a happy choice. So is Mic. 6:1-8 (Episcopal, NA), "the saving acts of the Lord." The second reading, I Cor. 1:26-31, transposes the motif of the Beatitudes into a different key. God has chosen the foolish and the weak (a partly ironical description of Christians) to shame the powerful and the wise, so that no one may boast except "in the Lord."

In no case does Jesus put conditions on the promises. They are the purest examples of grace. But, like all other gifts of grace, they are effective only for those who receive them in faith.

The real problem that confronts us as we hear these words is that there continue to be the poor, the hungry, the sorrowful, and the rejected. The Beatitudes can make sense to such persons only as God's People stand on their side and carry out the mission of the prophets and Jesus. The Church's role in this is not easy to define. What is a valid liberation theology? Revolutionary movements so often accomplish little more than to substitute one set of masters for another, and the benefits to the poor are ambiguous. The one thing certain is that the proclamation of the Good News, combined as it was in Jesus' ministry with deeds of mercy, is acceptable to God, and to us is a sign of the Kingdom's nearness.

Y10A. To suppose that Judaism in Jesus' time did not care for the poor would be to do a great injustice. Riches were considered a proper reward for a pious man, but the Pharisees were deeply concerned for the unfortunate and taught the duty of almsgiving. As in all societies, there were heartless people, and some of these were absentee landown-ers who belonged to the party of the Sadducees. The gospel reading for this Sunday (Matt. 9:9–13) shows that Jesus brought his message also to those whom pious people considered outcasts. Tax collectors, harlots, dice players, and sometimes shepherds were among these. In contrast to John the Baptist, who was an ascetic, Jesus and his disciples shared joyful meals with these people frequently enough for his enemies to accuse him of being "a glutton and wine drinker, a friend of tax collec-tors and sinners" (Matt. 11:16–19; cf. Luke 7:31–35, a passage not included in the lectionaries). This does not mean that Jesus was lax in his judgment on sin; it was a sign of the near presence of the Reign of God. It was not healthy people but the sick who needed a physician.

Matthew introduces a quotation from Hos. 6:3–6, which is part of the first reading for the day in most lectionaries.

Y11A. In the gospel reading for this Sunday (Matt. 9:35—10:8) the emphasis is on those who are "harassed and helpless, like sheep who have no shepherd." The Twelve are chosen to bring the message of the Kingdom to them and to heal the sick, raise the dead, cleanse lepers, and cast out demons. This pericope comes after a series of stories in chapters 8 and 9 that Matthew has brought together to illustrate Jesus' healing work, which is to be a model for the disciples. Today's reading is composite and Matthew has edited it extensively. A more primitive form of the mission discourse is found in Luke 10:1–20, part of which is read on Y14C.

The reading (except in NA) from Rom. 5:6–11 speaks of Jesus' work of reconciling human beings to God, and the first reading (Exod. 19:2–8) is part of the covenant story. Yahweh has carried his people on eagles' wings and promises to make them a kingdom of priests and a holy nation. The Hebrews had previously been semi-nomads, and no nation at all.

Y13A. The reading from Matt. 10:34–42 is also composite and con-sists of three separate groups of sayings. Verses 37–39 are partly Chris-tological; the disciple must take up his cross and follow Jesus. Verses 40–42 speak of the rewards given those who aid the disciples; this explains why the reading from II Kings 4:8–11, 14–16a is read by three lectionaries on this day. One should, however, note especially verses

34–36, which are based on Mic. 7:6 and warn the disciples that the message will bring dissension in families, which by the way is a mark of the troubles preceding the new age. The gospel tradition contains other sayings to this effect, such as Luke 12:49f. Jesus' ministry was in a time of crisis. For the epistle, see pp. 214f., 245f.

The Parables of Jesus

The art of story is common to people of all lands and ages. In our western cultural tradition the first outstanding examples of story tellers are the Hebrew author of the J document and the poet Homer among the Greeks. Jesus is sometimes called the greatest of all, but his is a special kind of narrative. In contrast to the epics the parables are very brief. They have analogies in Jewish tradition, but Jesus used the form in a unique fashion. We say that they embodied his teaching, but he was more a prophet than a teacher. These parables were part of the total action of his ministry, bringing judgment and hope and forcing his hearers to reflect and come to a decision.

Almost all the parables have one outstanding trait: they are drawn from everyday life, the household, farm, marketplace and law court; they do not speak of prophets, holy men, angels or heavenly occur- rences. They do have a variety of forms. What is often called a true parable may describe a typical situation or event (e.g., the Yeast, Mus- tard Seed, Lost Sheep, Lost Coin, Hidden Treasure and Costly Pearl), or it may tell of an interesting particular incident (the Dishonest Manager, the Two Sons, the Great Banquet, the Friend at Midnight). Other para- bles might be called illustrations or example stories (the Good Samari- tan, the Rich Fool, the Pharisee and the Tax Collector).

The parables are told with economy and conciseness; there is no interest in the surrounding circumstances or the possible sequel. As in much folk story, there are three characters or three episodes. The emphasis comes at the end, and it is believed that originally each parable had a single point; thus it is wrong to seek allegorical meanings in the details. Sometimes Jesus did not explain the point but left it to his hearers to ponder the story.

There are many sayings that are parabolical and so are closely related to the parables. "You are the salt of the earth . . . You are the light of the world" (Matt. 5:13f.). "When you give alms, do not sound a trum- pet" (Matt. 6:2).

The tradition also contains a few allegories, such as the parables of the Ten Young Girls (Matt. 25:1–13) and the Wicked Vineyard Workers (Mark 12:1–11 and parallels). Other parables that were not originally in this form have been transformed into allegories, and scholars are not agreed as to whether Jesus used this method at all. We cannot say dogmatically that he did not, but in every case the allegory serves the interest of the early Church's catechesis.

Certainly the parables as we have them have undergone modification in the oral tradition and through the editorial work of the evangelists. By distinguishing the original parable from the rather obvious changes that have been made, we can often see both what Jesus and the early Church were saying. This is important for the homilist and his hearers.

At an early stage the parables were translated into Greek, and the gospels were written for Greek-speaking churches in the Hellenistic world. As a result, some of the cultural details and even the meaning underwent some change. The setting of these stories was originally in the ministry of Jesus, but they were used for instruction in the Church. Parables that were at one time addressed to opponents or to a crowd of hearers were now applied to the needs of the Christian community. Some that dealt with the coming Reign of God and the judgment have been transformed into moral exhortations to church people, sometimes by making them allegories, at other times by giving them generalizing conclusions so that they acquire a universal meaning. The Church quite naturally emphasized the missionary motive and also the delay of the Parousia. In a few cases two parables were fused together, and the evangelist by placing a parable in a particular context in his gospel suggested an interpretation of it.

The Parables of the Kingdom in Matthew

Y15A. Matt. 13:1–23 is based on Mark 4:1–20. It consists of four parts.

(1) Chapter 13:1–9 is the parable of the Sower. Mark and Matthew do not call it a parable of the Reign of God, although it is that, because both evangelists use it as an example of parables in general in order to introduce a significant collection of them. The story is one of a group of Seed parables and tells what happens when the seed is sown. The several types of soil can be observed easily in Galilee near the lake, but this is subsidiary to the main point. When the seed falls into a very fruitful place like the plain of Gennesaret, which Josephus called "the ambition of nature," the harvest is beyond all expectations. The parable

has sometimes been understood as an encouragement to the disciples, who might become disheartened when the seed of the Word fell into infertile places, but nowhere in early Christian literature except in 13:18–23 and its parallels is seed used as a symbol of the preaching of the gospel. Paul uses it as an eschatological symbol of resurrection. The parable probably suggests the almost unbelievable glory of what Jesus is proclaiming and what God will do in his Reign. All the Seed parables strike the note of surprise and joy.

(2) Verses 10–15 are based on Isa. 6:9f., which Matthew quotes fully and which is implied in Mark. The disciples, who represent the Church, have been given the secrets of the Kingdom; to the evangelists this explains why most of the Jews have rejected Jesus, and also why some of the parables have been difficult to understand. Isaiah's original words were in the nature of shock treatment. It is not that God wills the rejection of his People but rather that this will happen if they persist in refusing to hear and see. If Jesus said something like this, it must have been to the same point, for the purpose of a parable is more to communicate than to conceal.

(3) Whereas Mark 4:11 says that the disciples have been given the secret, other parts of that gospel indicate that they often misunderstood. But in verses 16–17 Matthew includes a Q saying (cf. Luke 10:23) congratulating the disciples because they see; it is only outsiders who are blind and deaf.

(4) Verses 18–23 are an application of the parable that was probably traditional even before Mark's time. It transforms the story into an allegory of the soils, and its setting is in the second generation of the Church when zeal and enthusiasm have flagged and riches and good living are a temptation. It is a good early Christian homily even though a rather obvious one.

The first and second readings for this Sunday have a general application to the themes of the gospel. Isa. 55:1–5, 10–13 teaches that God's word will not return empty but will accomplish his purpose; Rom. 8:18–23 (8:9–17, Episcopal) is part of Paul's rhapsody on the glory of the new creation.

Y16A. Matt. 13:24–43 continues the collection of parables and interpretations. First comes the parable of the Weeds (verses 24–30). This replaces a parable in Mark 4:26–29 which both Matthew and Luke may have considered obscure. Some words are found in both the Marcan and

Matthaean parables, and the relationship between them is not certain. In its present form, the Weeds is a parable of the final judgment, but its point is that one should not try too zealously to separate the poisonous darnel from the wheat; thus it fits with Jesus' warning, "Do not judge, so that you will not be judged" (Matt. 7:1-5).

Matthew's version of the Mustard Seed (verses 31f.; cf. Mark 4:30-32; Luke 13:18f.) has traits drawn from Mark and also from that of Luke, which evidently reflects the Q form. It is one of the Seed parables, and the contrast is between the small and the great. As its introduction shows, it is a parable of the Kingdom, and there is an allusion to the great tree of Dan. 4:20-22 (symbolizing Nebuchadnezzar's Kingdom) or of Ezek. 17:22-24 (Israel) or 31:1-14 (Egypt).

Yeast is not a seed, but the parable of the Leaven (verse 33; cf. Luke 13:20f.) is a twin of the Mustard Seed. The way in which dough rises is dramatic—it can overflow the kettle or trough—and to the ancients it was mysterious. Jesus' choice of the metaphor may have been paradoxical and shocking, for elsewhere in Scripture yeast is a symbol of sin and evil influence (Mark 8:15; I Cor. 5:6-8). God's Reign is more powerful than evil. Like the new wine (Mark 2:22) it may even be a danger to the present order.

Verses 34f. are a rewriting of Mark. It is interesting that Matthew quotes Ps. 78:2, where a parable is equated with "dark sayings." Certainly parables, just because they are metaphorical, can sometimes be taken in more than one way, and the hearer must puzzle the meaning out for himself. This is particularly so with anything that refers to the Reign of God, for God's purposes are partly revealed, partly hidden.

Matthew breaks his parable collection into two parts. Verses 1-35 are addressed to the crowds; then Jesus goes into the house and at the disciples' request explains the parable of the Weeds. This is a completely allegorical interpretation which warns the Church's leaders against trying to purge the Church by excommunicating all sinners. Here a distinction is drawn between the kingdom of the Father and that of the Son. Commentators sometimes understand the latter as meaning the Church, but in Matthew's theology Christ is also king of the world (Matt 25:31-46; 28:18). The explanation is entirely in Matthew's style and must be his composition.

The lectionaries vary in their choice of the first and second readings. In the Roman and Episcopal rites (and in the Methodist as an alternative) the first is Wisd. 12:13, 16-19, which teaches that God cares for all;

though sovereign in strength, he judges with mildness. This is standard Jewish doctrine.

Y17A. In 13:44–52 the parable section comes to a magnificent conclusion. The twin parables of the Hid Treasure (verse 44) and the Costly Pearl (versus 45f.) present a different aspect of God's Reign; it is worth giving up everything else to obtain it. At the same time, as in the Seed parables, its note is surprise and joy. When the opportunity to decide is presented, there are those who like the rich man go away sorrowful (Mark 10:22), while for St. Francis of Assisi and many others it is unspeakable liberation and happiness.

The stories are drawn from life. The man who found the treasure was within his rights according to Jewish law; he bought the field and then its contents were legally his. The other story involves more risk; at the end of the transaction the merchant owned nothing but one pearl. As in other parables, there is no interest in the sequel, and it is idle to ask whether he then sold the pearl and became even richer, or simply enjoyed his priceless possession.

The parable of the Seine or Dragnet (verses 47–50) is a twin to that of the Weeds and makes a similar point. Its theology and style are those of Matthew.

Commentators have often seen in the little figure of the householder (verses 51f.) a self-portrait of the evangelist Matthew. Everything in his gospel suggests that he is something of a scribe educated for the Kingdom of the heavens. Perhaps, like the rabbis, he consciously sought new interpretations along with the old message.

The first reading for this Sunday, I Kings 3:5–12 (Solomon's prayer at Gibeon for wisdom) was evidently chosen to go with this final parable. Exod. 3:13–20 (NA) tells of Yahweh's self-revelation to Moses. As in the parable of the Pearl, something new and amazing occurs.

Y20A. The gospel reading (Matt. 15:21–28; see p. 202) does not speak of the Kingdom of God but has some relation to it. It is essentially the same story as the one in Mark 7:24–30, and a comparison discloses the habits of the gospel writers. They (and no doubt the oral tradition also) were relatively faithful in transmitting sayings of Jesus but took liberties with the stories. This tells of an exorcism, but the miracle is incidental to the dialogue between Jesus and the woman and to the tradition that on occasion Jesus healed a Gentile (of which there is another example in 8:5–13). Matthew knew that Jesus' ministry was mainly among his own people, and he transmitted a saying that forbade the Twelve to go among Gentiles and Samaritans (10:5f.). This logion was probably handed down by conservative Jewish Christians who disapproved of such a mission (Acts 11:1ff.), but Matthew himself believed that the gospel was destined for all nations. The stories of the woman and the centurion's slave supported Matthew's theology. The seeming abruptness of Jesus' remark, comparing Gentiles with dogs, has disturbed modern readers, but the ancients seem to have had no difficulty with it. What was important to them was that the woman answered with wit and faith, and that Jesus healed her daughter.

The first reading (Isa. 56:1–8) pronounces God's blessing on eunuchs and foreigners and proclaims that the Temple is to be a house of prayer for all nations. The epistle pericope (Rom. 11:13–16, 29–32) is part of the chapter in which Paul defends the mission to the Gentiles and expresses his faith in the destiny of Israel.

Parables of Response—Matthew

There are several ways of classifying the parables, but those we shall consider now can roughly be called parables of response; that is, they indicate the ways in which people may respond to God's action toward them. They also show that God's ways are not man's ways.

Y24A. The parable of the Unforgiving Slave (Matt. 18:21–35) comes at the conclusion of a chapter in which Matthew has dealt primarily with life within the Church. One must become like a child and must also be ready to accept children (18:1–5, 10); the greatest sin is to cause little ones to sin (18:6–9); and the parable of the Lost Sheep expresses God's care for everyone (18:11–14). After this comes a composite section on what is to be done if one brother sins against another; if this cannot be worked out, excommunication is the last resort, and the Church has the necessary authority (18:15–20). But then Peter, as usual the spokesman for the disciples, asks how many times he should forgive his brother, and the answer is seventy-seven times (18:21f.). This is climaxed by the parable, which in this context implies that both the Church and the individual must forgive as they have been forgiven.

So much for Matthew's setting. This is a King parable and therefore related to the ones that speak of God's Reign. The king is not to be equated with God; he is like the Persian monarch and his "slaves" are satraps who rule large provinces and are responsible for collecting taxes and tribute. The point of the parable is that we can expect no more mercy than that which we show to others. The first reading, from Sir. 27:30—28:9 (Roman, Episcopal, Methodist alternative) shows that Jesus' teaching on this subject has been anticipated: one is not to take vengeance but to forgive one's neighbor.

Y25A. The first reading (Isa. 55:6–11; Jonah 3:10—4:11, Episcopal) gives the real point of the parable of the Vineyard Workers (Matt. 20:1–16): "My thoughts are not your thoughts . . . says the Lord." Verse 16 is to be disregarded; although the story is a reversal, that is not the main point, and this is a floating saying that the evangelists use when they think it appropriate.

The story begins with the words "The Kingdom of heaven is like . . ." All such introductions mean "It is with God's Reign as with this situation."

The parable is wonderfully lifelike and its setting is Palestinian. We can see how unconventional it is when we realize that there is a rabbinical parable in which laborers complain that a man has been paid more than they, and the boss answers that this person has done twice as much work. Jesus' story does not teach that everyone should receive a living wage (though he would not have objected to that) or that the owner of a vineyard has a right to deal with labor as he chooses.

Certainly any boss who behaved as this one did would soon have labor troubles. But the point is that when God is in charge, what is conventionally considered proper is not appropriate at all.

In this parable we arrive at a fundamental aspect of the teaching of Jesus. There have been many attempts to identify the exact theological meaning. Often it has been interpreted in Pauline terms as a simple contrast between grace and the works of the Law. But in fairness it must be said that the rabbinic tradition has no single doctrine of reward; the rabbis understood that life is not as simple as it is made out, for example, in Ps. 37. They also recognized the grace of God. Therefore Norman Perrin drew the contrast between grace and a doctrine of mingled works and grace.[1]

In any case the parable teaches that God is generous and that no one can complain if he seems especially generous to someone else. Those who made a contract with the boss received their just due. Thus the parable has to do primarily with *attitudes.*

[1]N. Perrin, *Rediscovering the Teaching of Jesus* (New York: Harper & Row, 1967), p. 118.

Dominic Crossan has said something that applies to this and to some other parables. The question that arises here and lies behind St. Paul's doctrine of justification by faith has to do with the relationship of human beings with God. Good deeds and grace are both involved, but, as he says, in which way does the arrow fly? Do we establish this relationship as the result of our virtue, or does the relationship with God come first, and our virtues or good deeds arise out of that relationship? This is absolutely fundamental to the religious life. It is not a question of works or grace, or of Christianity versus Judaism; the issue cuts across both Judaism and Christianity and it touches every individual.[1]

Many commentators believe that such parables as this and the Prodigal Son and Great Supper were Jesus' answer to objections made by his opponents. Crossan makes a further point: it is more likely that the parables arose out of Jesus' religious life, his experience of the Father, and that the parables *aroused* controversy rather than resulting from it.[2] Certainly the parable forces its hearers, as it undoubtedly did the original disciples, to reflect on where they stand. Stories such as these, if they are really heard, shock a person out of his complacency and call him to examine his existence and the conventional attitudes that he has been taught.

Y28A. Matt. 22:1–14. The lectionaries prescribe this form of the parable of the Great Supper rather than the simpler pericope, Luke 14:16–24. The original parable can be easily recovered by leaving out what has been added in the two gospels.

Matthew's tendencies are apparent here. (1) He makes the parable Christological, for it is not just "a man" but a king who gives a marriage feast for his son (the heavenly bridegroom). (2) The story becomes an allegory of the killing of God's servants and the destruction of Jerusalem, which has already occurred when Matthew writes. (3) A second parable that is added (verses 11–14) introduces a moral idea. One who is invited must wear the proper clothing (deeds of righteousness). (4) Finally there is an eschatological judgment: the unworthy man is cast into the outer darkness. The language is in Matthew's style.

Luke did very little to the parable except that he (or the underlying tradition) added a second sending into "the highways and hedges" (14:22–24) which perhaps symbolizes the mission to the Gentiles.

---

[1]J. D. Crossan, *In Parables* (New York: Harper & Row, 1973), pp. 80–82.
[2]Ibid., p. 22.

Behind the parable is the metaphor of the messianic banquet (cf. Matt. 8:11f.; Luke 13:28-30). The first lesson, Isa. 25:1-10a, is chosen appropriately. Jesus pronounced a blessing on the hungry, and he ate and drank with sinners and outcasts. The messianic banquet was a feature of the Jewish future hope, and like the Feeding of the Five Thousand it is a symbol of the Kingdom of God. In God's order the starving are fed, but man does not live by bread alone, and the Kingdom's promises include all human needs. The main point of the parable, however, is that if respectable people do not accept the invitation because they are too busy with their own affairs it must be offered to those who are in greatest need.

As in the case of the Laborers in the Vineyard, it is a question of attitudes. When Jesus spoke the parable it was as much a challenge to his disciples as to his opponents.

On the last three Sundays of Year A the three parables of Matt. 25 are read in sequence, except in the Lutheran and Presbyterian service books, which interpolate other passages from Matthew which strike the note of judgment.

Matt. 25:1-13 is assigned to Y32A. This is the parable of the Ten Young Girls. It is possible that when Jesus originally spoke the parable it was not an allegory, and the point was similar to that of the Thief in the Night (Luke 12:39f.): one must be prepared at all times. In that case the attitude of the wise bridesmaids is simply a part of the story and has no hidden significance. Although the details do not altogether match what we know of ancient Jewish marriage customs, the story is rather lifelike, for the climax of the wedding comes when the bridegroom arrives to take the bride home.

But as the parable stands it is an allegory and one that fits with Matthew's theology. The bridegroom is Christ and the girls represent Christians. Both the foolish and the wise fall asleep (i.e. die). At the general resurrection, the arrival of the groom, they must have oil in their lamps (a righteousness appropriate to Christians). If they have not, it is too late, and there is no way that the wise girls can transfer their virtues to the foolish.

The other readings for these last Sundays vary greatly, but generally deal with judgment and the end of the age.

Y33A. The parable of the Talents (Matt. 25:14-30) has a rough parallel in the simpler story of Luke 19:13, 15-26, but another parable has been woven in with the latter.

The parable in itself is quite secular and we can understand its point better when we compare it with a fragment from the apocryphal Gospel of the Nazarenes that Eusebius has preserved. Here there are also three slaves. The first made money with his talent and was rewarded; the second hid the money and was only rebuked; while the third wasted it with harlots and flute-girls and was put in prison.

As everyone should know, when we speak of a talent for music or mathematics, we use a word that is derived from Matthew's parable. The surface meaning of the story is that a talent not used is a talent lost, and this is a good piece of secular wisdom.

Jesus often used such pieces of wisdom, but always to make a more profound point. We can only guess at what he had in mind here, but we do have such sayings as verse 29 and its parallel, Mark 4:24f., which Mark puts into a context on the hearing of parables. Did Jesus refer to our life, which God has given us, with all the graces that have been lavished on us? Or was he speaking to the disciples, to whom he committed the message of the Reign of God and all the rest of his teaching?

We have discussed the parable of the Last Judgment (Matt. 25:31-46, Feast of Christ the King) in the chapter on Advent.

·13

The Message of Jesus - Year B

Fewer pericopes will be discussed in this chapter because Mark contains a lesser amount of Jesus' teaching than do the other Synoptic gospels. This evangelist frequently speaks of Jesus' teaching activity, but he understands "teaching" as including the healings that he performed and his other works.

The Reign of God in Mark

Y3B.* Mark 1:14–20 is the actual beginning of the Good News and of Jesus' ministry, and verse 15 is the keynote. This is followed by the call of the first disciples. As we noted in connection with Matthew's form of the story, the emphasis is on their immediate response. The details are interesting, for the men were fishing with one of the two types of nets used at least until recently in the Sea of Galilee, the *amphiblestron* or purse-net, circular and with a draw rope around its circumference.

The kernel saying of Jesus promises to make them "fishers of men." When this metaphor is used in the OT it is ominous: men are caught

---

*In this book the Sundays "of the year" are numbered as in the Roman *Ordo,* which counts the First Sunday after Epiphany as the First Sunday of "ordinary time." See the table of conversion on page ix.

with hooks for their destruction (Jer. 16:16; Ezek 32:3). The idea of judgment cannot be excluded here, for in Matt. 13:47-50 the net catches the good and the bad, but probably Jesus turns an evil metaphor into a good one, as he does in the case of yeast. People are caught to be saved.

The accompanying reading from Jonah 3:1-5, 10 tells how the prophet was sent to Nineveh to preach repentance. I Cor. 7:29-31 (p. 224f.) points to the eschatological aspect of Jesus' message. 7:17-23 (Episcopal) teaches that the external circumstances of one's call are irrelevant.

Y8B. Mark 2:18-22 consists of two parts, verses 18-20 and 21f. The first verses are an apophthegm or paradigm which enshrines the essential saying of verse 19. The reference is not to obligatory fasts, such as the Day of Atonement, but to voluntary ones undertaken by particularly pious people. The disciples are not violating any law; it was just that they did not conform to what was deemed proper. But the days of Jesus' ministry were like a wedding celebration and not a time for penitence. Verse 20 is a Christian addition; at the time of the Crucifixion his followers will fast. Verses 21f. are brought in artistically; the old and the new do not fit together; indeed the new can be perceived as a danger to the old. These sayings could have been uttered on any occasion.

The first reading, Hos. 2:14-23, calls attention to the figure of the bridegroom, but it is important for another reason, for it is an example of Good News in the OT. Yahweh will woo his wayward bride in the wilderness and bring her back (see notes on Lent 1). She will no longer call him "My Baal," a word that can mean "husband" but alludes to the pagan practices of the northern kingdom; she will call Yahweh her "man," her husband. II Cor. 3:1b-6 (p. 211f.) prepares for the gospel message of newness by proclaiming that the apostolic ministry is the ministry of a new covenant. II Cor. 3:17—4:2 (Episcopal, Presbyterian) speaks of the spiritual and moral transformation that is the essence of this ministry.

Y15B. Mark 6:7-13 recounts the sending out of the Twelve. As compared with the mission discourse in Luke 10:1-20, which is read on Y14C (p. 251), this is a later form. The disciples may take a staff and wear sandals, a feature implying a long journey, and they are given explicit authority to exorcise demons. This is also one of the two places in the NT that mention anointing the sick with oil (cf. Jas. 5:14). Mark evidently reflects a mission outside Palestine. Although his geography is confused and somewhat artifical, he tells how Jesus healed the daughter of a woman in the neighborhood of Tyre (7:24–30), and some of the narratives that follow this at least as far as 9:13 are located in Gentile territory. At the cleansing of the Temple Jesus teaches that it is to be a house of prayer for all nations.

In Amos 7:7–15, the first reading, the prophet declares that Yahweh has sent him, though he was not a member of a prophetic guild. Like the apostles, he was non-professional. Eph. 1:1–14 is a rhapsody on the salvation brought by the gospel.

A Parable of the Kingdom

Y11B. Mark 4:26–29 is the one parable of the Kingdom that is found only in Mark. The picture is simple and beautiful. One should not ask who the farmer is; the point is that the seed is sown, the harvest is in God's hands and will surely come. The phrase "he puts in the sickle" is a reminiscence of Joel 3:13 and shows that the parable is eschatological.

The first reading (Ezek. 17:22–24, except Episcopal and NA) is meant to match the parable of the Mustard Seed (verses 30–32; cf. p. 155). It speaks of the coming kingdom as a noble cedar whose branches will provide nests for birds of every sort. Ezekiel 3:1–6, 10–14 (Episcopal) is a similar passage.

Christology and Discipleship in Mark

Y7B. It is generally agreed that the controversy over forgiveness of sins (verses 5–10) has been inserted into the story of the paralytic (Mark 2:1–12). The story itself is Palestinian, for the house was roofed with thorns and branches laid over poles, and plastered with mud, so that the men had to dig through the roof to let the sufferer into the room. Mark probably thinks of this as a sign of the faith exhibited by the friends of the sick man, but this is incidental to the story.

Like all healing miracles the narrative is a sign of God's action through the Good News of Jesus. What is distinctive about the passage is that Jesus pronounces the forgiveness of sins in a specific case when there is no mention of prior repentance. The position of the scribes was that only God could know that there was genuine repentance and amendment of life. Jesus' words are one of many examples of God's good will; the grace is there first and freely offered, repentance comes as a natural response.

In the Gospel of Mark both the healings and the controversies are told to disclose Jesus' divine nature. Here the term "Son of Man" is applied to him for the first time in this gospel. Its only other occurrence before Peter's confession at Caesarea Philippi is in 2:28, where it is said that the Son of Man is lord of the Sabbath. In these two places the phrase could mean "human being," as it always does in the OT. Thus it might be said that "Man is master of the Sabbath," which fits with 2:27, and "Man has power on earth to forgive sins," and Matthew evidently understands the latter saying in this way, for he remarks, "The crowds were in awe and glorified God, who had given such power to men" (Matt. 9:8). Mark, however, thought of the Son of Man as the one exalted to God's right hand (14:62) and was to come again in glory (13:26). The two uses of this title in chapter 2 are Mark's enigmatic signals of a revelation that is later to come.

Isa. 43:18–25 fits with the gospel reading in that Yahweh proclaims, "I am doing a new thing . . . I blot out your transgressions." Paul teaches that the promises of God find their Yes in Jesus Christ (II Cor. 1:18–22) (p. 210f.).

Y24B. Mark 8:27–38 is part of a composite section that runs from 8:27 to 9:1, and is bracketed by the healing of the blind man of Bethsaida (8:22–26) and the Transfiguration (9:2–8). Mark presents seeing in three ways: a blind man is physically and gradually healed; Peter, the typical disciple, sees partially but has to have his vision corrected; and a fuller vision of Christ in his glory is given on the mountain. The other evangelists are not conscious of this pattern.

The verses before us are in three parts.

(1) Verses 27–30. The geographical setting is significant. Caesarea Philippi is in pagan territory, an old center of worship of the god Pan, near one of the sources of the Jordan at the foot of Mount Hermon. Here Peter acknowledges Jesus as the Messiah of the One God. If our Lord on such an occasion had commanded silence it was because "Messiah" would ordinarily be understood as a conquering earthly king. But by the time when Mark wrote, this was the universal Christian confession, and Peter represents all the Church.

(2) Verses 31–33. It is altogether probable that Jesus warned his disciples of the danger of death that he and they faced in going to Jerusalem. 8:31, 9:31 and 10:33f. are, however, three stylized predictions that occur at significant points in Mark's gospel and have been

formulated in the light of later events. The prediction which, we repeat, is substantially historical, is introduced because in this passage Peter represents tendencies in the Church that existed in Mark's time. He rebukes Jesus because he can accept a Christ of glory but not a suffering Christ. Yet the true Messiah is both, and Peter is called Satan, the tempter.

(3) Verses 35-38 are addressed to the crowds as well as to the disciples. Such words are a message for the whole Church. A true follower of Jesus must deny himself—"deny" is a technical word, the opposite of "confess"—and take up his cross. *What is distinctive here is the teaching that one can save one's life only by losing it.* The Cross was only the climax of a life of self-giving. "For my sake" may be a phrase that comes from the Christian tradition. Curiously Matthew and Luke omit the words "for the gospel's." To Mark the gospel meant the news of salvation through the Cross and faith in Christ.

The first lesson is from Isa. 50:4-10 in which the Servant of the Lord tells of his sufferings and also of the sustaining word that he brings.

The story of Peter's confession appears in a different form in Matt. 16:13-20, which is read on Y21A. This is evidently based on the passage in Mark but contains significant changes and an additional tradition. We can ascribe to Matthew the changes in verses 13-15, which reflect that evangelist's desire to make the theology more explicit. Matthew preserves the command to secrecy in verse 20 (Mark 8:30) and Jesus' harsh words to Peter (verse 23; cf. Mark 8:33), but verses 17-19 are inserted before this. Thus in place of a simple command to silence, Peter is blessed for having received the revelation of the truth, and to Matthew messiahship implies the Church's Christology as it is developed throughout his gospel.

Verse 18 is a tradition that explains how Simon came to have the name *Kepha* (Aramaic, rock or stone; in Greek, *Petros*). There is a rabbinical story of how "a certain man" wished to build a house; he dug deeper and deeper and found only mud, but at last he struck a rock on which he could lay a foundation, and this rock was "our father Abraham." The allegory suggests Abraham's reliability and perhaps his faith; the same may be the thought in the gospel.

On this rock Jesus will build his Church. The word *ekklesia*, very common in the Pauline letters, is found in the gospels only here and in Matt. 18:17, though the *idea* of the Church is implied in many places, especially in the Fourth Gospel. The gates of Hades (the powers of death) will not prevail against this Church.

Y25B. Mark 9:30-37 begins with the second prediction of the Passion. This is the opening of a major section on discipleship that concludes with 10:35-45. Verses 33-37 are in fact an anticipation of the
pericope just mentioned. In the Church, as in all societies, there are
those who are ambitious for leadership. But the "first" must be last of
all and servant of all, and the example given here is that he accepts and
ministers to a child.

The passages prescribed as the first reading (Wisd. 2:12-20, Roman
and Episcopal; Jer. 11:18-20, other lectionaries) are related to the Passion prediction.

Y27B. Mark 10:2-16. The section on divorce belongs with Jesus'
teaching about the Torah, and will be discussed on p. 192f. Here we are
concerned with verses 13-16, which are part of his unique message.

Like other dialogues or apophthegms in the gospels, the story is told
essentially to enshrine a saying, and here the kernel is verse 15. Jesus
seems to have had a special concern for children as he had for women;
both were too often disregarded. But the point is that there is a special
characteristic in children which everyone must have to be fit for the
Kingdom of God. Matthew tends to think of this as humility (Matt. 18:4),
but children are not naturally humble; they are taught to be that. Some
commentators say that children do not bargain with their parents for
food and love and care, they accept them naturally. It is more likely,
however, that Jesus thinks of their openness; they are not sophisticated
or jaded. They have come into a wonderful world with infinite possibilities and so are able to have faith.

Y28B. Mark 10:17-31. The story of a rich man (he is a young man
only in Matthew, and a "ruler" only in Luke) was difficult to accept, as
verses 23-30 prove. Clement of Alexandria was not the last to write on
the question "Which rich man is saved?"

The pericope does not teach that Jesus made it a general rule that rich
men must sell everything and give to the poor; in another part of the
gospel tradition he is said to have accepted Zacchaeus (Luke 19:1-10).
On the other hand, Jesus distrusted wealth as one of the greatest of all
perils, and the kernel saying in the discussion with the disciples is verse
25: "It is easier for a camel to go through the eye of a needle than for
someone who is rich to enter the Kingdom of God."

Attempts to tone down this saying or explain it away are futile. It has
the hallmark of Jesus' paradoxical and pictorial language. But just

because it is metaphorical it cannot be taken with extreme literalness. Wealth and poverty are not absolutes; they are always relative to the condition of other persons. Most of the poor in America are well off in comparison with many in India, Haiti and parts of Africa.

Why was it necessary for this man to divest himself of his wealth? One suggestion is that Jesus saw special possibilities in him (he "loved" him) and was calling him to be an apostle. It may also be that wealth was his particular temptation and like a hand or an eye (Mark 9:43-47) had to be removed. This is one example among many that the word of Scripture must be read as a letter addressed to each individual in his or her situation. Only a few are called to make a complete renunciation, and only they can make the decision. Taken with all the other sayings of Jesus, this pericope is a call to everyone to make the acquisition and conservation of wealth secondary; what is primary is the Reign of God.

Verses 28-30 are from the point of view of the early Church. Its habit of sharing is somewhat idealized here and in the Book of Acts, but it was nonetheless real. Most modern people are stingy in comparison.

Y29B. Mark 10:35-45. As so often in Mark, there are two parts, the dialogue in verses 35-40 and Jesus' teaching to the disciples in the remainder of the pericope.

It is James and John, the "sons of thunder," who are ambitious, not their doting mother (Matt. 20:20). Essentially what they ask is to be Secretary of State and Secretary of the Treasury in the kingdom that Jesus is to establish. To Mark this must have symbolized the highest offices in the Church.

The evangelist frames much of his gospel with the baptism of Jesus and the Last Supper, but we cannot tell whether in this section there is an allusion to the two major sacraments, as they were later called. Jesus will drink the cup of suffering and be overwhelmed by the dark waters of death, and he promises the same fate to the sons of Zebedee, but he disclaims the power to give them honors that God alone can give.

In the following verses, true greatness is contrasted with the petty glory of princes. The ancient world always took it for granted that one who has authority will "lord it over" others, and it is not very different today. The key words in verses 43 and 44 are *diakonos,* servant, minister, deacon, and *doulos,* slave. The most magnificent title of the Pope is *servus servorum Dei.*

Quite properly, the first reading is Isa. 53:4-12, from the fourth of the Servant songs.

·14

The Message of Jesus - Year C

Y *3C, Y4C.** The narrative of Jesus' "inaugural sermon" in the synagogue at Nazareth (Luke 4:14–21, Y3C) has provided the title of this book and an illustration of its purpose. The pericope should be compared with the very different story in Mark 6:1–6 and understood in its context in the Gospel of Luke.

Luke 4:21–30 or 4:21–32 is the reading for Y4C. The saying "No prophet is acceptable in his own country" (4:24) is found in a fuller form in Mark 6:4. Luke also transmits the proverb "Physician, heal yourself" (4:23), and the two sayings are combined in Logion 31 of the Coptic Gospel of Thomas, "A prophet is not acceptable in his own country, neither does a physician heal those who know him." Many scholars believe that this saying, with its Semitic parallelism, is the original form, and it is certainly the point in the pericopes of Mark and Luke.

The traditions in Mark 3:19b–21, 31–35 and John 7:1–9 indicate that at some point in his ministry the members of Jesus' family did not

*In this book the Sundays "of the year" are numbered as in the Roman *Ordo,* which counts the First Sunday after Epiphany as the First Sunday of "ordinary time." See the table of conversion on page ix.

believe in him. If there is history behind this, James "the brother of the Lord" came to faith only after the Resurrection. The tradition may also point to rivalries in the early Church between the Lord's family and other leaders, and it is a further development of the theme that "he came to his own home, and his own people did not accept him" (John 1:11).

Luke places the pericope 4:16–30 after Jesus has returned to Galilee in the power of the Spirit. Mark 6:1–6, however, comes after five chapters in which there is both acceptance and controversy; the issue of whether "his own" will receive him has not yet been decided. Luke's position of the story removes the tension and tragedy; at the very outset it is clear that the mission must go to the Gentiles, who will be more ready to heed the message.

The first reading for Y3C, Neh. 8:1–10 or parts therof (five lectionaries), tells of the repentance that followed Ezra's reading of the Torah; here we have a typology of law and gospel. On Y4C the OT pericope is Jer 1:4–10 (in the Roman lectionary 1:4–5, 17–19, which is less poetic but makes the same point). Here the prophet objects that his immaturity prevents him from speaking, but Yahweh gives him power over the nations (see p. 50). Like Jesus, he will suffer rejection; unlike Jeremiah, Jesus is fully secure in his authority.

Y6C. Luke 6:17–26. Matthew's form of the Beatitudes has been discussed on p. 150. The striking features in Luke's pericope are the direct address to the hearers, the unconditional form of the promises, and the woes which pronounce judgment. This last is the other edge of the two-edged sword of the prophets. The first reading, Jer. 17:5–10, contains an OT beatitude and also a curse on the one who trusts in human beings.

Y13C. Luke 9:51–62. Other examples of the call of disciples have been examined. This reading (actually two separate pericopes) has as important a function in the structure of Luke's gospel as the story of Jesus' proclamation at Nazareth. On this occasion Jesus decides to go to Jerusalem where he will be "taken up"—Luke sees everything as pointing toward the Ascension—and here begins the great central section of the gospel that runs from 9:51 to 18:34. Very little of this, except toward the end, is derived from Mark. What Luke has done is to collect and place here most of Jesus' important teachings. No chronological or geographical sequence should be expected in the central section. The impression that Luke leaves is that Jesus starts near the border between Samaria and Galilee and the journey ends at Jericho.

This is the first place in Luke where Samaritans are mentioned. Both Luke-Acts and John are very much interested in the Samaritan mission, which began very early after the Resurrection, and was validated by the fact that Jesus had had occasional contacts with these people. The lesson here is that even if a Samaritan village rejects him, the disciples are not to call down fire on it, as Elisha had done (II Kings 1:9–12).

The other pericope gives three examples of the call of disciples. Luke would have understood the saying "The Son of Man has nowhere to lay his head" as a paradox: he who is destined to sit at God's right hand has no home on earth. But as Jesus originally spoke it, there may be a contrast between foxes and birds and himself, a human being.

The third saying recalls I Kings 19:14–21, which is the first reading for the day. When Elijah calls Elisha to be his successor, the latter requests permission to say good-bye to his father, and this is granted. But nothing can take precedence of the Kingdom of God.

"Leave the dead to bury their own dead" has been called one of Jesus' most radical sayings, for burial of the dead was an absolute obligation, and honor to father and mother one of the most important of all commandments. We must once more recall that Jesus' speech is hyperbolical. It is the attitude, rather than literal following of the command, that counts, but he speaks in extreme terms so that no one will fail to take it seriously.

Y20C. Luke 12:49–56. These hard words have already been mentioned in connection with the parallel in Matt. 10:34–36. Jesus' prophetic vocation is to cast fire on the earth, and it was to consume him and some of his followers. Forms of this saying are found in Thomas 10 and 16, and in Thomas 82 there is a logion quoted also by some Church Fathers: "Whoever is near me is near the fire, and whoever is far from me is far from the Kingdom." The first reading in three of the lectionaries is Jer. 38:1b–13, which tells of the persecution of that prophet; in the Episcopal and Lutheran orders it is Jer. 23:23–29, which contains the awesome words, "Is not my word like fire, says Yahweh, and like a hammer that breaks the rock in pieces?" NA reads Jer 20:7–13, the prophet's lament that in his heart there is a burning fire. Heb. 12:1–13 speaks of the great cloud of witnesses and the danger of persecution that Christians will face.

Forgiveness and Response in Luke

Y11C. Luke 7:36—8:3. As happens sometimes in the gospel tradition, a controversy (and in this case a parable also) is interwoven with another story. Most hearers will remember the genuine penitence of this poor anonymous woman and not be concerned with the theological and historical difficulties of the story as it now stands. Simon the Pharisee is simply a lay figure who represents the self-righteous who objected to Jesus' free offer of forgiveness. The woman should not be identified with Mary Magdalene (8:2), as so often in later ecclesiastical tradition, or with the woman in the house of Simon the Leper (Mark 14:3–9), or with Mary of Bethany (John 12:1–8). The relations between the various stories are obscure and should not concern us here.

It is certainly true that the greatest of sinners can become one of the greatest of saints. Of course Jesus does not teach that one can do evil so that good may come (Rom. 3:8; 6:1), only that those who are in the greatest need are more apt than the "righteous" to recognize their true condition. When we come upon the word "Pharisees" in the gospels we can usually substitute "good church members"; it is not a question of Jews and Christians, or Pharisees and other Jews, but of two kinds of people in all religions. The passage chosen for the first reading is II Sam. 11:26—12:10, 13–15 (or parts thereof), in which Nathan confronts King David with the parable of the ewe lamb.

Because of his concern for women, Luke brings in at this point (8:1–3) the story of the women who followed Jesus and served him. Mary Magdalene, who had suffered from various illnesses, perhaps neuroses ("seven demons"), later became a witness of the Resurrection. Joanna came from the court of Herod Antipas. Since the rabbis frowned on too much familiarity with women, however innocent, Jesus' acceptance of them as disciples probably caused scandal.

Y24C. Luke 15:1–32. The evangelist understands these three great parables as Jesus' answer to the criticism that he accepted sinners and ate with them. This may be so, but as we have remarked, the stories could have aroused the criticism. Note how Jesus challenges his hearers: "What man of you . . . ?"

The first two are parables of forgiveness, or rather of the grace of God which precedes all repentence. The Pharisees said beautiful things about repentance and taught that God's pardon always follows it, but they did not seek out sinners.

Luke's form of the parable of the Lost Sheep is lifelike and more detailed than its parallel in Matt. 18:12-14. The shepherd may have owned the flock, but probably he was a hired man who would have been held responsible if he did not find the sheep. When Jesus speaks of "joy in heaven" the word "heaven" is the devout substitute for God's name. While God does not disdain the just ones who need no repentance, he actually rejoices over the saved sinner.

As elsewhere in Jesus' teaching, the righteous and the sinners are broadly defined groups, and at the moment he is not concerned with the fact that no human being is perfectly virtuous. Other sayings show that Jesus was aware of the universality of sin.

The story of the woman with the lost drachma is equally poignant. She has in cash only the equivalent of ten days' wages for a laborer, and to lose one coin on the earthen floor of her one-room house is no small loss.

The first two parables are twins. The story of the Prodigal Son starts out as though it would be the third of a series, though far more personal (verses 11-24), but the episode of the elder brother (verses 25-32) makes it much more disturbing.

From the point of view of an oriental family, the younger son has insulted his father scandalously. To ask for the wealth to be divided before the death of the father was as much as to wish that he were dead. The other brother is just as culpable, because apparently he did not protest this but accepted the division. From now on, legally speaking, the father might have been considered a guest in his elder son's household.

When the boy came back, the father forgot all his dignity and *ran* to meet his son, called for the best garment, and gave him the ring which is a token of lordship. What the elder brother said in his anger was no doubt true; he had stayed home and served and obeyed his father. But his attitude destroyed the bond of family life; every commentator notes the contrast between his words "this son of yours" and the father's "your brother." The point of the story is in this contrast. The father of the parable is a human being, not God; he was foolish to let the younger son go in the first place, but his generosity and love are like the love of God. Hosea had taught that God goes out to reclaim Israel, his adulterous wife (Hos. 2:14-23). Jesus understood this grace to apply to individuals.

The first lesson for this Sunday in most lectionaries tells of Moses' intercession for the people after the sin of the golden calf (Exod. 32:1, 7-14); Hos. 4:1-3; 5:15—6:6 (NA) speaks of repentance. The second lesson teaches that Christ came into the world to save sinners (I Tim. 1:12-17).

Y25C. Luke 16:1-13. The parable of the Unjust Steward or Dishonest Manager is unusually interesting. It was puzzling enough so that Luke, or perhaps the earlier tradition, added sayings out of various contexts in an attempt to make it acceptable. All of these deal with "mammon" (the Aramaic word for money or property) in various ways. (1) Use money, unrighteous though it is, for good purposes so that you may get into heaven (verse 9; cf. Matt. 6:19-21). (2) Verses 10-12 are three separate proverbs that could be applied to the parable. (3) "No servant can serve two masters . . . you cannot serve God and mammon" (verse 13; cf. Matt. 6:24).

Only verse 9 fits in any way with verse 8, which consists of two parts. In verse 8a, does *ho kyrios* mean "the master," i.e. the owner of the farm, as the RSV and most versions render it, or "the Lord," i.e. Jesus? The point of verse 8b seems to mean that wordlings are more shrewd in dealing with their affairs than "the sons of light," who should be at least as intelligent in matters of religion. But is 8b part of the original parable? If not, it is simply the story of a rascal who got himself out of a difficult situation. It has even been suggested that the original prices on the receipts for oil and wheat were exorbitant and that by reducing the debts the manager gave his boss a (perhaps undeserved) reputation for generosity. In any case the parable is secular in tone; it could be Jesus' ironic and realistic observation of what life so often is like. If the application he made has been preserved, it can only be verse 8b.

Amos 8:4-12, the first reading, speaks of one of the abuses of riches, the oppression of the poor. It fits more or less with verse 13. The NA reading, Hos. 11:1-11, would have been more appropriate for the preceding Sunday.

Y30C. Luke 18:9-14, the parable of the Pharisee and the Tax Collector. The introduction (verse 9) is Luke's, and the conclusion (verse 14b) is a saying found in other contexts; here it tends to generalize the point too much.

The Pharisee is not a bad man and we can assume that what he says about himself is true. The Monday and Thursday fasts were not obligatory, and he tithed more than the OT required. When we preach on the passage we must remember that there is a very thin line between self-satisfaction and an honest prayer of thanksgiving that one has been preserved from temptation and given God's grace. The *Alenu* prayer of the synagogue service expresses this kind of humble thankfulness; on the other hand, there are passages in the Dead Sea Hymns of Thanksgiving and the rabbinical literature, contrasting the pious person and the wicked, that resemble the prayer of this Pharisee. It is also true that the rabbis speak of various kinds of Pharisees, good and bad. The man in the parable represents a tendency to be found among all religious people.

The tax collector went home "justified," vindicated. There is no reference to the feelings of either man. Justification is not a matter of subjective religious experience; it denotes the believer's objective right standing in the sight of God. The parable is related to the Laborers in the Vineyard and the Prodigal Son.

The first reading in the Roman *Ordo* is Sir. 35:12–14, 16–18, which speaks of the prayer of the humble; three of the other lectionaries employ Deut. 10:12–22, referring to what God requires. Jer. 14:1–10, 19–22 (Episcopal) is a prayer of penitence.

Y31C. Luke 19:1–10. Zacchaeus is called a chief tax collector, i.e., he was a tax farmer who employed agents to do the collecting and so must have been wealthy. One notes immediately the vividness of the story and Jesus' courtesy in offering to visit a man who might hesitate to ask him into his house (cf. Luke 7:6). The Torah commanded that illicit gains he restored twofold, and Zacchaeus offers to do twice this much. Jesus accepts him completely; "son of Abraham" is a title of honor.

The theme of Wisd. 11:23—12:2 is God's mercy to sinners. The Lutheran, Presbyterian, and Methodist lectionaries prescribe Exod. 34:5–9, the magnificent passage in which Yahweh proclaims his grace. The Book of Common Prayer reads Isa. 1:1–20, a call to radical repentance.

Samaritans and Gentiles in Luke

Y9C. Luke 7:1–10. Solomon's prayer (I Kings 8:22–23, 27–30, 41–43) is read with the story of the healing of the centurion's slave. The former includes a petition that the prayer of a foreigner (*ger*) may be heard. The *ger* was a non-Israelite who lived in the Hebrew community. In later Judaism the term usually means a proselyte or convert to the national religion. There was an active movement in Jesus' time to win proselytes

(Matt. 23:15), but the attitude toward them was sometimes ambiguous, and some rabbis held that a member of a proselyte's family could not be trusted till the third generation.

There is no suggestion in the gospel story that the centurion was about to become a proselyte. He is more like the *ger* of the OT or the God-fearing Gentiles of Acts 13:16; 17:4 who had not yet become Jews. The account here and in Matt. 8:5-13 is the only miracle reported in the Q tradition (except for the brief verse Matt. 12:22; cf. Luke 11:14) and it is evidently included because of the dialogue with the centurion. As in the narrative of the Syrophoenician woman (Mark 7:24-30) the faith of a Gentile is praised and rewarded. Luke adds some vivid touches. At first the army officer is reluctant to approach Jesus, for a holy rabbi might not wish to speak with a Gentile. The Jewish elders explain that the man has built a synagogue for them. In Capernaum there are ruins of a fine third or fourth century synagogue; the one built by the centurion would have been much more modest.

This story and that of the Canaanite woman (Y20A) were probably used by the early Church to defend its mission to foreign nations.

The second reading (Gal. 1:1-10) touches the Gentile mission in a different way. The Galatians were Gentiles whom Paul had converted to Christianity and were being upset by Jewish Christians who demanded that they be circumcised and keep the Torah. St. Paul regarded this as a false gospel that would divert them from the essential faith in Christ which was the basis of their salvation (see p. 206f.).

Y15C. Luke 10:25-37. The evangelist has framed the parable of the Good Samaritan with Jesus' dialogue with a "lawyer," i.e. scribe or rabbi. Luke assumes that the question was asked in order to put Jesus to the test, but this man had insight and it is he rather than Jesus who gives the Summary of the Law, which was probably already a part of Jewish tradition. At the conclusion Jesus does not answer the question "Who is my neighbor?" Instead he asks, "Who showed himself to be a neighbor?" This is an example of Jesus' emphasis on positive righteous action: What do you do that is more? (Matt. 5:47).

Rabbinical literature contains parables of the response of three persons: the priest, the levite, and the Israelite (the ordinary layman), and it is always the third who, like the Little Red Hen, is the hero. When Jesus began the parable his hearers might have expected such a story. The substitution of a Samaritan was disturbing if not actually insulting.

The Samaritans were a remnant of the old ten tribes and their Bible contained only the Pentateuch. The oral Torah treats them in some respects as though they were Jews but otherwise as Gentiles. Jewish people in general held them in contempt as mongrels and had as little to do with them as possible (see Sir. 50:25f.). Like the centurion of Capernaum, this man is the example of a righteous non-Jew, but there is more than this in the parable. What he does shows the Good News in action.

The first reading, Deut. 30:9–14, speaks of God's commandments. They are not merely in a book but in the mouth and heart of a true Israelite.

Y21C. Luke 13:22–30 consists of three sayings groups. The narrow door (verses 22–24; cf. Matt. 7:13f.) has a clear and obvious meaning. Because the door is mentioned, the next saying (verses 25–27; cf. Matt. 7:22f.) became associated with it in the tradition. Matthew applied this to false prophets in the Church; Luke's form is more primitive and refers to any who have been in Jesus' company and therefore presume on his favor. Matthew inserted the substance of verses 28f. into the story of the centurion (Matt. 8:11f.). In the messianic banquet of the future Gentiles as well as Jews will be with the patriarchs. Mere membership in the religious community will not guarantee this, as John the Baptist had already warned (Matt. 3:9; cf. Luke 3:8). Isa. 66:18–23, the first reading in four lectionaries, promises the new heavens and new earth in which people of all nations will come to worship Yahweh. Isa. 28:14–22 (Episcopal) contains a warning to those who trust in lies and a promise of "a precious cornerstone." Jer. 28:1–9 (NA) gives an example of a false prophet.

Wealth and Power in Luke

Y18C. Luke 12:13–21. It is only Luke who transmits the parable of the Rich Fool, and this is one indication among several that he shares to an unusual degree Jesus' distrust of wealth. Verses 13–16 are his introduction, and the words "Man, who made me a judge or divider over you?" echo Exod. 2:14. At the same time, this exemplifies one of Jesus' traits: he sweeps aside what he perceives as irrelevant in order to concentrate on a deeper problem.

The wealth of a Palestinian landowner was largely in his crops. This is a wisdom parable. It has been proved countless times in history that "you can't take it with you." When, however, Jesus uses proverbs and other commonsense pieces that were part of the rich stock of Judaism, it is never for a secular purpose alone. Even being "rich toward God" must be more than doing good deeds and being saved; to be a child of God is another way of putting it. So far as we can tell, Jesus left the interpretation to his hearers. We may suggest that the life worth living is modelled on his life of outreach to others and risking everything for the pearl of great price.

Eccl. 1:2, 12:14; 2:1-7, 11, 18-23 (various parts of which are read) is from the wisdom literature; wealth and even toil are nothing but vanity. "Koheleth," the author of that book, pictures himself as an over-achiever.

Y26C. Luke includes the parable of the Rich Man and Lazarus (16:19–31) for the same reason that he transmits other sayings on wealth and poverty, but this is incidental to what Jesus is teaching here.

The parable reflects a conventional Jewish idea that in the age to come or the after-life the roles are reversed. Pious men who suffer unjustly will be rewarded later, and prosperous sinners will get their punishment. This concept appears here only for the sake of the story.

Nor is the parable intended to explain to us what the after-life is like. Here, as in other parts of Luke, we find Gehenna and Paradise, which also are features of Jewish eschatology along with the majority belief that reward and punishment come only after the general resurrection. But all of this is only conventional.

Jesus' point has to do with the five brothers for whom the rich man was concerned. As he has taught on other occasions, no miraculous signs will be given to force unbelievers and evildoers into obedience and faith. "If they do not listen to Moses and the prophets, they are not going to be convinced if someone should rise from the dead." We Christians might add that one did rise from the dead, and still there are those—sometimes including ourselves—who do not listen. Amos 6:1-7 is a denunciation of the heartless rich, but it speaks also to us who are "at ease in Zion."

·15

Jesus and the Judaism of His Time

In his brief ministry Jesus' principal purpose was to proclaim the Reign of God by word and action. His deeds of forgiveness, healing and pastoral concern for other human beings were signs of the near presence of the Kingdom. As we have said, he acted out concretely what he said God was doing and was about to do. The Reign of God was also a judgment on the contemporary world; and although he taught that one must judge with the mercy that one hopes to receive, many sayings have been preserved to us that express condemnation of evil.

The sins that aroused his fiercest indignation were heartless cruelty to "little ones" and hypocrisy.

The "little ones" are those who are weak, defenseless and disregarded; some were outcasts from respectable society. Too often stumbling blocks that were put in their path caused the "little ones" to sin or lose confidence in God. To such people Jesus brought a message of liberation. He regarded the Torah, as then interpreted by the strictest experts, as putting heavy burdens on their backs by making requirements that went far beyond the OT law.

Jesus sometimes used the word "hypocrites" as we do, to refer to those who pretend to be better than they are. But sometimes they are people who are inconsistent: they tithe even the herbs used for seasoning but neglect the basic principles of Torah, justice, mercy and love.

Thus there is a large element in Jesus' teaching that interprets the law and piety of the OT. It occurs in positive statements but often in the form of controversies with opponents. We find most of the controversy dialogues in the Gospel of Mark and a few in Q passages where Matthew and Luke run in parallel. Mark evidently had access to a collection of these and they are now found in chapters 2, 3, 11 and 12 of his gospel. They tend to have a similar form, in which Jesus (or his disciples) is criticized, and he answers with a crisp saying.

When Jesus was in dialogue with opponents it was a dialogue *within* Judaism not unlike the debates between "houses" or schools of the Pharisees that have been preserved in the rabbinic tradition. The early Church had a different perspective. Mark and Matthew still had some contact with Judaism but only as outsiders, and by their time Pharisaism was the only important force in the old religion. The evangelists read the controversy dialogues and sayings as expressing the criticism of Jesus *and the Church* against Judaism as such, and the controversies got their present form in the light of this interpretation. At the same time they understood very well that Jesus had not merely denounced tendencies within Judaism; they were real and present dangers within the Church. They still exist among us and we must read and preach them as though we ourselves were sometimes the opponents of Jesus.

Matthew and Luke edit and include most of Mark's controversy stories. In addition, Matthew has a rich tradition of Jesus' legal teaching. Luke transmits rather little of this, for he writes for a largely Gentile church and evidently regards such issues as irrelevant to its needs. Rabbinical disputes belong only to the past, so it is the moral and theological teaching that interest Luke, as one can see by comparing Luke's Sermon on the Plain with Matthew's Sermon on the Mount.

The lectionaries contain a selection of pericopes from Matthew and Mark that illustrate Jesus' teaching about the law, but nothing from Luke. The single pericope from Year C to be discussed below is a controversy over the resurrection.

Year A—The Sermon on the Mount

Y6A. Matt. 5:17–37 (Y6A and 7A in NA). The Sermon on the Mount is a collection of sayings that Matthew has put together artistically and with a definite theological purpose. Its two themes, the Kingdom of God and righteousness, are closely correlated. Thus it is a Torah in the original full sense of the word; not just law, but also teaching and tradition, intended for the true Israel. The Sermon begins with the Beatitudes, then come sayings regarding the disciples as salt of the earth and light of the world. The pericope before us is in two parts: a statement about the authority of the Torah (verses 17–20) and four contrasts between the old Torah and the new (verses 21–37).

The authority and permanence of the Torah are stated in the strongest terms possible. Jesus does not come to destroy it but to fulfil it (perhaps enforce it in its true meaning). Whoever breaks (or tries to annul) the least of the commandments will be called least in the Kingdom of the heavens. The disciples' righteousness must be greater than that of the scribes and Pharisees.

The principle is applied in the contrasts that make up the rest of the chapter. At first glance there is a paradox here, for although verses 21–30 strengthen the law (anger and lust are sins, not merely murder and adultery), the OT provisions for divorce and oaths appear to be abrogated.

Oaths are, however, forbidden because a child of God should tell the truth at all times and need swear no oath. The reason for the saying is illustrated by Matt. 23:16–22, which shows how the religious oath can be misused. The Scripture says often that Yahweh is a God of truth and equity, and the Jesus of the Fourth Gospel declares that "the truth will make you free" (John 8:32). The standard expected of a child of God is in contrast to the ways of the world. Advertising and propaganda are necessary in economic and political life and when used properly benefit the public. But often we are given half-truths and hear claims and comparisons that are dishonest. The image and not the reality is presented to the reader and television viewer, and in our culture we are taught every day that we must project the right image. Thus the Christian must be warned not only to tell the truth and make the image correspond to the fact—anything else is hypocrisy—but also to examine critically what is said by politicians and salesmen.

Jesus also forbade divorce, but Matthew's community admitted one exception, perhaps because one of Jesus' reported sayings gives the Church power to bind and loose (18:18), and the ruling in this pericope is similar to that of the Pharisaic rabbi Shammai (cf. 19:1–9). The matter will be discussed further in connection with Mark 10:2–10, which is read on Y27B. In fact, rabbinic tradition gives instances of the abrogation of specific commandments based on scriptural exegesis.

The first lesson in the Roman and Episcopal lectionaries (and as an alternative in the Methodist and NA) is Sir. 15: (11–14) 15–20, which sets forth the standard Jewish idea that anyone who is willing can keep the commandments. Christians have not found, however, that it is easy to observe the Sermon on the Mount, although Jesus is quoted as saying that his yoke is easy and his burden light (Matt. 11:30). That is so in the sense that the new law is not complicated like the Pharisaic oral tradi-tion, but the moral demand is so high that Jewish scholars, among others, regard it as unrealistic.

The commands are stated in extreme form, but they cannot be dismissed as examples of hyperbole, because more than once Jesus makes it clear that his disciples are expected to be more just and merciful than the best examples of accepted piety, and he puts the accent on positive doing of good rather than on avoidance of evil. When rightly heard, these commands can be a refreshing and liberating call to lead a new heroic life.

Perhaps the most important thing to realize is that Jesus' ethic is the ethic of the Reign of God. But the Kingdom is not a nation-state or an organization; it is God's just and loving dominion over his People, individuals in community and in relation to their Father. The good life under this Reign, which the Sermon calls righteousness, is first of all this family relationship with God, and from it flow the desire and power to do what we cannnot do by ourselves. The commandments are signs of the potentiality of redeemed human nature and of God's love flowing through us.

The other lectionaries prescribe Deut. 30:15–20a, which sets forth the two ways of life and death, and interestingly calls heaven and earth to witness (the covenant lawsuit theme).

The second lesson in lectionaries other than the Episcopal and NA, I Cor. 2:6–13 (see p. 212f.), can be related to this theme. Paul speaks of a wisdom which the rulers of this world did not know when they crucified the Lord of glory, and also of that which eye has not seen and ear not heard, which God has prepared for those who love him. The lesson in the Episcopal and NA lectionaries, I Cor. 3:1–9, cannot be easily harmonized with the gospel, except that partisan strife would not exist if the spirit of Matt. 5:21–26 were to be observed.

Y7A (Y8A in NA). Matt. 5:38–48 completes the group of antitheses. We should not criticize the OT law of retaliation too sharply, because in contrast to certain other ancient codes and to the severity of the song of Lamech (Gen. 4:23f.) it limited revenge to *only* an eye for an eye. Jesus goes further to abolish revenge. He has in mind the attitude of the person who has been wronged and does not deal with the need to protect others who are attacked. The one who presses another into service to walk a mile might have been a Roman soldier compelling a peasant to bear a load. If so, the oppressor is regarded as a person and not as the mere agent of a foreign government.

Love of enemies goes beyond any OT law but it does have anteced-ents there, for example in the Book of Jonah. Nineveh was the supreme example of a brutal oppressor. The reason that Jesus gives here is bold: one must imitate God, as a child imitates its father. The rain falls indiscriminately on good people and bad, because Jesus understands this apparent blindness of the natural order as God's loving kindness. His joyful acceptance of God as Father suggests that in his own experi-ence Joseph had been such a father.

A Christian interpreter should never forget that God is Father in the OT also. Jesus did not discover this truth, and many synagogue prayers address God as "our Father, our King." If there is any difference, it is that Jesus made this filial relationship more personal and concrete. The Lord's Prayer in Aramaic evidently began, as in Luke 11:2, with the single word *Abba,* not a liturgical salutation or even the usual form of the word, but the speech of a small child addressing its father.

The first lesson, Lev. 19:1-2, 9-18, includes the command to love one's neighbor as oneself. This chapter is from the Holiness Code, which is designed to set forth the requirements for being a holy people. NA reads this on Y8A, and here substitutes Isa. 49:8-13 (day of salvation, release of prisoners). I Cor. 3:10-11, 16-23 teaches that Christ is the only foundation that can be laid. In the liturgical context it suggests that allegiance to him implies loyalty to his teaching on love of enemies.

Year A — The State

Y29A. Matt. 22:15-22. The discussion regarding payment of taxes to the emperor is taken over from Mark 12:13-17 with few changes. The mention of the Herodians shows how politically sensitive the question was, for these were supporters of Herod Antipas, tetrarch of Galilee, who held his office as a client of Rome. The Pharisees were originally a political as well as a religious party and were only now beginning to disengage themselves from politics and to concentrate solely on keeping the religious law. But one group, who are called zealots in the gospels, were like the Pharisees except that they rejected Roman rule and held that it was disloyal to God to pay imperial taxes because only God could be king over the nation. From the year A.D. 66 on the zealots got the upper hand and precipitated the revolt that led to destruction of the Temple.

The denarius was a Roman coin used to pay the troops. To use this coinage, and especially to pay taxes with it, implied obedience to Roman rule. For whatever reason, Jesus did not possess a denarius on this occasion. His answer shows that he did not side with the zealots; it is no sin to pay a tax that after all is exacted from one. Give Caesar what is his! But this does not imply actual allegiance. As on other occasions, Jesus shows a certain contempt for the petty glory of the kingdoms of this world. Caesar's power, such as it is, is only derivative and temporary, like that of the Assyrian and Babylonian empires of the past, but God's authority is all encompassing. Give God what is his! On this occasion the Phariseees would have been in general agreement with Jesus. Certainly at a later time they taught the Jewish people to obey, except when the civil authority demanded idolatry, murder or some other heinous sin, and to have as little as possible to do with the government.

The pericope raises the issue of civil disobedience and demands an examination of attitudes toward the state in the NT. Like the words of Paul in Rom. 13:1-7 it has often been misused to teach that the state is supreme in its own sphere, while the sphere of religion is quite separate and the Church should be concened with individual morality and spirituality. Such a notion is based on a philosophy that contrasts soul and body, matter and spirit, and is foreign to biblical thinking. As Judaism also recognized, a situation can arise when, as Peter said, "One must obey God rather than men" (Acts 5:29).

When Paul wrote to the Romans the choice had not presented itself in an extreme form. The Book of Acts tells of his troubles with the authorities (e.g., 16:16-40), and he himself says that three times he had been beaten by the rods (probably of Roman lictors). He was a Roman citizen, and coming as he did from Asia Minor he knew how much the empire had improved public safety and economic life. Nevertheless the Gentile world was idolatrous and corrupt (Rom. 1:18-31), and the rulers of the age were demonic powers (I Cor. 2:8; Col. 2:15), belonging to an order soon to pass away (I Cor. 7:31); despite all the benefits that they brought, they were not absolutely good.

The NT is in general favorable to the empire. The First Epistle of Peter calls for good citizenship even when the Church is faced with persecution. Let the only charge against you be that you are a Christian! (I Pet. 4:12-19). The Apocalypse, however, sees the empire as totally evil. Persecution of Christians is only part of this; Roman wealth is based on greed, exploitation and the enslavement of human beings (Rev. 6:6; 18:1-13). The prophet John of course does not preach a human revolution; it is God himself who will destroy the demonic empire.

The NT, like the prophetic books of the Hebrew Bible, looks on the state as it does on all human institutions. They are subject to the sovereignty of God, and such value as they have is to be tested by God's standard of justice and mercy. Assyria is used by Yahweh as the rod of his anger and the staff of his fury, but it will be brought down because of its arrogance (Isa. 10:5-19). The other side of the coin is the enthusiastic reception of the Persian empire. The first lesson for this Sunday (Isa. 45:1-7) is an oracle spoken by the Second Isaiah which announces Cyrus the Great as God's messiah and instrument. He and his successors not only tolerated but actually encouraged the local religions, and the Jews were generally happy under Persian rule, which was ended only by Alexander the Great.

The Modern Political Problem

The writers of Scripture could not envisage a professedly democratic society in which Christians and others can influence their governments through the ballot box and pressure groups. The nearest analogy to our situation is the relatively free tribal life of the early Hebrew period.

The framers of the American Constitution were deeply influenced by the biblical concept of the covenant and almost equally by that of the social contract and other ideas of the 18th century enlightenment. Jefferson and others who signed the Declaration of Independence aimed to form a polity that would foster security and domestic tranquillity, justice and order, together with freedom for the several states and individuals. Freedom and order are not easy to reconcile, and the endurance of the American framework for more than two centuries has been due to the good will of the electorate and a relatively independent judiciary. The American legal system is based on Germanic and Roman law but it has been influenced also by the law and spirit of the OT.

The judiciary and the legal system are only a check and balance on other forces of power. Our representative democracy is so complicated that it can only slowly and approximately reflect the will of the elector-ate. On the other hand, an autocratic, authoritarian state like the Byzan-tine Empire, which sometimes relied on brute force, has its ultimate strength, as the Declaration of Independence says, in the "consent of the governed." When this fails, force sooner or later becomes futile. The society of the middle ages in western Europe was often a balance of powers, lord and vassal, Church and empire, empire or kingdom against free towns, a more or less stable adjustment of conflicting interests. The continual wars of the middle ages show how fragile this adjustment was.

A Christian needs to look at his community, as the OT prophets did, in the light of the realities of power. Our society is controlled by a multitude of interests that often conflict. It is not, for example, a matter of simple competition between capital and labor. Management and the owners of capital do not have identical interests, nor do labor leaders and the work force. Everyone is a consumer, and there is no single motive for consumers except to pay as little as possible for the best goods that are to be had. Those who have power in government are assailed by the demands of various parts of their constituencies, and the only common factor is that each, however much he desires the public good, seeks to protect his own power and influence. There are centers of power, and certain individuals exert great power in politics, econom-ics and society generally, but they are as much controlled by the system as they dominate it.

It was not very different in the feudal middle ages, and even modern despotic or totalitarian states are systems that to some degree control their rulers. The difference is that they are relatively less responsive to criticism and dissent than more democratic governments. Sometimes people can live in such a system without too much unhappiness. A concentration of political power is not totally bad, except in the view of minorities within it (many blacks and Chicanos in America, Slavs in the former Empire of Austria-Hungary, people of many former colonies of the old British Empire) who have little share in determining their own destiny. The "greatest good to the greatest number" may easily leave out "the least of these my brethren" and thus such a system cannot be the Reign of God.

Every political system, even the best, therefore has some demonic element within it. When we say "demonic" we have to remember that the personified Satan or any other mythical demon has to have certain attractive characteristics. No demon can survive if he does not promise something that is desired, however ephemeral it may be. It may be the pleasure of alcohol or drugs, or cheap money to pay back hard money that has been borrowed, or "peace in our time" in exchange for a worse time for our grandchildren. Perhaps nothing can be promised beyond the stability of the situation in which we live, and most human beings will settle for that.

When we consider our obligations in a free society, we turn to the Hebrew prophets. Justice and mercy are the marks of a good society (Mic. 6:8), and it is the duty of the Christian to work toward these, but the specific choices are often difficult. The Scriptures hold forth the promise of freedom, but it is always liberty under a standard. John 8:31-36 contains an ironical dialogue that might apply to any nation. The "Jews" or "Judaeans," who symbolize the opponents of Jesus, claim that as descendants of Abraham they have never been in bondage to anyone. The answer given in the Fourth Gospel is that no one can ever be free unless the truth as it is in Jesus frees him or her from sin. We cannot imagine a society without sin until the Kingdom of God arrives completely, but insofar as a nation moves in the direction of justice and mercy it is free.

Year A—Religious Leaders

Y31A. Matt. 23:1-12. The readings for this Sunday (in the Lutheran lectionary on Pentecost 26) are chosen to emphasize the responsibility of religious leaders to guide the people to salvation by their teaching and to behave with humility (verses 4-12). The first lesson (Roman, Presbyterian, Methodist), Mal. 1:14b—2:10, condemns the priests because they "cause many to stumble" and because they show partiality. "Do we not all have one father?" the prophet asks. "Has not one God created us?" Malachi was written late in the post-exilic period when the nation was ruled by high priests and the priests were responsible for teaching Torah. It was only later that "scribes," lay experts, took over this function. Other evidence for disillusionment with the "shepherds" of the nation is found in Zech. 10 and 11.

Mic. 3:5-12 (Episcopal) is directed against wicked prophets and priests. The Lutheran reading, Zeph. 1:14-16, is the basis of the *Dies irae* hymn: "the day of the Lord is a day of wrath" (cf. Amos 5:18-20).

In I Thess. 2:7-13, 17-20, the second lesson for the day, Paul reminds the Thessalonians that when he was among them he was gentle like a father and worked with his own hands so as not to burden them. The

Apostle's behavior was in contrast to that of Malachi's corrupt priests and the holy men and philosophers of the Hellenistic world in his own time who too often exploited their followers.

Verses 1–3 of the gospel pericope are surprising. According to this tradition, Jesus affirmed the authority of the rabbis and taught his followers to observe their rules. This does not fit with the many passages in which he rejects the authority of the oral Torah. On occasion he may have advised people to respect the rabbis, but it is possible that here "scribes and Pharisees" are symbols for teachers in the Christian Church whose moral teaching is correct but whose behavior is not to be imitated.

The function of chapter 23 as a whole is to warn against tendencies that Jesus observed in some (not all) Pharisees and that could arise in the Christian community or any other religious group.

Although the Pharisees in some cases adjusted the law so as to make it less burdensome for ordinary people and adapted it to changing circumstances, one has only to read the Mishnah to see how complicated it could become. The Pharisees deliberately "built a fence around the Torah to keep one far from transgression." The result was to make the observant Jew dependent on tutelage by the legal experts, and Jesus regarded this as a burden (verse 4) that kept people out of the Kingdom (verse 13). He rejected the oral law in principle and left many issues to individual judgment and common sense.

It is not true that all the Pharisees did everything in order to be seen by others; the great rabbis criticized such people in their own party, and verse 5a may be Matthew's comment. But it is certainly the case that clergy sometimes pride themselves on their vestments and are concerned for their rank. Verses 7–9, if taken literally, would forbid calling anyone not only "Father" or "Rabbi" but "Doctor" and "Professor" also. It is a question of attitude. Christ is our supreme teacher, and as Malachi had said, we all have one Father.

Chapter 23 is carefully constructed with its refrain, "Woe to you, scribes and Pharisees, hypocrites!" It is partly based on an earlier collection of sayings that lies behind Luke 11:39–52. Matthew alone has the section in which Jesus ridicules the distinction between binding and non-binding oaths (23:16–22) and the saying about converts to Judaism (verse 15). The fanaticism of certain new converts is a distressing problem, as most pastors know; the Quakers, for example, speak of the "over-convinced."

It is unfortunate that the lectionaries do not include verses 23-25 or their parallel, Luke 11:39-42, for these are essential for understanding Jesus' interpretation of the Torah. The "fence about the law" led to the tithing of more than the agricultural produce prescribed by the OT. Jesus did not object to tithing, but justice, mercy and faith (in Luke, the love of God) came first. Rabbinical rules about cleansing the cup are complicated and need not concern us here. The point is that here Jesus speaks figuratively: outward cleanliness is of no use unless the moral life of the individual is clean. A saying to much the same effect is found in Mark 7:15 (read on Y22B). The logical result of this radical saying is to sweep away the laws of ceremonial cleanliness. To the Pharisees this would have been intolerable, for it destroyed "holiness," the fundamental distinction between Jews and Gentiles. The Christians of Antioch, who evidently began the mission to Gentiles (Acts 11:20), and the Apostle Paul drew out the implications of these words of Jesus (cf. also Peter's conversion of Cornelius and especially Acts 10:28).

Luke's word "give alms" in 11:41 is evidently a mistranslation of an Aramaic word; Matt. 23:26 has the proper rendering, "cleanse."

Year B—Controversies

Jesus took great freedom in interpreting the Torah. It is often asked, what principle did he employ in making his decisions? In general, one may say that he aimed to discover the spirit that lay behind the letter of the OT law. Sometimes it is suggested that he tested everything by the twofold commandment to love God and neighbor. Another possibility is that the specific commandment or an interpretation of it was judged as to whether it fostered or hindered the mission committed to him to proclaim the Reign of God. This understanding is supported by Matt. 23:4, 13 and by some of the controversy dialogues in Mark.

Y9B. Mark 2:23—3:6. The first lesson (Deut. 5:12-15) sets forth the Sabbath law, which Jesus of course accepted. The question is about its detailed interpretation. Rabbinic tradition lists 39 classes of work prohibited on the Sabbath, and harvesting of grain was one of them. It is Jesus' disciples who are criticized on this occasion; thus in its present form the story reflects the Church's defense of its Sabbath practices in controversy with the synagogue. Jesus might have said that "the law does not concern itself with trifles," but instead he justified the action on the basis of human need. Furthermore, David was regarded as righteous, and if he could eat the sacred loaves of presentation the disciples could not be in the wrong.

Two sayings are placed at the end. The rabbis also said something like "The Sabbath was made for man, and not man for the Sabbath" (verse 27). Verse 28 is, however, Christological; as in 2:10, Jesus has authority as Son of Man.

In 3:1-6 the healing is incidental to the controversy. The Pharisees permitted healing on the Sabbath but only if human life was in danger. Jesus' saying implies that failing to do a deed of mercy merely because it is the Sabbath is in fact to do evil. The early Church considered the issue so important that the gospels contain several stories of Sabbath cures. In Luke 14:1-6 Jesus argues on the basis of inconsistencies in the oral tradition, and in Luke 13:10-17 there is the added point that the crippled woman is a daughter of Abraham and therefore should be set free (cf. Luke 19:9; John 8:33). John 9:1-41, which most of the lectionaries read on the Fourth Sunday in Lent, deals with the question on Christological grounds, and the emphasis is on the conversion of the man born blind. John 5:1-18 also rests the case on the authority of God's Son.

Christians gradually replaced the Sabbath by Sunday, the day of the Lord's Resurrection. Paul essentially abrogated the Sabbath law and obligatory observance of "days, months, seasons and years" (Gal. 4:8-11; cf. Col. 2:16f.), but for a long time, at least in certain places, the Church observed the Sabbath along with the Lord's Day. Some Christian denominations teach that Sunday is the Christian Sabbath, and a very few abstain from work on Saturday. It is difficult to require strict Sabbath keeping in the light of St. Paul's teaching, but a day of rest and worship is entirely in the spirit of the NT. Times and seasons are not absolute, but it is practical and proper for the churches to set aside times for consciously and deliberately resting in God's presence.

Y10B. Mark 3:20-35. The section is composite. As in other places, Mark seems to have framed a pericope with the beginning and end of another story. In this case his family or relatives (*hoi par' autou*) hear that Jesus is beside himself (possessed or in ecstasy) and come to take him away (verses 20f.), and after the dialogue (verses 22-30) his mother and brothers come and ask for him, whereupon Jesus utters the saying that identifies his true family (verses 31-35).

Some scholars relate this pericope to 6:1-6 and believe that it reflects a struggle for power between members of the Lord's family and others in the Church, with Mark on the side of the latter. This is not of great importance to us, though we know from Paul's letters as well as Mark 10:35–45 that competition existed. Verses 31–35 are a complete pericope, and verses 20f. may be no more than Mark's introduction. Jesus does not imply that he rejects his family; he simply states that God's Reign and will take precedence over all other obligations, as in Luke 11:27f. and Matt. 10:37–39; cf. Luke 14:26f.

The controversy over casting out demons is found also in Matt. 12:22–32 and Luke 11:14–23 in somewhat different forms. Luke derives his story from a source other than Mark (i.e. Q), and Matthew has woven the Marcan and Q pericopes together. The accusation against Jesus strikes at the very basis of his ministry; the greatest gift that he can give, the rescue of human beings from demonic power (insanity or other illnesses) is ascribed to a demon and not to God. Jesus' answer is that this is absurd; Satan or Beelzebul would be acting against his own interest and his kingdom would fall. The Q tradition adds another important saying; if one were to accept what the opponents say, then the Pharisees ("your sons") who perform exorcisms are also instruments of the demon; but if it is by the Spirit (or finger) of God that Jesus casts out demons, the Reign of God has overtaken them (Matt. 12:27f.; Luke 11:19f.).

Mark 3:27 is an independent saying on the necessity to bind the "strong man" (Satan). Verses 28f. should be compared with Matt. 12:31f. and with Luke 12:10, which Luke has in a different context. The latter form of the saying, from the Q tradition, says that abusive speech against Jesus can be forgiven (because his true nature has not yet been disclosed) but blasphemy against the Holy Spirit (God himself) is unforgivable. Mark writes from the perspective of the Church; blasphemy against the Son of Man is also against the Holy Spirit, therefore he changes the saying to make it refer to sins forgiven "the sons of men." He also puts it in the context of this controversy so that the unforgivable blasphemy is ascribing to Satan what is really God's work. Whether we read the saying in Mark's context or in that of Luke 12:4–12, the most heinous sin is the overturning of all values, saying that good is evil and that God's work is the work of a demon.

In the first lesson, Gen. 3:1–21, God curses and punishes the serpent that tempted Adam and Eve. The story can be used to typify the casting out of demons, or the serpent may be thought of as the counterpart of the malice and presumption of the opponents.

Y22B. Mark 7:1-8, 14f., 21-23. The first lesson, Deut. 4:1-8, is a beautiful panegyric on the Torah and Israel's privilege in having received it. This sets the right attitude for reading the gospel pericope, which strikes at misuse of the law. Mark has combined verses 1-8 with the controversy over the Corban vow (verses 9-13). The lectionaries omit the latter, but its point is that the duty to honor father and mother overrides a vow taken to their detriment, and it is a good example of the superiority of the moral commandment over the cultic. In Jesus' time some scribes evidently took the strict view of the force of vows, but later rabbinical tradition ruled just as Jesus did.

The controversy in verses 1-8, 14f. concerns ceremonial cleanliness, and in verses 3f. Mark explains the Pharisaic oral law for the benefit of his Gentile readers. Verse 15 is the most radical legal saying of Jesus in the Synoptic tradition, and should be compared with Matt. 23:23-25 and Luke 11:39-42, discussed above (Y31A). This effectively abolishes the purity laws. Verses 21-23 are a list of vices similar to those found in the epistles. Such catalogues are common in the catechesis of the Hellenistic Church, and Mark presents this one as a private teaching of Jesus. This is his device for explaining a saying or a parable.

Y27B. Mark 10:2-16. The pericope in 10:2-12 is in two parts, a dialogue on divorce and a general saying about the marriage of a divorced person. Matthew, by adding "for any cause" in 19:3, makes it clear that it is like a rabbinic debate between two schools of Pharisees. The house of Hillel held that a man might divorce his wife for any reason, that of Shammai that it must be for adultery or gross immodesty. The answer of Jesus is that the law of divorce was a concession to the "hardness of heart" of a primitive society. In fact the Pharisees protected the wife's interests to some degree by ruling that when the husband divorced her he must set her free by giving her an instrument of divorce that he could not retract. But God's will is not divorce but a lifelong union, and Jesus gives two quotations, one from the priestly source (Gen. 1:27) which point to the equality of the sexes, the other (Gen. 2:24) from the J source. It is interesting that the Essenes forbade both divorce and polygamy, citing Gen. 1:27 and 7:15.

Verses 11f. are in the form of a private explanation to the disciples. Mark has in mind Roman law, in which a wife could divorce her husband. This was not possible in Judaism, and the saying in Luke 16:18; cf. Matt. 5:32, which is closely related to the Marcan logion, illustrates this. There were, however, a few extreme cases in which the wife might go before the court and compel her husband to divorce her. Matthew's form of the saying presupposes that a divorced woman has no recourse but to marry again; thus by divorcing her the husband forces her into adultery.

Jesus' aim is to set forth the purpose of God for man and woman. From the beginning the Church has had difficulty in applying this in hard cases, as can be seen by the exception clause in Matt. 5:32; 19:9 and Paul's rule given in I Cor. 7:10-16. Both of these principles have been invoked in the discipline of various communions.

The first lesson for the day, Gen. 2:18-24, tells of the creation of Eve. It is one of the passages quoted by Jesus.

Year C—The Resurrection

Y32C (Roman, NA; Pentecost 25). Luke 20:27-38. The Gospel of Luke contains other controversy dialogues, but this is the only one prescribed in the lectionaries and it does not concern a strictly legal problem. The Pharisees taught the doctrine of a general resurrection of the dead. This seems to have arisen in the Maccabean period when many people were martyred because of loyalty to the law, and only their future reward could seem to vindicate God's justice. II Macc. 7:1-2, 9-14, which illus-trates this, is given in the Roman lectionary as the first reading, and in the Methodist lectionary as an alternative.

The Sadducees rejected the resurrection doctrine, evidently because it was not found in the books of the OT that they accepted, and in this story they bring up the absurd hypothetical case of a woman who had married seven brothers in accordance with the levirate law of Deut. 25:5f., which was designed to ensure continuance of the deceased brother's family. Jesus could have answered the Sadducees on their own legal basis by arguing that the first brother was the woman's only husband, since his brothers were only acting on his behalf, but he dealt directly with the issue of resurrection.

The life of the coming age does not repeat the conditions of this present life. The resurrection faith rests on the power of God (Mark 12:24), and in the Torah God speaks of Abraham, Isaac and Jacob as living. "All live to him" (God); a similar phrase is found in IV Macc. 7:19; 16:25, where it is taught that the martyrs of the Maccabean period are alive in heaven with the patriarchs.

The NT concept of life after death usually takes the form of belief in resurrection, but along with it there is the faith that the righteous are already with God (Luke 16:23; 23:43; Phil. 1:23). In either case the faith is not in the innate nature of humanity but in the creative power of God, the Resurrection of Christ, and the love of God as shown in Christ Jesus (Rom. 8:38f.).

All the lectionaries employ II Thess. 2:13—3:5 as the second lesson. This is in the context of the expected return of Christ, and it exhorts Christians to stand fast in that hope. The first readings vary widely. The Episcopal and NA schemes employ Job 19:23-27a ("I know that my redeemer lives"). II Macc. 7:1-2, 9-14, which teaches the resurrection of the dead, is the Roman reading and an alternative in the Methodist lectionary.

·16

The Mighty Works

Many people in our churches are able to accept without difficulty what we call the miraculous element in the gospels, but many others cannot. The vast development of science has created an intellectual revolution. Although the chain of cause and effect is not as simple as philosophers of science once thought it to be, the doctrine of the uniformity of nature is generally accepted, and everything that can be ascribed to natural causes is traced to them. It is sometimes said that whereas the reported miracles of Jesus were at one time an aid to faith, the Christian who now accepts them does so because he or she first believes in Jesus.

Miracle stories appear in the lectionaries in about the same proportion as in the gospels themselves. Since this is so, they ought to be dealt with in preaching with sensitivity toward believers with various kinds of world views.

All of us tend to approach the miraculous element with a built-in distinction between the natural and the supernatural. This does not correspond altogether to the outlook of ancient Jews and Christians. There was of course a Greek scientific and philosophical tradition that tried to trace all events in the created world to what we call natural causes, and in the time of Jesus this was represented by Epicureans like Lucretius, but this point of view was not widespread in the population.

The word miracle itself (*miraculum*) originally meant a marvel, something to wonder at, not necessarily a by-passing of the laws of nature.

The words used in the NT to denote such events were *dynameis,* deeds of power; *sêmeia,* signs; and occasionally *terata,* warnings or portents. Much that to us is natural and ordinary was mysterious and wonderful to people of the first century—yeast, the generation of seed, the falling of rain, the voice of a prophet. Every birth of a child was a new creation, for *God opens the womb.*

Although ancient people had a world view different from ours, it would be a mistake to suppose that all of them were credulous. Stories of wonderful deeds were told about Greek philosophers like Pythagoras and Apollonius of Tyana, of Moses, and of certain rabbis, and these resemble to some degree the miracles of the gospels. Some people accepted marvels of all kinds, while others were more skeptical. One story in the Talmud tells of a rabbi who performed all kinds of signs to convince his colleagues that his interpretation of Torah was correct, but they agreed with him only when he said that he had received the tradition from an earlier sage.

The gospel tradition is relatively reticent about miracles. In several passages Jesus refuses to perform signs in order to convince unbelievers. When the gospels are compared with such apocryphal books as the Gospel of James and the Acts of Paul, the miraculous element in them is seen to be modest.

The Apostle Paul never alludes to the miracles of Jesus' ministry; the supreme wonders are for him the Incarnation, the Cross and the Resurrection. His opponents, the "super-apostles," claim to have miraculous powers, and he is forced to remind the Corinthians that the "signs" of a true apostle had been displayed among them, signs and portents and mighty deeds (II Cor. 12:12). Paul considers it folly to boast of visions and revelations that he had received. As to healings, he ironically compares the success of his competitors with his own failure to be healed. Three times he prayed to the Lord that the thorn in his flesh might be removed, yet he received only the answer, "My grace is sufficient for you" (II Cor. 12:9). The real seal of his apostleship was his identification with Christ in his Cross and Resurrection. One might have sufficient faith to move mountains, but without love this was of no use (I Cor. 13:1-3). Miracles by themselves are no proof of the truth of the gospel or of an apostle's validity, and he understood from his own experience that although God often grants healing it cannot always be guaranteed, even by faith and prayer.

The NT has this balanced attitude toward miracle, but the tradition affirms that many remarkable events occurred in the course of Jesus' ministry. The stories are numerous and varied and the cumulative effect is great. When we approach them from a historical perspective, each narrative has to be considered separately. We have no way of strictly verifying them, but physicians reading the accounts have often believed that they could recognize psychosomatic diseases, such as hysteria and other neuroses. Evidently there were also cases of the manic-depressive psychosis (Mark 5:1–20) and epilepsy (Mark 9:14–29).

Throughout Christian history and in our own time there have been healings following prayer for which no scientific explanation has been discovered. Modern theologians do not invoke the concept of miracle when an event can be understood in the light of ordinary processes, and Scripture itself regards the created world as orderly. Nevertheless, faith in God as creator and sustainer of the world holds open the possibility that God has ways of working that we do not and cannot understand.

The gospel tradition does not ask many of the questions that we raise. In Mark, from which most of the miracle stories are derived, most of the wonders occur in the first half, and the emphasis in the latter part of the book is on discipleship, the Cross, and the return of the Son of Man. Mark tells the stories with delight and faith, but they are not told solely to arouse wonder. Their purpose is to show Jesus' divine power and the results of his proclamation of the Reign of God, and they also serve to instruct the disciples, who represent the Church for which Mark wrote. Thus they exhibit Jesus' compassion, his authority as Son of Man, his teaching about the Sabbath, prayer and faith, and the mission to the Gentile world. The baptism of Jesus and the feeding of the multitudes are related to Christian baptism and the Eucharist, and the cursing of the fig tree is a parable of judgment connected with the cleansing of the Temple.

The position of Mark seems to be similar to that of Paul. The marvels truly occurred and are signs of divine glory, but the Cross is the greatest glory of all. Both are necessary for comprehending the person of Christ. In the Gospel of John the understanding that is implicit in the other gospels comes to clearer expression. The first two of the great narratives are called "signs" (2:11; 4:54), but at least four others belong to the same category. The word is not used in the sense of the signs that Jesus, according to the Synoptics, refused to perform. Instead they point to a deeper theological meaning which is sometimes brought out in the discourse that follows them.

Year B—Mark

We begin with Mark, because most of the miracle stories read in Sundays of the Year are to be found in that gospel.

Y4B. Mark 1:21–28. The pericope comes at a dramatic moment, immediately after the call of the first four disciples. The first act of Jesus' ministry involves a conflict between the demonic world and the Kingdom of God. The demon attempts an exorcism in reverse, calling Jesus by name and disclosing his true identity. Our Lord uses no form of exorcism and simply commands the demon to be muzzled and to come out of the man.

Mark has, however, put the story in a particular setting. Jesus is teaching in the synagogue of Capernaum and the people are astonished by his message. The evangelist does indeed give many examples of Jesus' teaching, but not nearly as many as do Matthew and Luke, and it has been said that he is more interested in the fact that Jesus taught than in the content. Here it seems that the exorcism is an essential part of the "new teaching with authority" (or power, *exousia*). All of his action is instruction for the Church. The first reading for the day is the prophecy that a prophet like Moses will arise (Deut. 18:15–22). Moses, like Jesus, combined Torah with deeds of power.

Y6B. Mark 1:40–45. The first reading, Lev. 13:1f., 45f. (Roman, Presbyterian), gives part of the law of leprosy; the Episcopal, Lutheran, and NA lectionaries, however, read the story of Naaman the Syrian (II Kings 5:1–15ab). "Leprosy" in Scripture refers to several skin ailments and also to conditions due to fungus on walls or clothing. The leper, once healed, was still excluded from society until he could be declared clean by the priest and offer a sacrifice. There are two peculiarities in the story. A variant reading in verse 41 says that Jesus was moved by anger (not compassion, as most MSS. have it), and in verse 43 he speaks harshly to the man and drives him or sends him away. The thought may be that the anger was directed against the demon causing the disease. Verse 45 is usually taken to say that the man who had been healed spread news of the cure, but it can mean that Jesus preached and spread the "word," i.e. the gospel. In any case, such crowds gathered that Jesus stayed outside the towns. The story is intended to illustrate the power of the Good News and Jesus' willingness to heal.

Y12B. Mark 4:35–41. The narrative of the storm at sea is related somehow in the underlying tradition to the walking on the water in Mark 6:45–51 and John 6:16–21 and also to Ps. 107, part of which is used on this Sunday as a responsorial. Mark has placed the stilling of the physical storm as a prelude to the exorcism of the wild demoniac in 5:1–20; at the end this man is clothed and sane. The latter pericope is included in the Methodist reading and in the Episcopal as an option.

Jesus' words to the sea, "Silence, be muzzled," were such as he might address to the demon. Thus the story has the Christological purpose of exhibiting the Lord's divine power over hostile forces and incidentally the disciples' lack of faith. It is lifelike because such storms arise and cease quickly on the Sea of Galilee, which is between hills on the east and the west. In the first reading, Job 38:1–11, 16–18, Yahweh speaks to Job out of the whirlwind and announces his dominion over the sea.

Y13B. Mark 5:21–43. Mark sometimes encloses a story within two parts of another, perhaps to indicate a lapse of time. The style of verses 25–34 (the woman with the haemorrhage) is somewhat different from that of the story of Jaïrus's daughter, which is more Semitic. The story of the woman indicates Jesus' sensitivity (which Mark probably thought of as supernatural) and his compassion. "Your faith has saved you" does not mean that faith was the primary cause of the healing, rather it is the condition for receiving the power of God. Thus it is like the function of faith in the sacraments.

In many miracle stories outsiders are skeptical at first, the cure is performed in private, and the words of healing are quoted (in this case in Aramaic). The healing of the little girl also reminds one of those in which Elijah (I Kings 17:17–24) and Elisha (II Kings 4:18–37) raise children from the dead. Jesus' compassion is implied by his whole bearing and the practical command that the girl be given something to eat.

The Roman *Ordo* prescribes Wisd. 1:13–15; 2:23–25. This teaches that God did not make death; he created human beings for incorruption. Lam. 3:22–33 is used by the Lutheran and Methodist lectionaries: God does not willingly afflict or grieve the children of men. The second reading, II Cor. 8:1–15, speaks of the condescension of Christ and thus relates the healing stories to the gospel. For our sake, though he was rich he became poor, so that through his poverty we might be rich.

Y16B. Mark 6:30–44. The miraculous feeding was so important to the early Church that it has been preserved in two other forms, Mark 8:1–10 (the four thousand) and John 6:1–15. Matthew and Luke are dependent on Mark. T. W. Manson suggested that the story originally told of how Jesus ate with and taught a large body of men, grouped like a Hebrew army in hundreds and fifties, who were about to begin a revolt. They were like sheep without a shepherd; this is an OT figure for an army that has lost its commander (I Kings 22:17). In John 6:15 the crowd wishes to take Jesus by force and make him king. Thus the story was an example of his refusal to use military methods.

But as it stands in all the gospels the symbolism is eucharistic. Jesus as father of the assembly blesses the loaves and fishes, and the disciples act as deacons. Mark, as in 1:21–28, adds his own interpretation: the miracle is an example of Jesus' teaching activity. Matthew and Luke ignore this, but John makes the story the setting for a significant discourse in which the bread from heaven is the principal theme.

The evangelists and the underlying tradition assume that a miraculous multiplication of food took place, but this is not the principal reason for telling the story. It is rather to proclaim Jesus as Lord and the host at the Eucharist. In Mark, Matthew and John the pericope is coupled with the walking on the water. This is a sign that the Lord is present with his people even in the midst of storms and at the darkest hour of the night. In that narrative the words of Jesus (6:50) are usually translated "It is I," but *egô eimi* also means "I am," as Yahweh proclaims himself in Exod. 3:14.

The first lesson, Jer. 23:1–6 (all lectionaries except the Episcopal and NA), promises a "righteous branch" from the family of David. It is read here because God promises to set faithful shepherds over his People.

Y23B. Mark 7:31–37. The story of the deaf mute is a twin to that of the blind man of Bethsaida (8:22–26) and has the same form. In contrast to certain other narratives in Mark, nothing is said about faith or Jesus' compassion; it is only an example of his power to heal. If it had not been told about Jesus it would not be different from many other miracle stories. Physical means are used and "Ephphatha" is quoted in the original language. The motive of both pericopes is to show that such prophecies as Isa. 35:5; 29:18 have been fulfilled; cf. the proclamations in Matt. 11:5 and Luke 4:18, which are read on Advent 3 and Y3C respectively. The first lesson for the day is Isa. 35:4–7a, which is echoed in the gospel reading.

Y30B. Mark 10:46–52. Blindness and deafness are always symbolic in the Gospel of Mark. The evangelist has placed this pericope at a dramatic moment when Jesus and the disciples are leaving Jericho and are about to undertake the long uphill trip to Jerusalem. Bartimaeus addresses our Lord as "Son of David"; he thinks of him as Messiah with the supernatural powers that, according to Jewish tradition, Solomon had. As Mark will later teach (12:35–37) "Son of David" is an inadequate interpretation of Christ's person, but in this instance Jesus commends such faith as the man has (cf. 5:34; 9:23f.). Bartimaeus's eyes are opened and he follows Jesus on the road; perhaps the thought is that he becomes a true disciple, like the man born blind (John 9:35–39).

The first reading, Jer. 31:7–9 (all lectionaries except the Episcopal) is a promise that God will gather his People, including the blind and the lame, from the north country and the farthest parts of the earth.

Year A—Matthew

Y18A. Matt. 14:13–21. This is Matthew's rewriting of the story of the feeding of the five thousand. He omits any mention of Jesus' teaching and instead says that he healed the sick. The crowd includes women and children along with the five thousand men. The first reading in three lectionaries is the magnificent call of Yahweh for the thirsty to come to the waters and to eat milk and honey without payment (Isa. 55:1–5). Neh. 9:16–20 (Episcopal, Methodist) speaks of manna in the wilderness, and Exod. 12:1–14 (NA) recounts the institution of the Passover. The second, Rom. 8:31–39, is Paul's affirmation that nothing can separate us from the love of God in Christ. The theme of the day is therefore the free offer of Good News.

Y19A. Matt. 14:22–33. Mark's form of the story and its symbolism were mentioned in connection with Y16B. Matthew adds the incident of Peter's attempt to emulate his Lord. As so often, Peter is the typical disciple. He has faith but in a crisis he becomes terrified. Yet Jesus has compassion on the doubtful and saves them. The first reading in four lectionaries, I Kings 19:9–18, is the great story of Elijah at Mount Horeb. Yahweh is not in the wind, the fire and the earthquake but in the gentle voice of command and encouragement. Jonah 2:1–9 (Episcopal) is the prophet's prayer in the belly of the great fish. Rom. 9:1–5 enumerates the unique privileges possessed by the Jewish people and expresses Paul's concern for them; it actually introduces the theme of the follow-ing Sunday.

Y20A. Matt. 15:21–28. This is not essentially a miracle tale but a dialogue, although it involves the expulsion of a demon. Matthew seems to have revised the story of the Syrophoenician woman of Mark 7:24–30. That she is called a Canaanite identifies her with the ancient enemies of Israel. She addresses Jesus as Son of David, and is persistent even after he says, "I was sent only to the lost sheep of the house of Israel" (cf. Matt. 10:6). In the conclusion the woman's faith is praised explicitly (cf. 8:10); thus for Matthew the point of the story is faith and persistence in prayer, both of which are familiar themes in Jesus' teaching.

The heart of the narrative, however, is the part that modern readers often find disturbing. Their mental image does not permit a Jesus who can refer to Gentiles as dogs. Sometimes it is observed that the word for "dogs" is a diminutive, but to call them puppies does not mitigate the apparent harshness. Ancient Christians seem not to have been troubled; the woman's response showed not only humility but also spirit and wit. It is of course true that Jesus' principal mission was to the lost sheep of the house of Israel—the emphasis should be on "lost"—but his compassion extended to Gentiles and Samaritans when he came in contact with them.

One example of his attitude is suggested by the first reading of the day, Isa. 56:1–8, in which God promises to bring foreigners to the Temple. At the cleansing of the Temple Jesus quotes from this pericope: "My house shall be called a house of prayer for all the nations." The second reading, Rom. 11:13–16, 29–32, states God's purpose for Israel after Paul has interpreted the Gentile mission as the grafting of the wild olive shoot onto the good olive tree. Christians can never forget that the gospel came out of Judaism.

Year C—Luke

Y5C. Luke 5:1–11. This is Luke's form of the calling of the first disciples (cf. Mark 1:16–20, read on Y3B). One theory is that this was originally a resurrection narrative related to John 21:1–14. For early Christians the story was an example of the divine power and knowledge of Jesus, but it was used primarily to enshrine the saying "Henceforth you will be catching human beings."

The first reading in four lectionaries is the call of Isaiah (Isa. 6:1–8). Just as the fishermen seemed to be unlikely candidates for such a vocation, so the prophet acknowledges that he is a man of unclean lips. But the miracle is that he can be cleansed for God's service. The Book of Common Prayer substitutes the call of Gideon (Judg. 6:11-24a). The epistle (I Cor. 15:1-11), in which Paul gives his witness to the resurrection, fits with the others. He had persecuted the Church of God, yet he was called to be an apostle.

Y9C. Luke 7:1-10. The pericope was discussed on p. 175f. with respect to its main point, the faith of a Gentile. The early Church was also interested in it as a miracle story because it told of a healing from a distance. The second of John's signs (John 4:46-54) is a tale closely related to this. There it is not a slave who is healed, but the son of a royal official.

The belief in Jesus' power to heal is only the beginning of faith, but when it is genuine it can lead to more. This centurion, blunt and straightforward, puts it in military terms; he knows how to be commanded and to command, and he has no doubt about Jesus' authority.

Y10C. Luke 7:11-17. The story of the young man of Nain is coupled with that of Elijah raising the widow's son from the dead (I Kings 17:17-24). No more beautiful story is to be found in the gospels. It is simply told and completely satisfying. There is no need to ask whether here or in the case of Jaïrus's daughter whether the man or the girl was only apparently dead. It illustrates Jesus' compassion and contains the joyful announcement "A great prophet has arisen among us! God has visited his People!" Except for the Messiah, the Jews could ascribe no higher rank than prophet to any human being.

Y28C. Luke 17:11-19. This narrative has some similarity to that of the healing of the leper in Mark 1:40-45 (Y6B), and it is sometimes thought that the two acounts go back to the same incident. Here Jesus sends the lepers to the priests and they are healed as they are on their way. The lesions of a skin disease do not necessarily disappear at once.

The apparent difficulty in the story is that Jesus had told the men to go, and the nine who do not return are not necessarily disobedient. The original tellers of the story would have found the problem trivial; the emphasis is on the impulsive thanksgiving of the Samaritan. Jesus does not make any claims for himself. The nine should have given glory to God; healings come from God's Good News, of which Jesus is the bearer.

The distinctive feature of the story is that, as in the parable of chapter 10, the hero is a Samaritan. Members of a religious community often feel more hostility toward people who share a common heritage with them but are dissidents than toward those of a totally different religion, and the Jews regarded Samaritans as not much better than Gentiles.

The first reading of two lectionaries, II Kings 5:9-17, is the delightful story of the leper Naaman the Syrian, who at first scorned the prophet's word and later obeyed. The Episcopal, Lutheran and Methodist lectionaries substitute the account of Ruth's loyalty to Naomi and her people and God (Ruth 1: 1-19a). Ruth was a Moabite who became ancestress of David.

·17

The Message of Paul

The gospels are so important that the epistle readings may be considered only subsidiary and even neglected in liturgical preaching. Since they usually occur in modified course reading, they cannot always be easily related to the other lessons, and they should not be forced into an artificial harmony. Yet the epistles, particularly those of St. Paul, provide important insights, and sometimes the homily should be centered in the second reading.

The great Apostle was difficult for the Church to digest in his own time and he has been a somewhat controversial figure ever since. Devout Jewish thinkers who can appreciate Jesus usually regard Paul as a renegade with a distorted interpretation of Judaism and they question whether he understood its spirit at all. He left his mark on all Christian literature after his time and yet St. Augustine was the first Church Father to penetrate deeply into his thought. It is sometimes said that "Marcion was the first to understand Paul—and he misunderstood him."

The perspective of the Apostle to the Gentiles was different from that of Jesus. Paul was a Jew but also a Greek from Asia Minor. It is doubtful that he had seen our Lord before the Crucifixion, and he knew him as the risen Lord and to some degree through the tradition of the Church. He claimed that the Church's pillars had added nothing to his gospel, yet note I Cor. 15:1-7. He understood the human character of the earthly Jesus and knew something of the gospel tradition. On the other hand, Paul had a fixed apocalyptic eschatology, while it appears that

205

Jesus was reluctant to make definite predictions about the future. That was in God's hands.

Paul's letters are baffling at times, because we can reconstruct the situations with which he dealt only by reading between the lines of them. They are only fragments of his teaching, written for specific occasions and sometimes at the height of passion. Yet many parts of the letters are carefully constructed and the result of much thought and previous preaching. He was a theologian but not a systematic one, and not all of his statements agree perfectly. To build a system out of his letters distorts them somewhat, yet certain basic ideas are consistent throughout. As a writer he was brilliant; he used the Greek language with freedom but seldom like a Hellenistic literary man. He was above all a preacher and a missionary.

Conscious of his unique authority as apostle to the Gentiles, not conferred on him by any human being, he expected his churches to accept no gospel other than his own. As a pastor he could be severe, but his weapons were those of persuasion, and we often observe him as warm, gentle and tactful. He contended fiercely not for his own sake but for his message. Without him we would not be able to apprehend the full meaning of the Cross and would find it difficult to know what Jesus was really about in his parables and his controversial teaching. It requires Paul's perspective, with its slight difference in time and space, to understand the gospel fully.

Paul's Gospel: Galatians and Romans

As the homilist prepares to deal with the Apostle's message, he may well begin with Galatians and Romans, which are read in course in Years A and C. The themes of the two are closely related. Galatians discloses Paul's position *vis-à-vis* Judaism and his Judaizing opponents in its sharpest and most radical form. Romans discusses the question of justification, the believer's standing before God, more calmly and thoroughly.

Y9C. Gal. 1:1–10 was mentioned briefly in Chapter 14 in connection with the healing of the centurion's servant. The full force of what the Apostle says here can be felt only by reading the rest of the letter. Paul had previously converted the Galatians. Now Jewish Christians have evidently told them that Jesus was a Jew who observed the Torah and that in order to be within the covenant they must be circumcised and converted to Judaism. Later in the letter Paul was to argue that the basis of relation with God is faith, such as Abraham had, and that the Mosaic law does not annul the earlier and basic covenant. Here he declares that his apostleship came directly from Jesus Christ. No pretended authority can supersede it.

Y10C. The argument is carried further in Gal. 1:11–24. His message was not derived from the other apostles or from any human being. This is the primary account of Paul's conversion. It is sometimes thought that he speaks of the same experience in II Cor. 12:1–5.

Y11C. Gal. 2:11–21. It was in Antioch that the admission of Gentiles to the Church first became a critical issue. Acts does not tell of the incident in this pericope and gives a very different impression of Peter's attitude. The strict Jewish Christians in Antioch (Paul calls them false brethren who slipped in, 2:4) retreated to the next line of defense; they would not have table fellowship with the Gentile converts and they temporarily won Cephas (Peter) and Barnabas to their side. But this would have divided the Church into two groups out of communion with one another. Acts 15:22–29 tells of a compromise reached at a council in Jerusalem, according to which the Gentiles need only keep a few rules, but there is no indication in Paul's letters that he accepted this or had even heard of it.

Here he sets forth the principle that no human being can be justified (acquitted, vindicated, put in the right relation with God) by works of the law, but only by faith in Jesus Christ. Justification, important as it is to Paul's theology, is however only one way of looking at the relation-ship. Another way of putting it is that Paul, and by implication every other Christian, is identified with Christ. The believer is dead to the law—in Romans he will add that he is dead to sin—and the life in him is that of Christ.

The gospel reading (Luke 7:36–50, p. 172) tells of the sinful woman whom Jesus forgave. The Pharisee symbolizes the legal approach to morality, the woman represents faith and love.

Y12C. Gal. 3:23–29. Paul's manner of doing theology is an example of what Amos Wilder calls the new language of the gospel. Paul is like a wrestler trying to get a hold, not only on his readers but also on a way to express the truth. He now uses a different set of metaphors. He does not despise the Torah; it is holy, just and good (Rom. 7:12), but at its best it is the slave in a Roman household who takes care of the children and brings them to the schoolmaster, who is Christ. In the next chapter he uses two other metaphors: the minor who comes of age and now needs no guardian, and the person adopted into a new family. Adoption in Roman law was more than a legal status; it meant a new name and new emotional and religious relationships.

When speaking of baptism, Paul affirms boldly that in Christ there is no distinction between Jew and Greek, slave and free, male and female. This must remembered when one reads the puzzling passage I Cor. 11:2-16.

The gospel reading (Luke 9:18-24) tells of Peter's confession. The epistle pericope thus explains the implications of saying "You are the Christ."

Y9A. Rom. 3:21-28. Few parts of Scripture have been discussed so constantly and thoroughly. Justification is the primary metaphor but there are others: redemption (being bought out of slavery) and expiation (*hilastêrion,* removal of a pollution or tabu).

Justification is a metaphor of the law court. The accused is brought in, and by ordinary standards he would be found guilty. But in this case he trusts in God through Christ, and on this basis God is able to declare him innocent and does so. For three reasons this is not a fictitious righteousness. (1) Whatever God decides is right; he is justice itself and by definition he cannot judge unjustly. (2) Through faith a goodness has been established in the person. He is by no means perfect, but he can grow. (3) Elsewhere Paul personifies sin as an alien force that tempts and oppresses human beings, and in the contest between sin and the believer, the latter is in the right.

This rests on the OT concept of righteousness or rightness, which is more than what we usually think of as justice. The biblical writers have no illusion about sin, corporate or individual. Yet there are degrees of culpability, and in a lawsuit one party may be relatively more in the right than the other. The OT sees the rightness of God as an active force, not an abstract principle, which *vindicates* sinful and partly repentant Israel against the nations that oppress it. So God also vindicates the helpless person who trusts in him through Christ.

Looked at from another angle, this is God's steadfast love (*ḥesed*), the love expressed in his covenant. When Paul uses the word grace (*charis*) he means almost the same thing.

Justice is one aspect of a new state of affairs, which can also be described as being bought out of slavery so that henceforth one is slave only to Christ; as purification from defilement; atonement or reconciliation; adoption; and coming into one's inheritance. It can be summed up in the phrase Paul constantly uses, "in Christ Jesus," for the believer is now taken out of the sphere of law, sin and death, into the sphere of salvation and new life. This is an identification with Christ, both directly and individually, and through the Church, which is his Body.

This is not a matter of feeling, although the realization of it arouses emotions. It is objective and not dependent on what we call "religious experience." It rests on the act of God and this is supremely expressed in the Cross. Paul speaks of the blood of Christ, using the sacrificial terminology of the earliest Palestinian church. In discussing the meaning of the Cross in an earlier chapter we observed that while it can be seen as the Son offering himself to the Father, it is best described as the action of God in Christ reconciling the world to himself.

When the gospel pericope for the day (Matt. 7:15-29) is considered in the light of the epistle reading, two points emerge. (1) True faith is contrasted with false profession. (2) Faith is more than what we often mean when we say "belief"; life must be built on firm foundations, and the result of faith is right action.

Y10A. Rom. 4:13-25. As in Galatians, Paul argues from a principle that many ancient people accepted, namely that the oldest form of a religion is its truest. Abraham did indeed accept circumcision, but this was a seal and sign of the faith in God's promises that he already had. We may remind ourselves that the covenant with Abraham was an unconditional act of grace. The gospel (Matt. 9:9-13, p. 151) tells of the calling of the tax collector Matthew (Levi in Mark and Luke). All vocations summon one to follow God into an unknown land.

Y11A. Rom. 5:6-11. This pericope resumes the argument of Y9A. Paul does not say that God demanded the death of Christ. It is enough to say that he *did* die for us and that this has reconciled us to God. The wrath of God is spoken of as an impersonal force; it is the inevitable result of sin because God is just. His wrath or anger is only another aspect of his love and grace. God did not need to be reconciled to us; it is we who are reconciled to him. Here the homilist may wish to review pp. 107-111.

Because of the results of sin are so serious, there can be only a radical remedy. As on the following Sunday, Y12A, the pericope explains how sin came into the world and Christ has reversed the process.

The gospel reading for Y11A (Matt. 9:35—10:8, p. 151) tells of Jesus' commission to the Twelve. The message of the Reign of God reconciles his People to him.

Y12A. Rom. 5:12–21. "Adam" means "human being." The first man sinned, and the habit of sinning became universal; the Greek does not say that all sinned *in* Adam. The second man, who represents humanity as God purposes it to be, has brought the free gift of grace.

The language has to be understood as mythical. Because of our scientific tradition we cannot imagine a single man who committed the first sin against God's command. But there must have been some point in prehistory when humanoids became *Homo sapiens*. This change of nature, whether sudden or gradual, brought with it the art of speech; these men and women remembered the past, projected themselves into the future, made plans and felt failure. As they made tools they developed the capacity to transcend themselves, and the tools could be used for constructive or destructive purposes not hitherto possible. A sense of right and wrong came into being, and sometimes an individual chose what he knew to be wrong. Imitation, if nothing else, would ensure that the process of sin continued and infected the community. This is at least one way of looking at the phenomenon that St. Augustine called "original sin."

The Message to the Church in Corinth

Y7B. II Cor. 1:18–22. As we have seen, St. Paul's apostleship was challenged in Galatia. In Corinth there were two threats to his authority and his gospel. Second Corinthians shows him in competition with "false apostles" or "super-apostles." There is no suggestion that they preached circumcision, as the intruders in Galatia had done; rather, they claimed to have more superhuman power and eloquence than Paul and better credentials as apostles. The dangers he dealt with in First Corinthians were of a still different nature.

It is not always realized that in Second Corinthians Paul discusses some of the issues raised in Romans but from another angle. Among these are the basic problem of the relation of the new to the old, and the meaning of the new life in Christ.

The background of this Sunday's pericope is that Paul was criticized for delaying a visit to Corinth that he had promised. He answered that he was not vacillating like a worldly man ("according to the flesh") but that like Jesus Christ he was reliable. This led him to say that Jesus' response to people was not Yes and No but always Yes. God's promises are always positive and for the good of mankind; this is an aspect of the covenant, which is the theme of later parts of his letter. The Jewish and Christian liturgical response Amen is an affirmation like Yes; it confirms and guarantees (verses 21f.) and is related to the word translated as "truth."

Viewed from this point of view, the healing of the paralytic (Mark 2:1-12, p.164f.) is God's Yes to the need of the helpless man.

Y8B. II Cor. 3:1b-6 (four lectionaries). In the gospel reading (Mark 2:18-22) Jesus says that the voluntary fasts common among strict Jews are not appropriate while the Good News is being proclaimed; this moment is like a wedding party. The epistle pericopes demonstrate the fundamental difference between the new and the old; the latter (the law of the Old Covenant) kills but the Spirit gives life.

This is a radical antithesis between Law and Spirit that most pious Jews would have rejected. But when the law, or rather what claimed to be the Torah, stood in the way of the new relationship with God, its effect was nothing less than death.

The background of this pericope is that Paul had not come to Corinth with a letter from some other church certifying that he was a valid apostle, while his opponents evidently had such credentials. He speaks of "commendatory letters" (verse 1) and the need to be "competent" or "qualified" (verses 5f.). His response is that the Corinthians them-selves, who are now sound Christians in spite of their imperfections, are the only credentials that he needs.

The Church throughout its history has never been able to do without evidences of ordination for its ministers. This protects the people from imposters and individualists. Paul's situation was entirely different. There was little or no ecclesiastical structure, though he could have argued as he did in Gal. 2:7-10 that the Jerusalem apostles had accepted him and his gospel. But even so his commission came directly from the risen Lord. The point that is important for us to realize is that no matter how valid the ordination of bishops, priests or deacons may be, the effective-ness of their ministry depends on the integrity of their personal life and the truth of their message.

The Episcopal and Presbyterian readings for the day are an essential part of Paul's argument. By using a complicated typology he contrasts the old covenant (the veil on the face of Moses, which now lies on the faces of unbelievers) with the new, in which Christians with unveiled faces see the glory of God in the face of Christ and are transformed into the likeness of what they see. This is a bold interpretation of the new life. Paul (and by implication all true apostles) have received the ministry of this new covenant.

Y9B. II Cor. 4:5–12. The message which Paul bears in his ministry is like a hoard of gold contained in an earthen pot so that its power and glory can be seen for what they are, and no one can boast about being the vessel. Identification with Christ and the new life that flows from this also involve being under pressure, perplexed, persecuted and struck down, but nevertheless surviving. Here and in 6:3–10, in words of powerful eloquence, Paul describes the true triumph of the Christian which elsewhere is expressed as justification, redemption, adoption, and so on.

Y12B. II Cor. 5:18—6:2. No one who is bearer of such a treasure can live henceforth for himself or herself alone. The meaning of verse 16 is often debated, but probably Paul is not speaking of knowing Christ in his earthly ministry, as though the events of that story were of little consequence. The words "after the flesh" should be taken with "we have known" rather than with "Christ"; that is, we know him with the revelation of his full person and purpose and do not regard him from the world's point of view. A new creation has occurred when one knows him truly. The truth is that God was in Christ reconciling the world to himself and he has committed to his apostolic followers the message of reconciliation. God made the one who was without sin to be "sin" and to receive its full consequences so that in him we might become "righteousness," i.e. justified, acquitted, vindicated.

The gospel pericope read with this is the storm at sea (Mark 4:35–41, p. 199). This can suggest the changed situation that the gospel brings.

Y5A. I Cor. 2:1–11. In the gospel pericope, Matt. 5:13–20 (pp. 179–182), Jesus tells the disciples that (like Israel in the OT) they are the light of the world; and, as its salt, it is unthinkable that they should allow themselves to be saltless. The epistle reading shows what it is to be salt and light.

First Corinthians discloses problems that are different from those addressed in Romans and Second Corinthians. The church is split into factions, and the enthusiastic "wise" and "spiritual" group is the one that causes the most trouble. These people pretend to a wisdom or philosophy that some scholars identify as an early form of Gnosticism. They "know" that as Christians they are free from the law, they can eat foods that have been offered to pagan gods; some of them are ascetics who despise marriage, while others pay scant attention to morality and the conventions. They pride themselves on their ability to prophesy and speak in tongues, and in general look down on others who do not have their "wisdom."

In this pericope Paul reminds them that he did not come to them with eloquence and a high-flown philosophy. His message was simply Christ crucified; it is only this that carries the power of God, and its truth was justified by the concrete results. His behavior among them was not that of the spectacular, successful preacher, but modest, "in weakness and fear and trembling." No one can carry such an awesome message and at the same time promote himself.

Y6A. I Cor. 2:6–13 (all lectionaries except the Episcopal and NA). The argument is carried further in these verses. There is wisdom and a mystery, but it is not what the Corinthians think. The forces that rule the present world cannot understand it; otherwise the glorious Lord would never have been crucified. The "spiritual people" among the Corinthians claim to have the Spirit, but it is the Spirit that has revealed this paradoxical truth, the very depth of God's purpose. The test of having the Spirit is that one accepts the humility and weakness of the Cross. The Episcopal and NA reading is I Cor. 3:1–9, in which Paul says that the partisanship of the Corinthians shows their spiritual immaturity.

The gospel pericope (Matt. 5:17–37) seems to be related to Paul's themes only in that it sets forth the equally paradoxical nature of God's true law. His ways are not our ways. The extreme demands made here force humility upon us.

Y17C. Col. 2:6–15. Colossians is often considered a post-Pauline letter, but it fits so well with Paul's theology that at least in this pericope the question need not concern us. We discuss this reading here because it calls attention to another aspect of the message of the Cross. As in Romans, the new life begins with the death and resurrection of the believer in baptism. The old law is portrayed as though it were the legal document certifying that one is a slave. Christ cancelled it and nailed it to his Cross. And this Cross is his triumph over the powers and authorities that are hostile to God and his People.

The New Life

Y13A. Rom. 6:1-11. The act of God in Christ that results in new life for the believer is the principal subject of chapter 8. Chapters 6 and 7 lead up to this, but the pericope before us is the only one in these chapters that all lectionaries include. Here the thought is that baptism is a complete identification with Christ in his death and Resurrection, so that the life we now live is not subject to the conditions of our prior existence.

Anders Nygren understands Rom. 1-11 as a unit whose unifying theme is the two aeons, this age and the age to come, and interprets Paul's thought as strictly eschatological. The new age is entirely in the future, after the resurrection. The new life portrayed in chapter 8 is thus a potentiality rather than an actuality, and chapter 7 refers to the present condition of the believer, who is still struggling with sin "in his members." This line of thinking runs from St. Augustine through Luther and Calvin to Karl Barth, Reinhold Niebuhr and other recent theologians who stand in the tradition of the Reformation. But the Greek fathers and some modern commentators, Lietzmann, Sanday and Headlam and Dodd among them, regard chapter 7 as referring to the human situation before faith in Christ, and chapter 8 as a portrayal of the life of the redeemed.

The issue is important for the interior life of the individual, who might lose hope of realizing God's promises in his lifetime or alternatively be complacent about his salvation. We do not always find ourselves living on the high plane of chapter 8, and the Augustinian position appears to be more realistic. But if we accept it fully, we may forget that both Jesus and Paul expected their followers to lead a radically new life. If we have no hope of this during our mortal existence and it is only to be in tension between the Holy Spirit and the sin that dwells in us, if we can live only in expectation, we may despair and give in to sin too easily.

Paul never claimed that he was perfect. He says that he has not yet achieved but is striving forward to the goal (Phil. 3:12-14). At the same time, as he is thinking about the moral and spiritual life he moves back and forth between the indicative—you *are* different persons, baptized, justified, made into God's holy People—and the imperative—you must be what you really are (I Cor. 5:6-8; 6:11).

We propose this solution of the dilemma. The normal existence of the Christian, according to Paul, is what theologians sometimes call the state of grace, living in the Spirit, open to the grace of God. From time to time we may fall out of this into the realm of law, sin and death, but this need be no more than a temporary lapse. There is the possibility of repentance and restoration. The future is always open to the Christian. In secular terms, "this is the first day of the rest of my life."

We said in Chapter 3 that the function of the liturgy is to take the participants out of ordinary space and time into God's world and his true time. This thought can be applied to our ambiguous existence. The Christian must live in this world and participate fully in it, but he or she needs continually to be restored to the true nature that God has intended. By returning to him, not only in public worship but also in solitary prayer and contemplation, we are refreshed, guided and empowered.

Y14A. The Methodist lectionary, the Episcopal, and the NA (in part) prescribe Rom. 7:14—8:13, which permits explication of the problem we have just discussed. In the Roman *Ordo* the reading is Rom. 8:9, 11–13. Verses 1–6 announce freedom from sin and death. The right demands of the law can be fulfilled in us because we "walk," i.e. conduct ourselves, not "according to the flesh" but "according to spirit." One should not suppose that by "flesh" Paul means matter or our bodily life. The "mind" or bent of the flesh is something like what the rabbis called the evil impulse. To walk according to the flesh is succumbing to temptations to which our mortal nature is prone, and sometimes it means thinking and acting on a purely worldly level.

A Christian, however, can have the Spirit of Christ within him (verses 9–13), and this is an assurance of our resurrection which in a sense has occurred already. At the same time we are under obligation to lead the new life. The gospel pericope (Matt. 11:25–30) is an affirmation that even "babes" have been given the new revelation, and the burden that Jesus lays on them is gentle and light.

On the next four Sundays most of Rom. 8 is read, and with it several parables from Matt. 13 as well as the narrative of the feeding of the five thousand (Matt. 14:13–21). The cumulative effect of these readings is to assure the worshippers by proclamation and parable that they do indeed live in a new world and that all things are possible through God in Christ.

It is sufficient to mention only a few points. Creation itself is to be redeemed from its present bondage (Rom. 8:18–25, Y15A, three lectionaries). Thus all of God's purpose is to be achieved and we have an eschatology that reminds one of Teilhard de Chardin's Omega point. To believe this requires faith since we live in an age when everyone is fearful of nuclear war; it requires also the resolution to act in accordance with God's design for preserving and glorifying the earth.

Every earnest Christian must be perplexed at times about how one should pray, but the Spirit within us prays for us when we do not know what words to use (Rom. 8:26–27, Y16A, three lectionaries, cf. p. 246). We have, further, the assurance that for those who love him God makes everything work toward good, and we are destined to be brothers of Christ, the first-born of the new age; called, justified and glorified (Rom. 8:26–30, Y17A). Nothing in life or death or in the whole creation can separate us from the love of God in Christ (Rom. 8:31–39, Y18A).

Although everything is possible with God, Paul never thinks of prayer as a magical technique. In the bitter ironical part of Second Corinthians (chapters 10–13) he has to confront the "super-apostles" who boast of their visions, revelations and miracles, and in contrast he tells of his "thorn in the flesh," some nagging chronic illness, and how three times he prayed to the Lord for relief, only to receive the answer, "My grace is sufficient for you" (II Cor. 12:7–10, Y14B). Jesus himself was rejected in his home village and not able to do any mighty deed there (Mark 6:1–6).

Paul's Hope for the Future: Romans
Chapters 9–11 of Romans complete the doctrinal part of his letter and are an essential part of his argument. In 1:1—3:19 he has shown that the judgment of God falls on Gentiles and Jews alike. The new way of salvation which rescues humanity from this situation and transforms it is set forth in the succeeding chapters, in which he also deals with the many objections that arise. There remains the problem that many Gentiles but very few Jews have accepted the way of faith; what therefore are we to make of God's promises to Israel?

The lectionaries do not include all parts of his answer, which can be summarized briefly. Many past debates on this subject might have been avoided had it been realized that Paul is thinking dialectically when he explains why Israel has on the whole rejected the gospel. In chapter 9 he sets up one possibility: God can choose as he will; like a potter he can make vessels for splendor or destruction and no one can question his purpose. This is the strict view of God's omnipotence that is to be found in Islam as well as in the OT. On the other hand, as Paul says in chapter 10, Israel has simply been disobedient and the fault is its own. Chapter 11 gives his final answer: the "hardening" of Israel is only temporary, the promises of God will never be broken, God will save both Jews and Gentiles and have mercy on all.

Y19A. In Rom. 9:1-5 Paul resumes his enumeration of the special privileges of Israel which he seems to have begun in 3:1f. The "glory" is the presence of God, who has manifested himself on many occasions. "Worship" refers to the service of the Temple, which was still standing when he wrote; it could include the festivals, which were celebrated in Jewish homes.

Y20A. Rom. 11:13-16, 29-32. Paul sees the rejection of the gospel by Israel as a part of the divine plan that made possible the Gentile mission. God's promises to his ancient People are, however, unchangeable. The lectionaries omit the passage in which Paul likens the Gentiles to wild olive branches grafted into a domestic olive tree and warns them not to feel superior to the Jews. The metaphor has been called clumsy, but it is intended to emphasize the seemingly paradoxical way in which God works. The story of the Canaanite woman (Matt 15:21-28) fits well with the epistle passage.

Paul's Hope for the Future: Other Letters

The Apostle usually interprets the future life in terms of the general resurrection of the dead. His most extended treatment of this is in I Cor. 15, which he wrote in answer to questions raised by the Corinthians. The Greeks in general thought of human beings as made up of body and soul, which were quite distinct from one another. They could conceive of the soul as immortal and regarded it as the essential person, but the thought of a resuscitated body was strange to them and some found it absurd. Paul shared with most Jews the idea that body and soul are inseparable; man is a body which God has animated, and he could not contemplate a disembodied existence.

Y5C. I Cor. 15:1-11 (all except the Lutheran, which reads this at Easter). Here Paul transmits the tradition of Christ's Resurrection that he had received, and adds his own testimony that he had seen the risen

Lord. This, he explains, is an essential part of the faith that the Corinthi-ans had accepted. Since Cephas (Peter) was the first to whom Christ appeared, it is interesting that the gospel pericope tells of the miraculous catch of fish and Peter's call to be the first disciple. Both of these are examples of the creative power of God, on which all belief in life after death must finally rest.

Y6C. I Cor. 15:12-20. The argument here is that there must be a resurrection of the dead, otherwise Christ did not rise; but in that case the foundation of the Christian faith would be destroyed and we would be without hope. On Y7C parts of 15:35-50 are read, and here some of the perplexities of the Corinthians are resolved. In the resurrection, like Christ we will have transformed and glorified bodies. The living stalk of wheat is different from the apparently dead seed that is sown in the ground. The "spiritual" body is not the same as the "animate" body of flesh, and Christ is the "last Adam," the first man of the new creation (cf. Rom. 8:29, "the firstborn of many brothers"). In I Cor. 15:50-58 (Y8C) the Apostle gives a picture of what will happen at the resurrection, using the words "incorruptibility" and "immortality," which would be congenial to the Corinthians, in describing the risen body.

Possibly Paul's thought underwent further development after he wrote First Corinthians, but scholars are not agreed on this. In II Cor. 4:13—5:1 (Y10B) he speaks of resurrection but says also that as the "outer man" wastes away the "inner man" is renewed day by day. This sug-gests a process, but it may mean only that he is being prepared spiritual-ly for the future life. He also speaks of the body as a house or tent to be replaced by one that is eternal in the heavens.

Y11B. II Cor. 5:1-17. Here the metaphor changes to that of clothing, and Paul wishes not to be found naked but to be invested first with the new clothing. He then expresses the desire to be away from the body and at home with the Lord, and this at least raises the possibility that the Apostle hopes to be united with Christ after death and before the resurrection; at the same time he speaks of standing before Christ's judgment seat.

Here he may approach the minority view which is also to be found in Judaism. There is a doctrine of immortality in the Book of Wisdom, and some Jews believed that the martyrs were taken up into heaven to be with the patriarchs in the presence of God. This, as we have noted, is explicitly stated in Fourth Maccabees. When Paul writes to the

Philippians (perhaps from Rome, toward the end of his life) he knows that it might be better for the sake of his churches to remain alive, but he has a great desire to "depart and be with Christ" (Phil. 1:1–11, 19–27, Y25A), and this does not imply a lapse of time before the resurrection.

Colossians may well have been written by Paul, but it does not add much more information about his eschatology. Believers had died with Christ and are risen with him (2:20; 3:1), but it is when Christ appears that we will be manifested in glory with him (3:4). The great credal passage 1:15–20 (Y15C or Y16C; cf. p. 115) proclaims Christ's headship in everything, and one of its aspects is that he is the "first-born from the dead."

Evidently the great Apostle can use a variety of symbols when speaking of the future. If he speaks occasionally of immortality, it is not a belief in the natural immortality of the human soul; it rests on faith in God as the gracious and loving Creator.

·18

The Ethic
of the New Life

The Christians to whom Paul proclaimed a new and incomparably more glorious life were at the same time under obligation to conduct themselves as part of the new humanity. Paul's moral teaching is essentially a translation into fresh language, partly Jewish and partly Hellenistic, of the message and commandments that Jesus had given the first disciples. For the Good News of the Reign of God which brought power was joined to commands stated in such extreme form that in effect they were parables of a converted life, a new relationship with God the Father. The allegiance that the disciples gave was later to be described by Paul as faith in Christ Jesus, and by the Fourth Gospel as believing and abiding.

The principle that runs through the teaching of Jesus and Paul is that the relationship with God comes first and the moral life follows as a consequence. We are not accepted as God's children by first pleasing him and winning this standard as a reward. He comes to us first, as Jesus did to sinners, and offers himself. To state it thus is to put it in prose; the NT expresses it dynamically in stories and figures.

Since Jesus and his first hearers lived within the Torah, he had no need, as Paul did, to repeat moral principles that are to be found in the OT. All this could be assumed; thus the moral teaching of Jesus goes beyond the letter of the law to its purpose, and puts the purely cultic commands of the law in a subordinate place.

The person who attempted to follow what we may call the ethic of the Reign of God had to make many moral decisions for himself instead of relying on the guidance of scribes. The purpose of the Good News, far from building a fence about the law, was to bring men and women to freedom and maturity.

None of us completely fulfils Jesus' moral teaching, but it transforms us. God's demands, which are far more than any purely human society asks, are a moral tonic, a challenge that liberates the spirit while at the same time it puts an end to complacency and self-righteousness. "If you love those who love you, what credit is it to you?" (Luke 6:32). "When you have done everything that is commanded you, say 'We are only slaves; we have done only what was our duty' "(Luke 17:10).

Repentance, humility, discipleship and love are words that sum up much of Jesus' moral teaching. Not only is one liberated from detailed legal rules; such institutions as the Temple and the authority of kings and high priests are only provisional. God alone is sovereign, and allegiance to his Reign determines everything else.

Paul and His Churches

Paul lived and worked in a very different social situation. His field was the Greek-speaking Mediterranean world and mostly among pagans. His practical problem was to guide a church composed of people who did not have the solid background of Jewish morality and family life. There were good influences in Hellenistic culture, especially Stoicism; and philosophy had many of the functions of what we call religion, but Greek and Roman popular religion was polytheistic, had many primitive elements, and could easily descend to superstition. Unwanted children were often exposed to die, and in Corinth prostitution was a part of the cult of Aphrodite. In this pluralistic culture any new religious teacher or philosopher could get a hearing. Paul had to teach his converts the fundamental principles of morality and the new faith, and his letters were written at a second stage of development when problems had arisen.

First Corinthians discloses Paul's principles and methods. Such moral guidance as his people had previously received came from a philosophical tradition that had been widely diffused in the population by the preaching of Stoics and Cynics. It is not surprising that the Apostle echoes the commonplaces of Stoicism. He says, for example, that there is a law of nature written in the hearts of Gentiles (Rom. 2:14–16), and in this passage he also uses the word that we translate as "consciousness" or "conscience." Conscience, as he speaks of it, is not a standard for behavior but a function of the rational mind, the capacity for moral judgment. It is not purely intuitive and does not provide automatic guidance. Like the Stoics, he also uses metaphors drawn from the athletic games to express the inevitable moral struggle (I Cor. 9:24-27; Phil. 3:12-14).

Thus Paul stands on a common ground with his readers and speaks their language. His letters show that ordinary folk wisdom and philosophy coincide at some points with Jewish and Christian ethics. Not everything "secular" is false; the difference lies in the motives and often in the applications.

The lectionaries provide readings from First Corinthians as follows: parts of chapters 1-4 in Y2A through Y8A; from chapters 6-10 in Y2B through Y6B; from chapters 12, 13, and 15 in Y2C through Y8C, thus in the time between Epiphany and Lent. 14:12b-20 appears in the Episcopal calendar on the fourth Sunday after Epiphany (C) and in the Lutheran on the fifth. We shall follow this order with a few variations and also discuss pericopes from other Pauline letters as appropriate.

The Partisan Spirit

Y3A. I Cor. 1:10-17. After an eloquent thanksgiving such as he offers in all his letters except Galatians, Paul responds to news that has troubled him deeply, that the Corinthians are split into factions, each of which claims to follow a favorite apostle. There is probably no "party of Christ," unless there are people who pride themselves on being non-partisan. As one reads through chapters 1-4 it becomes evident that behind this divisiveness is pride in possessing the Spirit and a hidden wisdom; the latter may be related to an early form of Gnosticism. When in chapters 12-14 the Apostle discusses spiritual gifts, he returns to this theme.

When this pericope is considered in the context of the whole letter we see that partisanship—which can easily arise in any congregation—destroys the basis of moral living. Jewish and Christian morality is never a private or individual matter; it always concerns relationship to others in community. Morals and faith are also organically related to one another. How one behaves discloses how one believes about ultimate reality and therefore about God. Breaking the unity of the Church is tantamount to dividing Christ. In this world we can never expect perfect unity of faith and action, since we "know partially and prophesy partially" (I Cor. 13:9), but the Christian, like Paul in this letter, strives to reconcile persons and opposing viewpoints in Christ.

Y4A. I Cor. 1:18–31. This pericope was mentioned in Chap. 12 (p. 150) in connection with the gospel reading of the Beatitudes (Matt. 5:1–12). Fear and pride are the principal roots of sin; they corrupt our best aspirations and virtues. Here Paul strikes at intellectual and spiritual pride, which are more subtle than the boast of riches, family, and political power. The "foolish," like the poor of the Beatitudes, can accept the Good News because they make no pretensions. The result of true faith is that one relaxes, lets go of oneself, one's status and one's fears, trusting in God and in other human beings. The latter will sometimes disappoint us, but to be suspicious and paranoid is a worse disaster than having one's trust betrayed.

Y5A and Y6A. I Cor. 2:1–13 (NA reads 3:1–9 on the sixth Sunday). These were discussed in Chap. 17 (p. 212f.). The message of Christ crucified puts an end to pride. The "fear and trembling" (2:3) are not the fear that leads to sin, for Paul was not cowardly; they are the awe one feels in the presence of God because of the message that Paul carries. Likewise the wisdom of God is not one that leads to intellectual pretension; we can boast only "in the Lord" (1:31).

Y7A. I Cor. 3:10–23. Here the theme is the same, but in verse 22 Paul prepares for what he will say in the next chapter by ranking Apollos and Cephas as equals to himself, the founder and father of the Corinthian church. The Corinthians can claim all three apostles as their own (cf. 3:4–9).

Y8A. I Cor. 4:1–13. Three lectionaries omit the bitterly ironical passage (verses 8–13) in which Paul likens the apostles to captives led at the end of a general's triumphal procession in Rome, "a spectacle to the world and angels and men." In the earlier portion, the apostles are stewards of God's mysteries, subject to God's judgment but not accountable to any human being. Paul's most significant statement illuminates the idea of conscience. He is conscious of nothing against himself (the verb *synoida* is related to the noun), but this in itself does not justify him. He has the highest possible confidence in his vocation and message but knows that this cannot be absolute. The gospel reading for the day is the passage on anxiety; what Paul says here matches it, because his confidence is in God.

The Moral Principle Applied to Sexual Life

Y2B. I Cor. 6:11b–20. Judaism had an ambivalent attitude toward the sexual side of human nature. Since it was part of God's creation, it was holy and good. It was also dangerous, and therefore subject to many tabus. Jesus upheld the sanctity of monogamous marriage and forbade divorce. He forgave persons guilty of adultery and fornication but taught that to harbor lustful imaginings was as truly a sin as the act itself. Jesus was in the company of women more frequently than the scribes thought proper, and this suggests that he rejected the tabus on women which kept them in a subordinate position.

Paul and other early Christians shared the Jewish horror of sexual offenses. The Corinthians lived in a culture where prostitution was accepted as part of the worship of Aphrodite. They had heard the Apostle speak of freedom from the law, and so some said, "Everything is lawful for me"; "Food is made for the body, and the body for food"; that is, we are endowed with sexuality so that we may enjoy it.

In this pericope Paul gives two answers. Our bodies are under God's protection and belong to him; this is the old Hebrew idea of tabu or holiness, which he restates by saying that we are members of Christ. To be joined to a harlot is to desecrate Christ's body.

The other answer is twofold. Everything is theoretically lawful, but not everything is fitting, beneficial, or expedient (*sympherei*). This is a Stoic concept that Paul takes over and applies to other issues such as the eating of foods sacrificed to pagan gods and to *charismata* or spiritual gifts. It is one way of expressing the principle of love, concern for others, that he sets forth in chapter 13. He also adds that even if a thing is lawful, he will not allow himself to be mastered by it. This suggests the Greek virtue of self-control or sanity (*sophrosyne*), to which he alludes in Rom. 12:3 and which lies behind the athletic metaphors in I Cor. 9:24–27.

Y3B. I Cor. 7:29–35. The lectionaries omit most of chapter 7, but the homilist should be aware of the context of this pericope. Paul is thankful that he is celibate, and he prefers this state of life to marriage, but he advises most people to marry, and he states clearly that the two partners have equal sexual rights (7:1–9). He forbids divorce except in the case when a Christian is married to a pagan who makes the relationship impossible. If such a marriage can be maintained, however, it is holy and it sanctifies the children and the unbelieving spouse (7:10–16).

He then sets forth the general principle that each person should remain in the state of life which he had when he first came to faith. The Jew should not become a Gentile or the Gentile a Jew. A slave should not aspire to freedom. If he can be set free, he may take advantage of this; but the Greek can be understood as saying, "make use of your present condition instead." In any case, a slave is the Lord's freedman and the free man is the slave of the Lord (7:17-24, the Episcopal reading for this day). So with marriage; it is better to stay as you are, married or not. It is not wrong to marry, but if you do so you will be under additional pressure (7:25-28).

Paul's reason for the foregoing judgments is given in verses 29-31. The time, God's moment for action (*kairos*), has been shortened, the end of the age is near; therefore one should sit loosely to the world and all its affairs. What the Apostle and many other early Christians expected did not occur, but it would be wrong to sweep his words aside as though they had no application. No one's life on earth is absolutely secure; a crisis may intervene at any moment. The Christian should enjoy life and make the most of it but always be willing to renounce it and find true security in God. The gospel pericope (Mark 1:14-20, p. 162f.) tells of the call of the first disciples; they too went out into an unknown future.

Y4B. I Cor. 7:32-35 (Roman, Methodist, Presbyterian). Paul now develops this theme by showing why he prefers celibacy; it involves fewer anxieties. Married people have to care for one another and can easily be distracted from their concern for the Lord. But the Apostle again explains that he is not putting a restriction on his people; this advice is for their benefit (*symphoron,* a word related to the one used in 6:12). The Episcopal, Lutheran, and NA lectionaries read I Cor. 8:1-13, which relates to the pericopes for Y5B.

The Principle Applied to Food

Y5B. I Cor. 9:16-23. Much of chapters 8-10 deals with a question raised by the Corinthians: may a Christian eat food that has been sacrificed to a pagan god? The best meats came from markets attached to the temples. Dinner parties were sometimes held in the temple itself, but such meat might also be served in a home. Members of the church were not agreed on what to do when invited to dinner. The "strong" relied on Christian liberty and their faith that there is only one God; the "weak" rejected any compromise with idolatry. Paul's answer can be summarized thus: There is no God but the Father and no Lord but Jesus

Christ; the heathen deities are demons and one cannot share the table of the Lord and the table of demons. If, however, you are invited to dinner, eat the food offered you without hesitation; but if someone makes a point of telling you that this is sacrificial food do not eat it, for you will set up obstacles to the faith of the "weak" person who regards the food as idolatrous.

The Apostle gives these reasons: "If food causes my brother to stumble" (lose his faith or commit sin) "I will never eat meat, lest I scandalize my brother" (8:13); "Everything is lawful, but not everything builds up" (the individual and the Church, 10:23).

This is the exercise of freedom, not its abridgement. Paul claims as much right as the Lord's brothers and Cephas to travel with a wife and to be supported by the churches, but he has not availed himself of this because he wants to be able to boast that he has preached the gospel without pay.

In the pericope before us, he says that it is this that he can be proud of, not of preaching the gospel itself, which is an obligation laid on him. Although he is free, he has made himself a slave to everyone. Therefore he identifies himself with both Jews and those who are "outside the law," and also with the "weak," so that in every way he may save some of them.

Y6B. I Cor. 9:24–27. The lectionaries (except the Roman and Presbyterian) use these next verses on this Sunday and in Proper 1B of the season after Pentecost. Paul shows how well he knows his readers by using these athletic metaphors. The Greeks were enthusiastic fans, and the Isthmian Games were held in the neighborhood of Corinth. American archaeologists have discovered the installations used in the races. In Phil. 3:12–14 he also describes himself as a runner striving toward the goal and its prize.

Other lectionaries read I Cor. 10:31—11:1, which sums up Paul's teaching on what is "fitting" or "beneficial." All is to be done to the glory of God and for the salvation of the many. To imitate Paul in this respect is to imitate Christ.

Y24A. Rom. 14:5–12. When Paul writes to the Romans, he discusses the problem of the "strong" and the "weak," but the issue was slightly different from that in Corinth. Vegetarianism was the rule in certain philosophical schools, and a few new converts still had scruples about eating meat. Jews observed the Sabbath and other holy days, while

Gentiles felt no such obligation. No one must judge his brother, and whatever practice one follows it must be with thanksgiving to God. The pericope for this Sunday makes the point that no one lives for himself; whether we live or die, we belong to the Lord. This is in harmony with the gospel pericope (Matt. 18:21-35, p. 157f.), the parable of the unfor-giving slave.

Spiritual Gifts

Y2C. I Cor. 12:1-11. The principle of consideration for others is applied here to spiritual gifts. In 8:1 Paul had said that "knowledge puffs up, but love builds up," and this is the theme of chapters 12-14. Here he also speaks of what is beneficial (12:7; cf. 10:33). All gifts are good and should not be despised. They come from the one Spirit, but some are more useful to the Church than others. It is interesting that he first mentions wisdom (philosophy) and knowledge (*gnosis*), perhaps because the Corinthians valued them so much. The order is not very significant except that speaking in tongues comes last, and this is the problem that he has in mind.

The gospel reading (John 2:1-12) is related to the epistle only in that the miracle of Cana suggests the lavishness of God's gifts.

Y3C. I Cor. 12:12-30. The Apostle now uses different metaphors. Hellenistic philosophers used the symbol of the body to describe the interdependence of persons and groups in society (specifically in the empire), and Paul transposes this into a higher key. The sharp point he makes is that there should not be any schism in the body; all members should be concerned for the others (verse 25). He then lists the members of Christ's Body in descending order according to the importance of the gifts. Apostles, prophets and teachers come first. Speakers in tongues come last; helpers and those who govern are near the end. Although administration is important, it is subsidiary to that essential apostolic work which Jesus is portrayed as doing in the gospel pericope (Luke 4:14-20).

Y4C. I Cor. 12:31—13:13 (all except the Episcopal lectionary, which reads this on the last Sunday after Epiphany, C). 12:31b introduces chapter 13 and shows that this pericope is the centerpiece of chapters 12-14. The famous rhapsody on love can stand by itself and was proba-bly composed by the Apostle on a previous occasion. It must have grown out of his prayer and meditation. In 14:26 he says that one member of the church may contribute a psalm, another a teaching, another a revelation, and perhaps this is Paul's "psalm." It is carefully constructed in chiastic form but follows no classical or Hellenistic mod-els. As the Homeric scholar Wilamowitz said, something new comes into Greek literature in Paul, the fresh and powerful rhetoric of a man who is thoroughly at home in the language. Speaking theologically, we may say that in this chapter divine inspiration and human artistic expression are joined together.

The reference to tongues in verse 13:1 looks forward to chapter 14. Without love they are so much pretentious noise. Even the higher gifts and the most extreme sacrifice that one might make for the sake of the gospel are of no use apart from love. Verses 4–7 describe what love is and what it is not. The first clause in verse 7, "love bears" or "covers" everything, may refer to endurance or to the charity which does not disclose the faults of others; but in Hebrew speech "to cover" is also to atone for sin and reconcile human beings to God. Faith, hope and endurance all spring from love.

All other gifts of God's grace belong to this age and this life with its imperfect sight, and when the direct beatific vision of God comes, love alone remains. There can be nothing in earthly existence more splendid than seeing the glory of God mirrored in the face of Christ, and this vision transforms us (II Cor. 3:18—4:4). It is the most complete knowl-edge of God of which human beings are capable, but it still contains riddles and can be spoken of only in parables. Paul claims no more than this for his own theology.

General Admonitions

Most of Paul's letters contain a section of ethical teaching toward the end. He was not personally acquainted with the Romans and Colossians, so in his letters to them the admonitions are in more general terms.

Y22A. Rom. 12:1–8. Many ideas in this passage, which begins the ethical section, will be familiar to those who have read First Corinthians. The most interesting new statement is that rational worship (service of God, *latreia*) consists in offering our bodies (i.e. our personalities) as a living sacrifice to God. This takes the place of the sacrifices of the Old Covenant. It is not a substitute for the complete sacrifice that Jesus Christ made, but it is offered in union with the Cross as part of our identification with Christ. The moral result of it is transformation, not conformity to this world (or this age). The gospel reading (Matt. 16:21–28) is part of the Caesarea Philippi section, and Paul's words are in harmony with it.

Y23A. Rom. 12:9—13:10. Paul's attitude to the Roman empire was discussed in a previous chapter in connection with Jesus' saying "Render to Caesar." This pericope reflects his observation of the real benefits brought by a stable social and political order, but it should be read in the context of the whole NT. The Christian pays his dues and tries not to evade his obligation to anyone; the debt that remains is to love others, and we never finish paying all of that. The gospel pericope (Matt. 18:15–20) speaks of one aspect of love in the community, the need to reconcile if possible a brother or sister who has offended.

Y13C. Gal. 4:31b—5:1, 13–25. Paul has just established the principle that Christians belong to the new covenant of liberty, not that of bondage to law. It is sometimes thought that in Galatia the problems were twofold: some members of the community heeded the demand to be circumcised and keep the law, while others were fanatical and rejected all norms and rules. But the Apostle may simply think of the common tendency of people to go from one extreme to the other. To do the "works of the flesh" is to yield to all the impulses of uncontrolled human nature. One can be free of the law only by being led by the Spirit, and the presence of the Spirit is known by its fruits (5:22–25).

Y16C. Col. 1:15–29. The language of much of this letter, like that of Ephesians, is solemn and almost liturgical, in contrast to much of Paul's muscular and impassioned rhetoric; therefore many scholars think that a later disciple of Paul has written at least part of it. But if the Apostle composed this passage, as is possible, its tone can be explained by the fact that he did not know the Colossians personally; he is also in a calm, reflective mood during his imprisonment.

Two points are especially important. (1) Paul's sufferings help to fill up the measure of the sufferings of Christ. It is not that the Cross was an incomplete sacrifice; it is rather that the Church is his Body and that the process of the Crucifixion goes on in it, as the Church suffers and its members join themselves to Christ. The mystery now disclosed is that not only are the members in Christ, Christ is also in them, and this is their hope of glory. (2) To apprehend this truth and to live it is to be fully mature (*teleios*) in Christ, and it is Paul's purpose to bring everyone to this maturity. The word *teleios* has wide associations. In Matt. 5:48 it has the Hebrew meaning of the integrity of Job (Job 1:1), while in Hellenistic speech it can refer to one who is initiated into the mysteries. The gospel pericope is the story of Martha and Mary (Luke 10:38-42). Are we too fanciful if we say that Mary's attitude shows her maturity?

Y18C. Col. 3:1-17. This portrayal of the risen life is in harmony with the passages from Romans and Galatians. It is particularly directed toward Gentiles, who are still in danger of being influenced by the culture in which they were brought up. But there is also encouragement; in Christ there is no distinction between Greek, Jew and barbarian (one who does not speak Greek). Scythians were considered the most cruel and uncivilized of all nations. The reference to slaves may have a special point, because 3:22-25 speaks of the duties of slaves at some length, while wives, husbands, children, fathers and masters are addressed only briefly. The letter to Philemon, which concerns the slave Onesimus, is closely connected with Colossians.

Y23C. Philemon. This short letter, about the length of many letters on papyrus found by archaeologists in Egypt, provides a charming insight into Paul's methods as a pastor. While in prison (at Rome, or possibly at Ephesus) he has evidently converted a runaway slave from Laodicea, near Colossae. He wants Onesimus to be forgiven and received as a Christian brother. With a pun on the name ("profitable") he says that though the slave was once useless he is now very useful (verse 11). Paul offers to pay whatever the man may owe but reminds Philemon that the latter owes the Apostle much more. The letter seems to be a gentle hint that the slave should be released and sent back to Paul, who wishes that he could stay with him (verse 13). Punning again, the Apostle says that he would like to make some profit (*onaimēn*) out of Philemon.

Since he believed that the end of the age was near, Paul could not contemplate the abolition of slavery (cf. I Cor. 7:21-24, Y3B). But if a slave can be a Christian brother, dear as the Apostle himself, the way is open for a new order. Slavery has no place in a Christian society; it ended in the Roman Empire mainly for economic reasons, and unfortunately the Church was at most only a contributing factor.

·19

Christian Life in a Settled Community

The first Jewish revolt of A.D. 66–73, in which the Temple was destroyed, was a crisis for both Judaism and Christianity. After this the Pharisees were the only vital force in the Jewish community, and they turned away from politics and concentrated on observance of the Torah. There were still many Jewish Christians, but the majority of the Church was Gentile, and Christianity and Judaism became distinct religions. Although apocalyptic hope did not die out altogether, it receded into the background, and most people realized that for an indefinitely long time they would have to live in the world as it is. Nearly all the apostles had now died, and the generation growing up knew Jesus and Paul only by oral tradition and a few written records. It was necessary to produce more Christian literature, lest the tradition be corrupted or lost.

We get indications of the changed situation and perspective as early as the Gospel of Mark (especially in 4:13–20). Jesus' standard of behavior, appropriate to the Reign of God, and Paul's morality of the new life, seemed easier to understand when the end of the age was believed near. As this hope waned, many Christians sought guidance for everyday life and adjustment to their social situation.

There were rather few directives in the teaching of Paul and Jesus. Paul's principles of freedom and love were to be found in a few fragmentary letters, and, as the author of Second Peter said, some things in them were difficult to understand (II Pet. 3:16). The OT was as yet the only authoritative Scripture, and it was often the principal source of moral instruction. Greek philosophical ethics and the conventions of the surrounding community as to what was decent and right also had some influence on Christians.

Two opposite tendencies that can be called formalism and rigorism developed in this situation. By formalism we mean the setting of a minimum standard to which all are expected to conform. Rigorism is the imposition of an extreme heroic standard on all believers. The first can lead to complacency and the belief that one has done all that God requires; the other may lead to despair except among an elite who tend to reject any who do not meet their standards. Both can result in self-righteousness. One issue that was not settled until the third century was the question whether those who had committed serious sin after baptism—apostasy during persecution, for example—could be restored to communion in the Church.

The Epistle to the Hebrews and First John move in the direction of strict discipline. Hebrews holds out no hope for those who, once converted, deliberately sin and forsake the faith (Heb. 10:26–31; 12:15–17).

The position that the Church has taken, by and large, regarding the forgiveness of sins is well illustrated by the Gospel of Matthew. In chapter 18 of that gospel the Church is taught to exercise discipline, but always with mercy. The erring brother or sister must be forgiven seventy-seven times (18:21f.). The interpretation of the parable of the weeds (13:37–43) teaches that no attempt must be made to make the community perfectly pure. The final judgment is in God's hands alone.

Acts 4:32–37 gives an ideal picture of the community in Jerusalem, where, like the Essenes, the disciples held everything in common, and Ananias and Sapphira were stricken dead because they lied about their possessions (5:1–11). This ideal could not be maintained, yet it must often have been true that those who left families found brothers and sisters, mothers and children in the Church—with persecution (Mark 10:29f.). There was a strong impulse to lead a perfect life.

First and Second Timothy and Titus, written in St. Paul's name but some time after his death, are a kind of church order that gives directions for leaders and people. These two disciples of Paul are pictured almost as missionary bishops or vicars apostolic in charge of a wide mission field. The Church is in danger from teachers of a false knowledge (*gnosis*) who insinuate themselves into the congregations, preying especially on women. This suggests Gnosticism and possibly the doctrines of Marcion. There are also vague warnings against Jewish "myths."

What the author calls "sound teaching" includes the message of the risen Christ (I Tim. 3:16), but it is mostly about morals and manners. The Church now has an organized ministry. Bishops and presbyters are not clearly distinguished, and there are deacons as well as a group of widows who are formally enrolled and supported by the Church. Sobriety, maturity, and honesty in the handling of funds are qualifications for one who is to be made bishop. All Christians are expected to live quiet, modest lives and to mind their own business.

The morality of the Pastoral Epistles can be called formalism; it in no way contradicts Paul's ethic of the fervent love that cares for others, but it seems to expect much less. What we have is a standard of decency appropriate to a Greek community in western Asia Minor. The place assigned to women is more subordinate than in the Pauline letters; in fact the passage I Cor. 14:33b-36, which breaks the context and does not agree with 11:2-16, is often believed to have been interpolated by the author of the Pastorals.

The lectionaries omit the most severe passages in Hebrews and First John, and also those in the Pastorals that are clearly influenced by the cultural prejudices of that time and place. The pericopes chosen are the ones most likely to be helpful to a modern congregation.

Ephesians and James—Year B

Ephesians is probably a summary of Paul's teaching written by a man who knew the Apostle's letters thoroughly; Goodspeed argued that he is the one who collected the correspondence. Chapters 4-6 are the ethical part of the epistle, and four selections from these are provided in the lectionaries.

Y18B. Eph. 4:17-25 (NA, 4:1-6). The admonitions are very general and contrast the old evil life of paganism with the new humanity in Christ. "Mind" or intellect (verse 18) is practically identical with "heart"; in Hebrew speech, thinking and emotion are not separate faculties. Licentiousness and uncleanness refer primarily to sins of the flesh, but they arise from the imagination (Matt. 5:28). The gospel pericopes for four Sundays are taken from the discourse on the bread of life. The reading for this day (John 6:24-35) shows that the "work of God" (behavior according to God's purpose) springs from faith in Christ, who gives the bread in which there is nourishment for the new life.

Y19B. Eph. 4:25—5:2. The Spirit of God has put its seal on the convert. The reference is evidently to baptism, and the seal marks the person as God's property and under his protection. Bitterness, wrath and anger grieve the Spirit and are the cause of other evils; kindness and forgiveness, after the example of Christ, are the marks of God's dear children. To be taught by God and drawn to Christ is possible only because it is the Father who has acted first (John 6:44f.).

Y20B. Eph. 5:15-20. Two thoughts in this section are especially noteworthy. (1) In evil days one must redeem, buy up the time, and make every moment count for good. Modern Americans have so much leisure that they often waste time instead of managing it. (2) But the time that is saved is not all to be spent in *doing* something. Psalms and hymns—and one may add prayer—give exhilaration to the human spirit. The author uses the figure of "sober drunkeness" that is common in Hellenistic philosophy and which refers to the ecstatic contemplation of the mystics. The gospel pericope (John 6:51-59) contains another bold symbol. Life eternal comes from eating the flesh of the Son of Man and drinking his blood; this is the true manna of which the OT manna was but a type. This idea is to be further explained in the pericope for the following Sunday.

Y21B. Eph. 5:21-33. Marriage is the very foundation of society and it is love that sustains it. The words on the obedience of wives reflect the Jewish and OT point of view, and one should remember that in First Corinthians Paul comes nearer to teaching the equality of men and women. Here, although the husband is head of the wife (as in I Cor. 11:3), she is his body and is therefore to be cherished as much as his own flesh. The example is Christ's love for his bride, the Church, for which he gave himself.

The gospel reading (John 6:55-69) discloses another aspect of Christ's body. The flesh and blood eaten and drunk in the Eucharist are those of the ascended Son of Man and thus belong to the realm of the Spirit. In the pericope for the preceding Sunday strong language (*trôgôn*, referring to the physical act of eating) was used to affirm that the eating and drinking are real; the metaphor is more than a mere simile. Here John answers the objection that the metaphor is too crass. Those who reject it do so only because they do not have faith. The same thinking can be applied to the union of men and women in marriage and that of Christ and the Church. The symbolic language expresses a reality.

Y22B. Jas. 1:17-22. The Epistle of James has been called "the NT Book of Proverbs." Its maxims are sometimes strung together by verbal links, as in this pericope (word, hearing, doing). James is based on a tradition of Hellenistic Jewish wisdom that goes back partly to the Testaments of the Twelve Patriarchs, and the epistle is also a commentary on certain parts of the Gospel of Matthew (for example, cf. 1:13f. with Matt. 6:13). The emphasis on doing and not merely hearing fits with Matt. 7:21-27.

The Book of Common Prayer and the Methodist and NA lectionaries substitute Eph. 6:10-20, the famous passage on the panoply of God, which needs no explanation. In recent years military metaphors may not be as popular as they once were, yet the tradition which sees the Christian life as a continual fight against evil has an honorable history throughout the centuries. All the resources of the Holy Spirit are needed in the moral life.

Y23B. Jas. 2:1-5 (Roman, Lutheran, Presbyterian). When the tractate was written there were clearly a few rich persons in the Church and therefore the temptation was to show them special deference. The name of James was attached to the epistle, apparently because the "brother of the Lord" was an example of holy poverty and prayer, as we know from the story of his martyrdom preserved in Josephus's *Antiquities* xx. 9. 1. These admonitions against partiality are applicable to all congregations. The other lectionaries substitute 1:17-27, which again emphasizes doing, and also contains the metaphor of the magic mirror. To look into this mirror is to see the perfect law that liberates. This idea is something like a Stoic story of a mirror into which one looks and as a result purifies himself. Elsewhere in the NT this seeing results in a transformation (II Cor. 3:18; I John 3:2).

Y24B. Jas. 2:1-5, 8-10, 14-18. Martin Luther called James "a right strawy letter" because it seemed to exalt works over faith. But there is really no disharmony between this passage and the letters to Rome and Galatia. The "faith" that is pictured here is not much more than a profession of belief, and Paul himself would have rejected it as inadequate. Faith, as the Apostle used the word, is also commitment and obedience. Good deeds are its natural result. The gospel pericope (Mark 8:27–38, p. 165f.) contains Peter's confession at Caesarea Philippi and the first prediction of the Passion. To believe in Jesus as Messiah requires that one take up the Cross and follow him.

Y25B. Jas. 3:13—4:6. The pericope consists of two parts, bound to-gether by the problem of jealousy and selfish ambition. 3:13–18 con-trasts the heavenly wisdom, which is basically moral, with high-flown philosophies which result in contentiousness. The point is much the same as in I Cor. 1:13—3:23. 4:1-3 can be thought of as a meditation on Matt. 5:21f.; 7:7-11. The gospel reading (Mark 9:30-37, p. 167), which speaks of competition among the disciples, fits well with the epistle.

Y26B. Jas. 4:7—5:11. The theme of the futility of wealth and its spiritual danger, so frequent in the gospel tradition, is strongly ex-pressed here. The passage echoes Matt. 6:19-21, 24 and fits with the parable of the Rich Fool in Luke 12:16-21, but it also resumes the teaching of the Hebrew prophets. All congregations need to be re-minded that riches and poverty are relative terms and that members of a consumer society who buy indiscriminately on credit may be greedy for wealth.

The Pastoral Epistles—Year C
Y24C. I Tim. 1:12-17. The homily for this Sunday will probably concentrate on the parables of Luke 15. The epistle reading, which is a thanksgiving in the name of Paul, is related to it in that the Apostle, who had been a persecutor of the Church, had received mercy and the abundant grace of God.

Y25C. I Tim. 2:1-8. The exhortation to pray for rulers is motivated partly by the desire of a church composed of middle class and poor people to live in a quiet, secure society in which piety and reverence can flourish. At the same time, those in authority need divine guidance and grace as much as any others because of the greatness of their tempta-tions.

But there is another motive, for it is God's will that *everyone* be saved and come to know the truth (verse 4). This thought leads to an eloquent statement of Christology: as there is but one God, there is a single mediator between God and humanity, the man Christ Jesus. It is not enough to affirm his divinity; in his manhood he gave his testimony, as all heralds and apostles must do, and made his redeeming sacrifice for all people without exception.

Y26C. I Tim 6:6–19. These noble words, with their exhortation to fight the good fight of faith, are in the style of the author of the Pastorals, but they express well what Paul might have said in his last letters. Philippians may have been his final farewell. The doxology in this pericope is much like the one in 1:17.

Y27C. II Tim. 1:1–14. Again the author writes what he believes Paul would have said to a disciple and successor. There are Pauline ideas here, especially in verse 9, but the language in general belongs to the post-apostolic age. There is a deposit of "wholesome words" that is to be preserved, and the charisma of ordination is committed through the laying on of hands. The admonitions to clergy are certainly appropriate; a gift has been given them that they themselves must stir up into flame. As an antidote to cowardice, God has given a spirit of power and love and self-control. This additional gift is available to all Christians.

The gospel pericope (Luke 17:1–10) contains a saying on the power of faith and also a warning to God's slaves (which when read with the epistle applies particularly to all who do apostolic work) not to pride themselves on having served well (cf. I Cor. 9:17).

Y28C. II Tim. 2:3–15. This is another part of the imagined valedictory of Paul. Even though it is in a rhetoric different from his, it is very moving. "Remember Jesus Christ" points to an essential aspect of the NT. The gospels are, as Justin Martyr said in the second century, memorabilia of Christ, but they are more. By remembering him we come into union with him; it is more than how we remember Socrates or Abraham Lincoln. An apostle can be bound with chains, but the Word of God cannot be bound. The pericope includes a "reliable *logos*," a word of faith, somewhat like a creed, and these verses (11–13) prove that in the post-apostolic period the essential proclamation (*kerygma*), which is the power of God for salvation (Rom. 1:16), has the strength that it had at first and still has today. Here it is expressed eloquently; another example can be found in I Tim. 3:16.

That God in Christ remains faithful is a way of saying that the covenant still stands. The theme of faith appears in the conclusion of the gospel pericope (Luke 17:11–19). It is Luke who attached the saying of verse 19 to the story of the ten lepers, the purpose of which is to teach thankfulness; but thanksgiving is an aspect of faith, and only a person of faith will recognize that it is God who gives healing.

Y29C. II Tim. 3:14—4:5. The admonitions in this passage are ad-dressed to anyone who like Timothy exercised the apostolic office, but they apply equally to all pastors and teachers. The sacred Scriptures mentioned here are the OT, but every inspired writing gives the true wisdom (as contrasted with much that claims to be philosophy) which leads to salvation. We have to remember that in the Bible there are various kinds of inspiration. Some parts are directly inspired in that they speak to us directly; some are the best of human wisdom; others, like the stories of Joshua, Judges and other historical books, exhibit the Hebrews' partial understanding of God's purpose. There is no part of Scripture that does not have something to teach the Christian, but one must read with discrimination. One who can do this is equipped for every good work.

Y30C. II Tim. 4:6–8, 16–18. If any fragments of a last letter of Paul are preserved in the Pastoral Epistles, this may be one of them. It does not matter greatly, for this is the valediction of any true disciple, such as Christian in Bunyan's *Pilgrim's Progress.* His life is now being poured out. The word translated "departure" is *analysis,* which suggests break-ing camp when one is about to undertake another stage of pilgrimage. Paul has fought the good fight. Keeping or preserving the faith is an expression that belongs to the post-apostolic Church, which looked upon "the faith" as a body of doctrine; yet Paul also handed on a tradition (I Cor. 11:23; 15:1f.). The "crown of righteousness" is the victor's wreath toward which he was straining in Phil. 3:12–14; I Cor. 9:24.

The preacher may be puzzled as to whether the homily should deal with this or with the parable of the Pharisee and the Tax Collector (Luke 18:9–14, p. 174f.). We have to remember that the language of military combat and athletic competition is, after all, metaphorical. So is the parable that tells how one man rather than the other went home vindi-cated. The one passage speaks of moral struggle, while in the other the tax collector has no good deeds but only a cry for mercy. The Christian victor cannot have confidence in himself or herself; the trust is in God through Christ, but this does not excuse anyone from the exercise of will. Cardinal Reginald Pole, in the days when justification was a subject of controversy, wrote to Vittoria Colonna that a Christian should always think that one can be justified by faith alone, but work as though everything depended on works alone.

The pericopes chosen by the lectionaries make it clear that although the post-apostolic age of the Church has a perspective of its own, and its writings are here and there limited by this, it has much to teach the contemporary Christian. The gospels contain very early traditions, but even they were written in the post-apostolic period. Every era of Christian history contains prophets and saints who, each in their own way, illuminate the Good News.

·20

Prayer and the Interior Life

The earliest surviving records of human history give evidence that prayer in some form is a universal practice. Christian prayer shares certain traits with the worship of other religions, but it is unique in that it is *through* Jesus Christ our Lord and *in* the Holy Spirit. This is what it principally adds to the rich heritage from Judaism, in which its Lord was nurtured.

When most of our people hear the word "prayer" they think of saying prayers as a quiet, solitary act, or as participation in an exercise led by a minister or a lay person. Traditionally we list its components as adoration, thanksgiving, penitence, intercession and petition. It is sometimes forgotten that a gesture can be an act of prayer: kneeling, standing, laying on of hands, giving the peace, coming to the communion rail, walking in procession, making the sign of the Cross. Meditation is an act of prayer, and there can be a wordless prayer in which the worshipper remains relaxed and alert in the presence of God.

That there is an unsatisfied hunger for the higher forms of prayer is proved by the recent popularity of Zen Buddhism, transcendental meditation, and various new cults that offer techniques for meditation and spiritual discipline. There have been swamis and gurus in America for a long time, but there are more of them now. Part of this phenomenon

240

can be ascribed to an American tendency to hanker after novelties. But it is also a clear sign that many who were brought up in Christian homes have never been given the opportunity to learn of the rich tradition of spirituality in their own religion.

Much of the needed guidance can best be given in small classes of instruction and in personal counselling. Public worship can, however, provide some instruction in prayer and suggest that the resources for inward development have always been available in Christianity. Our people will learn much from the style in which we conduct public worship, and if the pastor has a healthy personal devotional life, some- thing of this spirit will be communicated to others. The pericopes of the lectionary are designed for public worship, but they touch the interior life at many points, and the purpose of this chapter is to identify a number of such passages.

Prayer in the Old Testament

The OT gives many examples of prayer. The Hebrews no doubt formed some of their methods of praying when they were still pagans, but when the covenant was established and they were commanded to have no God other than Yahweh, the characteristics of monotheistic, covenantal prayer begin to develop.

An ancient Hebrew often shouted to God and wrestled with him. Prayer was a dialogue. Abraham is said to have pleaded with Yahweh for the people of Sodom (Gen. 18:22–33). Moses resisted his vocation (Exod. 4:10–17) and later asked pardon for the rebellious Israelites (Exod. 32:11–13, 31f.). Elijah at Mount Horeb poured out his despair (I Kings 19:4, 10, 14). All these passages show that the biblical writers regarded such dialogues as normal, and in Jeremiah we have the prophet's own "confessions" or "laments," in which he disclosed his inner struggles and was sometimes given an answer. More than a third of the 150 Psalms contain elements of lamentation; often they seem to be the cries of individuals, but sometimes laments on behalf of the nation.

We also find liturgical prayers, notably those of David (II Sam. 7:18–29) and Solomon (I Kings 8:23–53). These reflect the theology of the editors of the historical books. Ezra's prayers (Ezra 9:6–15; Neh. 9:6–37) are confessions of the corporate sins of the nation. A similar style is found in the prayers of Simon and Eleazar in III Macc. 2:2–20; 6:2–15, and this indicates that the tradition continued in Judaism.

The Psalms

It is in the Psalms that the full range of Hebrew and Jewish devotion is disclosed. Most of them are now thought to have been composed before the Exile, and some, notably Ps. 29, bear a striking resemblance to Ugaritic literature (14th century B. C. or later). Ps. 119 may, however, be very late. Scattered throughout the OT there are other psalms, hymns and fragments that belong to the same genres as the large collection. The Psalter is the hymn book of an entire people, and while many of the pieces were intended for public worship there is a large measure of individual piety. In Hebrew psychology the individual is never apart from his family and nation.

Songs of praise, both those sung on behalf of the nation and by the individual, are numerous. Many declare God's glory and offer thanksgiving (e.g., Pss. 34, 84, 103); others celebrate his power in creation and the natural order (8, 19, 104) and especially the redemption of his People and his fostering care for them (66, 135).

Several psalms that recite Yahweh's deeds in the past are examples of the sacred story that restores worshippers to the ideal time and makes them contemporary with its events. Ps. 78 emphasizes the covenant with David (verses 67-72); 114 is a highly poetic remembrance of the Exodus and its marvels, and 136 has a constant refrain, "for his steadfast love endures for ever." 105, 106 and 107, like 78 express the Deuteronomic principle that the nation is rewarded when loyal and punished when disobedient. One group of psalms proclaims Yahweh's kingship; these are often thought to have been sung at a festival of his enthronement (47, 93, 95-99).

Of the clearly liturgical psalms, some are related to sacrifice (66, 107). Ps. 118 was sung in procession and is known to have been used at the Feast of Tabernacles. Ps. 122 is a pilgrimage hymn, and the songs of ascents (120-134) are closely related to it, though their exact function is not certain. The songs of Zion (46, 48, 76, 84, 87, 132) celebrate God's presence in the holy city. There are many examples of blessings (24:5; 67; 91; 115:9-15; 118:26; 121; 129:8; 134:3).

The royal psalms (2, 20, 21, 72, 89, 101, 110, 132, 144) are essentially prayers and thanksgivings on behalf of kings descended from David, several of which appeal to the special covenant with that dynasty. There is one song celebrating a royal marriage (45). We have already mentioned the many laments (e.g., 16, 17, 22, 74, 79, 80, 60-64, 140-143), some of which contain curses on enemies. There are also wisdom psalms that give moral instruction (e.g., 1; 15; 111:10; 112; 128), psalms of confession (51), prophetic psalms (50), and still others containing reflective meditations (34, 73, 92:12–15; 139:1–18). Finally, certain psalms extol God's law (19:7–14; 119). The categories overlap, and many psalms, as they are now numbered, contain two or more elements.

The Psalter has always been used in Christian worship. It is the essential part of the daily office, and some schemes prescribe the recitation of all psalms. Certain churches of the Reformed tradition still sing only metrical psalms in public worship, and many familiar hymns are based on psalms ("O God, our help in ages past," Ps. 90; "Praise, my soul, the King of heaven," Ps. 103).

But the Psalter as a whole is not entirely suitable for Christian use. It is nationalistic, and it contains dreadful imprecations on enemies, personal and national (e.g., 60:6–8; 69:22–28; 137:7–9; 139:19–22). The cries for vindication are natural, but taken literally they seem to express an appalling self-righteousness (26; 17; 119:97–104). The traditional way of dealing with these problems is to reinterpret the "enemies" as our sins and temptations, but of course this was not the original meaning. To repeat the curses and protestations of righteousness year after year may have a bad effect on the subconscious mind. The lectionaries have wisely tended to choose only those psalms that are of positive devotional value for the Christian.

Jewish Worship in New Testament Times

The main lines of Jewish worship, as it was carried on in Jesus' time, were established after the Exile. The tradition was unbroken and developed continuously. The Temple service was elaborate, and with its sacrifices there were prayers, the singing of psalms, and the reading of other passages from Scripture. But many Jews could attend the Temple only seldom or not at all, and it was worship in the synagogue and the home that touched Jewish life most deeply. We know from the Mishnah that certain psalms were sung and other passages from the Bible read on specific occasions. Prayer was both communal and private; in some cases set forms were prescribed, but spontaneous and original prayer was also common. Several prayers now used in the synagogue service had probably attained something like their present form by the first century, for example the Kaddish, the Alenu, and the Eighteen Benedictions. The wording of the Lord's Prayer is related to these.

The examples of Christian prayer to be found in the NT and other early Christian writings are based to some degree on Jewish models, and the same is true of the preface and *Sanctus* of the eucharistic liturgies. Jesus learned to pray in the home of Mary and Joseph and in synagogues so small and modest that only one or two first century synagogues can be identified by archaeologists. Jesus' disciples learned from him; and Paul's thanksgivings, which he prefaced to most of his letters, exhibit the Jewish way of blessing and thanking God. Worship is the best part of any religion, and Jewish worship, which formed and fructified the prayer of early Christians, is the point at which the two religions are still most nearly one. This should become evident as we discuss various pericopes of the lectionary.

Passages Previously Discussed

Much of the entire lectionary has a bearing on the interior life and the spiritual development of the Christian. Several psalms and other passages that relate specially to these have already been noted, for example in the discussions of Advent 1A, 2A, 4A (Chapter 6); the Baptism of the Lord (Chapter 7); Lent 5A (Chapter 8); Passion Sunday and Good Friday (Chapter 9); the Vigil of Easter, Easter Day, and the Ascension (Chapter 10); and the Pentecost Vigil and Trinity Sunday C (Chapter 11).

We now call attention to passages read during Sundays of the Year, for it is on these days that the homilist has the best opportunity to discuss prayer directly.

Year A

Y10A. The readings for the day (pp. 151, 209) are beautifully harmonized. Ps. 50 (three lectionaries) is usually called a prophetic psalm, and it represents a special type of prophecy, the announcement of the covenant lawsuit, in which God proclaims his glory and calls heaven and earth to witness against his People (cf. Mic. 6:1-8). He cares for truth and honesty rather than sacrifice. This is reinforced by the first reading, Hos. 5:15—6:6 (cf. also Isa. 1:10-17 and Gen. 22:1-18, the sacrifice of Isaac, NA). The gospel pericope is Matt. 9:9-13. Here the evangelist has introduced the quotation from Hosea, not found in Mark; in rejecting tax collectors and sinners the Pharisees have ignored God's covenant love.

These passages, taken together, can be applied to the temptations facing the Church as an institution and to those of the individual. The second reading, Rom. 4:13-25, looks at our relation to God in another way. Abraham's faith was counted as righteousness. Thus the good life involves faith in God, which is implicit in the covenant, and justice and mercy toward others. Scripture everywhere demands actual perform-ance and not merely profession, but this can come only through the formation of right attitudes.

Y12A. The psalm and first reading are examples of the Hebrew prayer of complaint. Ps. 69 (three lectionaries) is the lament of a sufferer who feels himself stuck in deep mire and deep waters and who yet expresses hope of deliverance. It is one of the psalms traditionally applied to the Passion of Christ, but verse 21 is not in the selections used, and the curses of verses 24–30 are properly omitted. Jer. 20:7–13 is the actual cry of a prophet under persecution. Jeremiah would gladly avoid this, but the word of Yahweh is like a fire shut up in his bones, and he must speak. The gospel reading, Matt. 10:16–33, gives two answers to one who is persecuted. Do not fear those who kill the body but cannot kill the soul. To this is joined the promise of God's care; we are of more value than the sparrows whose destiny is in his hand.

Every pastor meets those who consider themselves rejected and wronged, and such persons are sometimes in danger of becoming para-noid. It is good if they can realize that their difficulties with personal enemies, real or imaginary, are seldom as serious as those expressed in Scripture. At the same time, emotions must not be bottled up. If we can express them to those who can be trusted and if we can learn to pray for enemies, we may be able to see the problems in a better light. It is not wrong to complain to God if one does not stop at that point.

Usually the most serious enemy is within ourselves. The second read-ing, Rom. 5:12–21 (p. 210) turns us to recall our sinful condition and its remedy.

Y13A. The lectionaries (except the Episcopal and NA) employ selec-tions from Ps. 89:1–18. This is a psalm of covenant love that appeals to God's special care for David, and in a time of national disaster implores God to restore the Davidic monarchy. The Roman *Ordo* omits the refer-ences to David and the selection focuses on praise to God and his covenanted love (*ḥesed*). The OT reading, II Kings 4:8–16 (Roman, Pres-byterian, Methodist), the story of how Elisha promised the Shunammite woman that she would bear a son, emphasizes faith in God's loving promises.

The other readings, Rom 6:1–11 (p. 214f.) and Matt. 10:34–42 (p.

151f.), give faith another dimension: it is more than simple trust in God's power to grant boons. These pericopes would actually fit better with the psalm and first reading of Y12A. Our identification with Christ ensures our resurrection, but this is possible only if we are united with him in his Cross and death. We have no reason to expect any more immunity from trouble than Jesus had.

Y16A. The verses chosen from Ps. 86 continue the theme of God's covenant love, which is our basis for trust. The Roman lectionary includes the missionary note of verses 9–10: all nations will bow down and glorify God's name. Verses 14–17 ask for deliverance from enemies. Wisd. 12:13, 16–19, read in Roman Catholic and Episcopal churches (and as an alternative reading in the Methodist lectionary), proclaims that there is only one God. He judges with mildness and teaches that the righteous person must be kind. The other OT readings, II Sam. 7:18–22 (Presbyterian) and Isa. 44:6–8 (Lutheran and Methodist) express thanksgiving to God and confidence in him.

An important teaching on prayer occurs in Rom. 8:26–27, read on this Sunday by three lectionaries (on the following Sunday in the Episcopal, Presbyterian, and NA). When we do not know how to pray as we ought, the Spirit intercedes for us. Prayer therefore is more than petition, intercession, or even confession; it is opening oneself to communion with God. Paul perhaps has in mind speaking in tongues, but the principle applies to all wordless prayer. Matt. 13:24–43 appears at this point because of course reading. The principal link with the other pericopes is found in the parables of the Mustard Seed and Yeast (Y17A Episcopal), which indicate the inevitability and wonder of God's Reign. The parable of the Tares in this context is a warning that those who know themselves to be justified must not presume to judge whether others are to be saved or condemned.

Y19A. All except the Book of Common Prayer and NA read parts of I Kings 19:8–18. (NA uses this at Y12C.) This is the magnificent story of Elijah at Mount Horeb, and the Roman lectionary includes only the part essential for the interior life of the worshipper. It is in the still, small voice, not in the wind, earthquake and fire, that God reveals himself to the prophet and gives him courage. Other lectionaries include the message that the prophet must take decisive action; this is the proper result of prayer and meditation. Matt. 14:22–33, the account of Jesus and Peter walking on the water, suggests the presence of God in Christ at times of peril.

The Episcopal lectionary prescribes the Mount Horeb pericope for the last Sunday after Epiphany. On Y19A it substitutes the psalm in Jonah 2:1-9 and uses Ps. 29 typologically ("the voice of the Lord is upon the waters"). This is a magnificent psalm of God's power over nature.

Y20A. Ps. 67 is a beautiful prayer for God's blessings and mercy which calls on all nations to sing for joy and also proclaims that God judges the peoples with equity and guides all the nations. The other readings are not concerned with prayer except in the sense that they teach God's care for all people.

Y22A. The Roman and Presbyterian lectionaries prescribe Jer. 20:7-9; verses 10-13 of this chapter have been used on Y12A. The other service books, which read the longer pericope at that time, substitute Jer. 15:15-21 on this Sunday. This is another lament or confession in which Jeremiah insists on his innocence and calls for vengeance. Will God, he asks, be to him like a deceitful brook, like waters that fail? As elsewhere in Scripture, God answers one who is in perplexity. Here he promises to make the prophet like "a fortified wall of bronze" against the people.

As many devotional writers have said, God does indeed answer prayer but not always in the way one has initially hoped that he would. The validity of Jeremiah's prophecy was established by the events of history and he himself survived the invasion, but he went into Egypt as an exile.

Ps. 63:1-8, which is provided by the Roman lectionary, expresses the psalmist's thirst for God, a theme found also in Ps. 42 (see notes on Y6b).

While Rom. 12:1-8 (p. 228f.) is not closely connected with the OT reading, it approaches prayer in another way. Spiritual (or rational) worship is to present ourselves as a living sacrifice, and not to be conformed to this world but rather transformed by the renewing of the mind. This renewal of the mind introduces one of the most important summaries of Paul's ethics, which echoes the ideas of I Cor. 12-13. Renewal of the mind results in the understanding of one's proper function as a member of Christ's Body. True worship always involves loving action in the community.

Y28A, The parable of the Great Supper in Matt. 22:1-14 (p. 159f.) occurs here because of course reading, but it is not as satisfactory as the parallel, Luke 14:15-24, because of the allegorical elements that Matthew has introduced. By adding the parable of the man without wedding attire he has taught that one cannot come to God's banquet without the garment of righteousness. Preachers have often used this pericope as a figure of the Eucharist, but it relates principally to the call to accept the Good News.

The other lessons are related to the gospel reading by enforcing the idea that God feeds and protects his People. Ps. 23 (Roman, Lutheran, Methodist) is found in various places in the lectionary. God gives suste-nance and rest, leads his People in right paths, and protects them even in the valley of deep shadow. At the end the figure changes to that of God as host, and the guest is confident that he can worship in God's house for the rest of his days.

Isa. 25:1-10a comes from one of the earlier apocalyptic passages in the OT and this selection is eloquent and interesting. The future is pictured as a banquet which God will prepare. He will remove the veil over all the nations—the veil of ignorance or perhaps of mourning—and death will be "swallowed up."

The lectionaries select various parts of Phil. 4:1-20 for the second reading. This passage is an example of how St. Paul could sit loosely to the circumstances of life and even to life itself. Here he says that he is *autarkês,* content or independent (verse 11). This was a word used by Stoics to say that they regarded external conditions—being an emperor or a slave, rich or poor—as irrelevant to the good life. But Paul's strength is not that of a Stoic; he can do anything through the one who strengthens him. He has learned (the verb can be used to refer to initiation in a mystery religion) how to accept either abundance or privation. These words were written while he was in prison facing death, and he was expressing his gratitude to the Philippians for the gifts they had sent him. Among his other graces, he had that of being thankful, tactful and courteous even when he was helpless and poor.

Year B

Y5B. Job's lament (Job 7:1-7, all lectionaries except the Episcopal) is part of the answer to his friend Eliphaz, who has stated the traditional doctrine that anyone who repents and obeys the will of God will be restored and blessed. The pericope here expresses part of the truth about the human condition, but it is not the best that could have been chosen to illuminate Job's point of view. Job is as upright a man as anyone could be, and his suffering is quite undeserved. In the end he was justified, partly because he stood on his feet like a man and would not accept easy theological answers. What justified him was that he heard the word of God and accepted the conditions of human life. In the conclusion of this wisdom book his fortunes are restored, but this is secondary to the fact of his communion with God, and one cannot forget that his first sons and daughters died in the wind from the desert.

The Book of Job looks forward to the NT message that it is God who puts the believer in the right. In the Roman, Lutheran and Methodist lectionaries, the psalm is 147, a paean of praise to God for his goodness. He "lifts up the downtrodden." The Episcopal lectionary has II Kings 4:18–21, 32–37 (Elisha raises the child of the Shunammite woman from death). For some reason the Book of Common Prayer uses a psalm of lament, 142, instead of 147.

Y6B. The gospel reading is the story of the healing of the leper (Mark 1:40–45), and the OT readings set forth the law of leprosy (Lev. 13:1–2, 44–46) or tell the story of Naaman's healing (II Kings 5:1–15). Ps. 32 (Roman, Lutheran, Methodist) is a penitential psalm of great importance in the Christian devotional tradition. The theme is repentance and restoration, and it begins: "Happy is the one whose transgression is forgiven, whose sin is covered" ("cover" translates a Hebrew word that corresponds to the NT verb "atone" or "reconcile"). But in the Marcan pericope there is no suggestion that the leprosy was a punishment for sin; leprosy, like demon possession, was an affliction that God wills to remove because of his loving kindness. Ps. 42 (Episcopal) perhaps fits the condition of an innocent sufferer, though it has no reference to illness. The psalmist is far away from the Temple, and he is overwhelmed by enemies and other troubles ("all your waves and storms have gone over me"). Like Job, what he longs for is the presence of God ("My soul thirsts for God, for the living God"). Sensitive and truly religious persons often go through times of "dryness" when they cannot sense God's presence, and the only counsel that can be given them is to hang on, persevere, and wait. Jesus' figure of the absentee master (Luke 12:35–38; Mark 13:34–37) addresses this problem. It is of course a metaphor: God is never absent, he only seems to be.

Y8B. Ps. 103 is both a communal hymn and the thanksgiving of an individual. For both purposes it is one of the most useful pieces in the Psalter, and it is a poetic masterpiece so transparent that it needs no explanation. One notes, however, that it extols the steadfast love of God revealed in his covenant (verses 8, 17). As we have previously remarked,

Hos. 2: 14–20 exhibits Yahweh's love in seeking out and restoring Israel, his wayward wife. He "will allure her . . . and speak tenderly to her" and "she shall answer as in the days of her youth." God does not always threaten and judge, even in the OT; he acts most often by invitation and persuasion.

The psalm and OT reading evoke confidence in God's love. II Cor. 3:1–6 (Roman, Lutheran, Methodist, NA) points to another aspect of the covenant relationship. Here Paul has to justify the validity of his creden- tials as an apostle, his *hikanotês* (sufficiency, qualification, competence). This does not depend upon letters of commendation from some other church or apostle, which would correspond to a certificate of ordination today, for his credentials come from God, and this is proved by the fact that the congregation in Corinth is a true and living church. In another place he has said that no human court can really judge him; though he knows nothing against himself (and in this he is like Job) this does not aquit him; only God can judge (I Cor. 4:3–4).

Paul was a unique apostle, commissioned only by the risen Christ, whereas in our churches a minister must be called by the Church as well as by God. But the principle does not apply only to apostleship or ordination. The thought is that the vocation of everyone, lay person as well as priest, in fact our existence as Christians, can only be tested by its results in the common life, and in the end only God can decide whether we are speaking and doing rightly.

Y19B. I Kings 19:4–8 tells how Elijah was miraculously fed on his way to Mount Horeb when he asked for death, feeling that his mission was a total failure. The rest of the story was told on Y19A. The passages should be read together, and unfortunately the Episcopal lectionary omits verses 4–8, substituting Deut. 8:1–20, which reminds the Hebrews of the manna in the desert. For the gospel pericope, various parts of John 6:35–51 are prescribed; here the manna is a type of the Eucharist.

This points to the best application of the Elijah narrative, for whatever position one may take regarding the feeding miracles, it is true that the one who fed his people and bade them pray for daily bread taught also that man does not live by bread alone.

Y28B. Ps. 90 has always been a favorite in Christian devotion. It is a lament in which the nation prays to be delivered, but it also has some characteristics of a wisdom psalm, in which believers remind them- selves of the shortness of their days and the uncertainties of creaturely existence. Hence the Roman *Ordo* (and the Methodist lectionary as an alternative) couples it with Wisd. 7:7-11, and two lectionaries read Prov. 3:13-20 (wisdom is better than silver or gold). The Episcopal and Methodist books substitute Amos 5:6-7, 10-15, evidently because of its denunciations of the rich. NA employs Gen. 3:8-19, the fall of Adam and Eve.

The gospel is the story of the rich man who came to Jesus (Mark 10:17-31, pp. 167f.). Ps. 90 and the section from Wisdom are the passages that harmonize best with it.

Year C
Year C is particularly rich in passages that nourish the interior life because the course reading is from Luke, and this evangelist has a special interest in prayer.

Y14C. Ps. 66 appears to consist of two separate psalms; verses 1-12 are a hymn praising God for a national deliverance, while verses 13-20 are the praise of a worshipper who is about to make a thank-offering. In Isa. 66:10-16 a prophet calls upon people to rejoice with Jerusalem, which will be restored to such prosperity that she will be their nursing mother. The connection of these with the mission discourse, Luke 10:1-12, 16-20, is not quite clear, except that the joy of the seventy over the triumph over demons is a sign of the present reality of God's Reign, which is typified by Isa. 66. The language is apocalyptic; the serpents and scorpions are symbols of the power of evil, and Satan has fallen (cf. Rev. 12:7-12).

One possible application is that spiritual triumphs and success in prayer should never make one proud; instead, "rejoice that your names are written in heaven," you are God's People, subject to his protection and rule.

Y17C. Three examples of prayer are provided on this Sunday. Gen. 18:20-33 is the dialogue in which Abraham pleads with God not to destroy Sodom if fifty righteous men are found in it; successively the number is reduced so that the city will be spared if ten righteous are there. This is actually a dramatic portrayal of mental prayer in which the theological principle is: "Shall not the judge of all the earth do right?"

Ps. 138 is a joyful thanksgiving for deliverance and would be suitable on many occasions. Verse 6 is to be noted particularly: "For though the

Lord is high, he regards the lowly," a theme of the Song of Hannah and the *Magnificat*.

The gospel reading, Luke 11:1-13, contains the Lord's Prayer, the parable of the Friend at Midnight, and some concluding sayings on prayer.

Countless books and articles have been written on the subject of the Lord's Prayer; two of the best treatments are those of Ernst Lohmeyer and Joachim Jeremias. Here it is necessary only to make a few observations.

1. Jesus may have spoken the prayer in more than one form, but it has come down to us through oral tradition, and Luke's version, with the brief address "Father" (*Abba,* a form such as a child might use; cf. Mark 14:36; Rom. 8:15), appears to be more nearly the original. Part of the differences may be due to separate translations from Aramaic, but Matthew's additions are mainly liturgical. The doxology does not occur in the earliest MSS. of Matthew or in Luke. Matthew's preface says "Thus you shall pray," as though the Our Father were a model for other prayers, while Luke reads, "When you pray, say . . ."

2. The prayer must have been known to Mark, because it is echoed in 14:36, 38. The *Didache* gives it, with a doxology, and in a form similar to that of Matthew, and directs that it be said three times a day, just as Jews said the *Shema'.*

3. The basic petitions can be analyzed as three. (*a*) Prayer for the sanctification of the Name and the coming of the Kingdom are related, because God's Name is hallowed (his renown is enhanced) when his Reign is accepted. "May your will be done" is an explanation of the double petition. (*b*) Daily bread (or bread for the coming day), that is, the sustenance needed just now; one does not ask for more. (*c*) Deliverance: the forgiveness of sins, protection in the time of testing (perhaps temptation also), and rescue from the Evil One. The *peirasmos* or trial may be eschatological, referring to the troubles of the end-time, but the word can apply to any crisis in life.

4. The prayer is completely Jewish. Here Jesus stands in the finest devotional tradition of his people, as we can see from the parallels in the Eighteen Benedictions, the Kaddish and the Alenu. This is particularly evident in Matthew's form. If Jews do not use it, it is because of its historical association with Christianity.

Verses 9-13 have a parallel in Matt. 7:7-11. The Lucan section consists of two parts. Verses 9f. are in poetic parallelism. As we have said, prayer is not always answered in the terms of the original petition; Jesus simply makes the point that one must pray, and an answer will surely come. The second part is also in Hebrew poetic form, but in Luke the bread and stone are replaced by the fish and scorpion (though some MSS. have all three members). The language is artistic: the flat bread of Palestine could be shaped like some stones, some fishes are long, like serpents, and a scorpion is somewhat oval in shape. In verse 13, Luke replaces Matthew's "good things" with the Holy Spirit, which is the greatest of all gifts.

The parable of the Friend at Midnight will be discussed with its twin, which is read on Y29C.

Y19C. The gospel reading is Luke 12:32–48 (some lectionaries omit verses 41–48). The whole passage is eschatological, and as it stands answers the perplexity of early Christians over the delay of Christ's return. It is, however, essentially the teaching of Jesus, who spoke originally not of himself but of the delay of God's Reign.

The pericope is in three parts. Verse 32 is actually the conclusion of the section on anxiety (12:22–31) and a transition to what follows. Verses 35–38 are complete in themselves, and verse 39 is the remnant of another parable. If verse 40 (cf. Matt. 24:44) is a saying of Jesus it has nevertheless been added in the tradition from a different context. The introduction in verse 41, in which Peter is the interlocutor, serves to bind together two separate but related parables, essentially verses 35–38 and 42–46. Both deal with waiting, but the former emphasizes the joy of the master's coming and the latter his judgment. The most useful homily might be on the first of the two, because it can deal with the sense of God's absence which was mentioned in connection with Ps. 42 (Y6B).

The other pericopes are related to this theme only in the matter of obedience and trust. They deal with the Exodus from Egypt and the covenant (Wisd. 18:6–9, Roman; II Kings 17:33–40, Presbyterian) or Abraham's faith (Heb. 11:1–3, 8–16; Gen. 15:1–6, Episcopal, Lutheran, and Methodist). Ps. 33 is one of the loveliest of communal hymns, exalting God as creator and Lord of history. As such, it expresses the spirit of the great prophets.

Y27C. The first reading is Hab. 1:1–13; 2:2–4, read by NA at Y29C. Chapters 1–2 of this book are another example of a dialogue between a prophet and Yahweh. Habakkuk may have written in the last days before Nebuchadnezzar invaded Jerusalem. Whatever the historical situation, the prophet, like the sufferer of Ps. 22, complains that God does not hear. 2:2–4 is the response to Habakkuk's second lament. The answer is twofold: one must wait, and meanwhile "the righteous shall live by his faith." Waiting in patience is not the complete solution to the suffering of the righteous, because while fortunes are sometimes reversed, it does not always happen so in this life. But it is true that the just person is sustained by faith, which here primarily means faithfulness, though trust is also an element. In the letter to the Romans (1:17) Paul takes up this famous verse and reinterprets the meaning of faith.

Insofar as the OT and gospel readings are linked, it is through the theme of fidelity. Luke 17:1–10 has three parts. In the second, verses 5f., Jesus tells his disciples that one who has faith can command a sycamine tree to be rooted up and cast into the sea. This hyperbolical language should be read in the context of all his teaching on prayer. The other saying (verse 10) deals with the attitude of God's People. It is true that the master who has been away at a wedding will serve a dinner to his loyal slaves (Luke 12:37, Y19C), *but they have no right to expect this.* When the slave has done all that has been commanded, he should say, "We are mere slaves, we have only done our duty." The Greek word here translated as "mere" seems to have been part of a stock phrase: "good-for-nothing slaves." The saying is not an allegory; a slave might follow orders, but a Christian can never do all that is commanded him.

Y29C. Many psalms express confidence in God's protection; Ps. 121 is in the form of a blessing on the worshipper. It has great poetic beauty and has been very important in Christian devotion.

As used here, it supplements Jesus' parable of the Unjust Judge (Luke 18:1–8), for it creates the mood in which one approaches God. The parable should be studied along with its twin, the Friend at Midnight (Luke 11:5–8, Y17C).

Both parables are typical stories of something that has happened or is likely to happen. In themselves they are purely secular and should not be allegorized. God is not like the surly peasant who does not want to get out of bed or the heartless judge, as the "how much more" principle of Luke 18:7 makes clear. The one point of comparison is that one ought to persist in prayer. And it is not because God is hard of hearing or the celestial switchboard is flooded with calls, for "your Father knows your needs before you ask him" (Matt. 6:8). Prayer is conversation and communion with God; it does not change him, but it transforms us.

But what wonderful stories these are! The homily will be more lively if the preacher portrays the peasant sleeping on the earth floor of a one-room house. Both he and his neighbor will lose face if hospitality is not shown to a suddenly arrived guest. The judge is an oriental who holds court in the open, and the poor woman keeps screaming until the magistrate can bear it no longer.

Christ the King (Last Sunday before Advent) C. The gospel reading, Luke 23: 35–43, is chosen because it expresses an aspect of Christ's Kingdom. The penitent bandit, who unlike the other is able to think of something beside his own sufferings, will not have to wait for the final establishment of the Kingdom; that very day he will be with Jesus in paradise. NA substitutes John 12:9–19, in which Jesus is welcomed as king by the crowds carrying palms.

Col. 1:11–20 is in a solemn liturgical style not often found in Paul's letters. It is a proclamation and a creed in the form of a thanksgiving. Since it celebrates creation, the Cross and Resurrection, and the Church, it provides a context for Christian prayer. Ps. 122, used only in the Roman *Ordo,* is a fitting preface to it, for it is a pilgrimage hymn, sung as the worshipper goes up to the city where the King of kings has his house. The Episcopal lectionary substitutes Ps. 46, which also speaks of God's presence; the Lutheran choice is Ps. 95:1–7a, a psalm used on many occasions, especially as an invitatory. It proclaims God as King.

Select Bibliography

I. Lectionaries

Roman Catholic: *Ordo Lectionum Missae*. Vatican City: Typis Polyglottis Vaticanus, 1969. This lectionary can be consulted in R. H. Fuller, *Preaching the New Lectionary*. Collegeville, Minn.: The Liturgical Press, 1971-74.

Presbyterian: *The Worshipbook: Services and Hymns*. Philadelphia: Westminster Press, 1975, pp. 167-175.

Episcopal: *The Book of Common Prayer*. New York: Church Hymnal Corp. and Seabury Press, 1977, pp. 888-931.

Lutheran: *Lutheran Book of Worship*. Minneapolis: Augsburg Publishing House, 1978, pp. 13-41.

United Methodist: *Seasons of the Gospel*. Nashville: Abingdon Press, 1979.

NACCL: *Table of Readings and Psalms Prepared by the North American Committee on Calendar and Lectionary* (mimeographed). Washington: Consultation on Common Texts, 1982.

II. General Orientation

A. Lectionaries

G. S. Sloyan, L. R. Bailey and E. Achtemeier, *Interpretation,* XXXI, 2 (April, 1977), 131-164.

B. Biblical and Liturgical Preaching

G. M. Bass, *The Renewal of Liturgical Preaching*. Minneapolis: Augsburg Publishing House, 1967.

O. C. Edwards, Jr., *The Living and Active Word*. New York: Seabury Press, 1975.

L. E. Keck, *The Bible in the Pulpit*. Nashville: Abingdon Press, 1978.

James D. Smart, *The Strange Silence of the Bible in the Church*. Philadelphia: Westminster Press, 1970.

C. Myth and Ritual

Mircea Eliade, *Cosmos and History: The Myth of the Eternal Return*. New York: Harper & Row, 1959.

Mircea Eliade, *Myth and Reality*. New York: Harper & Row, 1963.

Mircea Eliade, *The Sacred and the Profane*. New York: Harcourt, Brace & World, 1959.

Marion J. Hatchett, *Sanctifying Life, Time and Space*. New York: Seabury Press, 1976.

D. Religious Language and Worship

Paul Hoon, *The Integrity of Worship*. Nashville: Abingdon Press, 1971.

Amos N. Wilder, *The Language of the Gospel*. New York: Harper & Row, 1964.

E. Biblical Theology

Walter Brueggemann, *The Bible Makes Sense*. Winona, Minn.: St. Mary's College Press, 1977.

William Countryman, *Biblical Authority or Biblical Tyranny?* Philadelphia: Fortress Press, 1981.

Paul D. Hanson, *The Diversity of Scripture: A Theological Interpretation*. Philadelphia: Fortress Press, 1982.

David H. Kelsey, "The Bible and Christian Theology," *Journal of the American Academy of Religion*, XLVIII (1980), 385-402.

See also under "Other Helps," below.

F. Old Testament

E. Achtemeier, *The Old Testament and the Proclamation of the Gospel*. Philadelphia: Westminster Press, 1973.

Joseph Blenkinsopp, *Prophecy and Canon*. Notre Dame, Ind.: University of Notre Dame Press, 1977.

Paul D. Hanson, *The Dawn of Apocalyptic*. Philadelphia: Fortress Press, 1975.

James A. Sanders, *Torah and Canon*. Philadelphia: Fortress Press, 1972.

Claus Westermann, *Handbook to the Old Testament*. Minneapolis: Augsburg Publishing House, 1969.

H. W. Wolff, *The Old Testament: A Guide to Its Writings*. Philadelphia: Fortress Press, 1973.

G. Jesus and Paul

Günther Bornkamm, *Jesus of Nazareth*. New York: Harper, 1960.

Günther Bornkamm, *Paul*. New York: Harper & Row, 1971.

F. H. Borsch, *Power in Weakness*. Philadelphia: Fortress Press, 1983.

Raymond E. Brown, *The Birth of the Messiah*. Garden City, N.Y.: Doubleday, 1977.

J. Jeremias, *The Lord's Prayer*. Philadelphia: Fortress Press, 1964.

E. Lohmeyer, *Our Father*. New York: Harper, 1966.

Norman Perrin, *Rediscovering the Teaching of Jesus*. New York: Harper & Row, 1967.

Norman Perrin, *Jesus and the Language of the Kingdom*. Philadelphia: Fortress Press, 1976.

James D. Smart, *The Quiet Revolution*. Philadelphia: Westminster Press, 1959.

John Howard Yoder, *The Politics of Jesus*. Grand Rapids, Mich.: Eerdmans Publishing Co., 1972.

H. Other Helps

Articles on most of the above topics and related issues such as Hermeneutics, History of Interpretation, Biblical Criticism, Apocalypticism, Midrash and Typology, are to be found in the following:

The Interpreter's Dictionary of the Bible. Nashville: Abingdon Press, 1962. Supplementary Volume, 1976, which is especially important.

The Interpreter's One Volume Commentary on the Bible. Nashville: Abingdom Press, 1971.

R. E. Brown, J. A. Fitzmyer and R. E. Brown (eds.), *The Jerome Biblical Commentary*. Englewood Cliffs, N.J.: Prentice-Hall, 1968.

M. Black and H. H. Rowley (eds.), *Peake's Commentary on the Bible*, 2nd edition. London: Thomas Nelson & Sons, 1963.

III. Preaching from the Lectionaries

R. H. Fuller, *Preaching the New Lectionary*. Collegeville, Minn.: The Liturgical Press, 1971-74.

R. H. Fuller, *The Use of the Bible in Preaching*. Philadelphia: Fortress Press, 1981.

J. Gaffney, *Biblical Notes for the Sunday Lectionary*. New York: Paulist Press, 1978.

Marion J. Hatchett, *Commentary on the American Prayer Book*. New York: Seabury Press, 1980.

Foster McCurley, Jr., *Proclaiming the Promise*. Philadelphia: Fortress Press, 1974.

Proclamation: Aids for Interpreting the Lessons of the Church Year. Philadelphia: Fortress Press, 1973-76. 26 small paperbound volumes.

Proclamation 2: Aids for Interpreting the Lessons of the Church Year. Philadelphia: Fortress Press, 1970-82. 24 small volumes.

Special attention should be called to the Proclamation Commentaries, edited by Gerhard Krodel, published by the Fortress Press. These cover most books of the Old and New Testaments.

Index of Scripture References

The pericopes frequently overlap in the several lectionaries. Therefore many references given below combine them and also include references to individual verses. Entries in **boldface type** refer to the principal discussions.

Old Testament

Deuterocanonical Books

New Testament

Gospel of Thomas